BIRDWATCHING
FOR BEGINNERS

BIRDWATCHING
FOR BEGINNERS

Rob Hume

DORLING KINDERSLEY

LONDON, NEW YORK, MELBOURNE, MUNICH, AND DELHI

Senior Editor Angeles Gavira
Senior Art Editor Ina Stradins
DTP Designer Rajen Shah, Anita Yadav
Production Controller Melanie Dowland
Managing Editor Liz Wheeler
Managing Art Editor Phil Ormerod
Category Publisher Jonathan Metcalf

For cobalt id
Editors Marek Walisiewicz, Kati Dye
Art Editors Paul Reid, Darren Bland,
Pia Hietarinta, Lloyd Tilbury

Produced for Dorling Kindersley by cobalt id,
The Stables, Wood Farm, Deopham Road,
Attleborough, Norfolk NR17 1AJ
www.cobaltid.co.uk

First published in Great Britain in 2003
by Dorling Kindersley Limited
80 Strand, London WC2R 0RL
Penguin Group (UK)
2 4 6 8 10 9 7 5 3
002-188092-Mar/2013
This edition first published in 2013
Copyright © 2003, 2006, 2013
Dorling Kindersley Limited, London
Text copyright © 2003 Rob Hume

A CIP catalogue record for this book is
available from the British Library

978-14093-6449-8

Reproduced by Colourscan, Singapore
Printed and bound in China by South
China Printing Co. Ltd

See our complete catalogue at
www.dk.com

Contents

Preface

Birds are free, in both senses of the word. They live independently of us, wild and free: the epitome of wild nature for most of us. They are also free to watch: birdwatching is free to all, with no equipment needed, no memberships of any clubs or societies required, no rules to follow.

True, it helps to have binoculars and a book or two, and you can help birds if you join a society such as the RSPB that works to conserve them. But watching birds is still a cheap hobby if you want it to be. This book helps you get more out of it, with a little investment and a good deal of very enjoyable practice. Birdwatchers are always learning, however long they have been doing it. It could be said that all birdwatching is, in a sense, about practice: by putting in the time to learn and to understand more, the more you will see.

While birds do live independent lives, they are not by any means free from our influence. The way we use the land and seas on which they depend affects them immensely and that affects how and where we can find them, and how we can enjoy watching them. There are,

fortunately, many more nature reserves than ever before, where we can see birds close up. Many have footpaths and hides, and, in such places, "field craft", even so much as getting closer for a better view, is necessarily somewhat limited: birdwatchers' habits have changed over the years.

Now, many birdwatchers carry cameras as readily as binoculars, and the results of digital photography have revolutionized birdwatching for many people. You can now see a bird and go back home to study photographs of that very individual on a website. In places where birds tend to be a bit more distant, such as lakes, gravel pits, and the coast, tripods and telescopes are more the norm than the exception. Keeping notes has moved towards computer-based systems, away from the old-fashioned notebook (but notebooks still have a place!).

This book looks at all the ways that you can watch, study and learn about birds, but strips away the myths and jargon that tend to go with any such hobby. In the end, it is all about enjoyment – and an appreciation of the amazing lifestyles and abilities of the most mobile and some of the most dramatic life forms on the planet.

Rob Hume

What is a bird?

Birds are warm-blooded, lay eggs, and, in most cases, fly, but what makes them unique is their covering of feathers and two-legged stance. Their adaptations for flight, including incubating their eggs externally, centre on reducing weight and optimizing aerodynamic efficiency.

Evolution and diversity

WITH THEIR FEATHERS, toothless bills, bipedal locomotion, and their remarkable flying ability, birds are physically quite different from any other living animals. Most scientists agree that the first birdlike creatures evolved from archosaurian reptiles – a group that includes the dinosaurs and crocodilians. From their origins some 230 million years ago, they have diversified into around 10,000 living species.

Alternative evolution
The kiwi is sometimes considered to be a primitive bird, but in fact it has just followed a different evolutionary path.

Prehistoric origins

A biologist would have no trouble in listing the features that characterize a bird. A bird is a vertebrate with a highly modified skeleton that allows flight; its flying surfaces are elongated feathers on the forelimb and tail; its digits lack claws; and the bones of its forelimb are fused together in a very specific manner. A host of other anatomical features differentiate birds from other animals, but to really address the question "what is a bird?", it is necessary to delve into evolutionary history.

Winged, feathered, birdlike animals first appear in the fossil record about 150

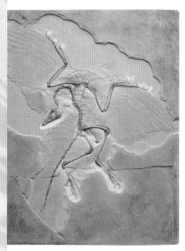

Only six complete *Archaeopteryx* *fossils have been discovered. They were found in Jurassic limestone deposits in Germany.*

million years ago, in the Jurassic Period. These crow-sized creatures, called *Archaeopteryx*, were essentially feathered dinosaurs. Scientists speculate that they evolved from small, scurrying, bipedal ancestors that had long tails and long, flexible necks. The ancestral dinosaurs would have been very active creatures that needed to keep their body temperature high, and it is possible that feathers first evolved from scales to help retain heat. Some descendants of these animals may then have taken to the trees, developing an arboreal lifestyle in which the ability to glide would have been valuable. The rudimentary scale-feathers on the extended forearms

may have provided some lift, and flapping would have extended the animals' trajectory. Further enlargement of the wing and tail feathers may have produced an *Archaeopteryx*-like animal, capable of gliding and possibly weak flight. *Archaeopteryx* may or may not be the direct ancestor of modern birds, but it is certainly not far from the main line of bird evolution and it gives vital insights into the early development of the group.

Flight is the *most obvious characteristic of birds; even flightless birds evolved from ancestors that could fly. The birds alive today represent only a fraction of total diversity; scientists estimate that over 150,000 bird species have lived and disappeared.*

Birds have evolved *to occupy almost every niche. Flamingos, for example, are filter feeders, straining food from water.*

Grebes appear *primitive and are unable to walk on land, but they are superbly adapted for their lifestyle on and under water.*

Chaffinch

Goldfinch

Bullfinch

Hawfinch

Pine Grosbeak

Siskin

The shape of a finch's bill indicates its food preferences: Chaffinches are generalists, eating insects and seeds; Goldfinches probe into flower heads with long, fine bills; Bullfinches have rounded bills with cutting edges for tackling soft buds; Hawfinches crack heavy fruit stones; Pine Grosbeaks eat softer buds, shoots, and insects; Siskins probe for seeds in the cones of larch and alder.

Early diversification

Bird skeletons are fragile and do not easily withstand the rigorous process of fossilization. For this reason, the early evolutionary history of birds remains sketchy. It is clear, however, that birds diversified widely early in the Tertiary period, about 65 million years ago; and by 15 million years ago, most of the contemporary groups had evolved. It is difficult to be sure of the relationships between the 28 living and extinct bird orders, but most specialists divide them into two larger groups – the Paleognathae and the Neognathae (both members of the sub-class Neornithes) – on the basis of differences in the anatomy of the mouth. The paleognathous birds are mostly flightless, and are sometimes called ratites; living species include the Kiwi, Cassowary, Ostrich, and Emu. Neognathous birds make up the majority of land birds and waterbirds with which we are familiar.

Within the Neognathae, it is likely that waterbirds split off from land birds at an early stage in evolutionary history, with the cranes, coots, and rails representing the most primitive group. Amongst land birds, groups such as swifts, kingfishers, owls, songbirds, and woodpeckers are seen as more advanced than pigeons, grouse, parrots, hawks, and eagles, because they have lost one thigh muscle (the ambiens), which is present in reptiles and primitive birds. Most advanced are the perching songbirds, of which there are more than 5,000 living species.

Finches have *adapted to a wide range of foods and habitats. Crossbills, for example, have bills specialized for spruce seeds.*

Radiation and convergence

Birds have diversified astonishingly to exploit a vast range of different foods and habitats. The basic bird body plan has proved sufficiently adaptable to colonize the air, land, and the sea, and natural selection has acted on this body plan to produce animals as different as the ostrich and the penguin. Natural selection is the engine of evolution. It is the process by which "successful" designs or useful behaviours are passed on from one generation to the next, while deleterious characteristics are eliminated from the population. Natural selection drives diversification – such as the small changes in beak design that allow closely related species of birds to coexist in the same area by feeding on different foods (see above). It can also have the opposite effect of "convergence", in which quite unrelated species of birds evolve to show similar structural features – a situation exemplified by swifts and swallows. Sometimes, natural selection produces change for reasons that are hard to fathom – for example, the Treecreeper and Short-toed Treecreeper are different species, yet they are exceptionally hard to tell apart, they live apparently identical lives, and even occupy the same habitats.

SPECIES FORMATION

A species is any group of animals that can interbreed and produce viable offspring. New species are usually created when part of the group becomes isolated from the "mother" population by a geographic accident. This population follows its own evolutionary course, and eventually a new species is created. The Hooded Crow was derived from the Carrion Crow, and is now considered a separate species.

Carrion Crow

Hooded Crow

Anatomy

To conquer the challenges of an aerial life, birds must be light in weight. Any anatomical feature that increases weight for no useful gain is reduced. Their bones are honeycombed for lightness combined with strength and rigidity. Their skulls are light, there is no heavy musculature for chewing food, and no heavy teeth. Their outer surface is streamlined for easy movement through air or water; even their legs can be tucked away to reduce drag in flight.

Meat eaters
Birds of prey, such as the Short-toed Eagle, have hooked bills for tearing flesh.

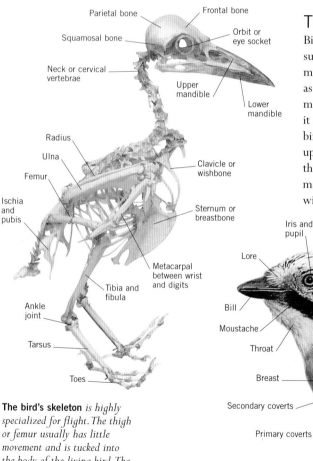

Parietal bone

Frontal bone

Squamosal bone

Orbit or eye socket

Neck or cervical vertebrae

Upper mandible

Lower mandible

Radius

Ulna

Femur

Clavicle or wishbone

Ischia and pubis

Sternum or breastbone

Metacarpal between wrist and digits

Tibia and fibula

Ankle joint

Tarsus

Toes

The bird's skeleton *is highly specialized for flight. The thigh or femur usually has little movement and is tucked into the body of the living bird. The upper leg, visible on long-legged birds, is actually the shin, with tibia and fibula fused. The main joint is the "ankle" above the tarsus (equivalent to a human foot). It is the toes that make up a bird's "foot".*

The skeleton

Birds are vertebrates, with a long, central spine that supports the head, limbs, and body. The backbone is made up of as few as 39 vertebrae in songbirds and as many as 63 in swans. It is more rigid than in most mammals, except in the neck, which is flexible because it is made up of between 11 and 25 bones. This means that birds can rotate their heads through large angles, making up for a lack of mobility in the eyes, which are fixed in their sockets. The breastbone provides an anchor for the main flight muscles; it is deep on birds with powerful wingbeats, shallow on those that glide. The forelimbs are much like ours (see opposite) but the upper arm, the humerus, is often hidden in the body feathers. The "inner wing" is the forearm; the "outer wing" the digits beyond the wrist, with its complex carpal and metacarpal bones.

Iris and pupil

Nape

Lore

Ear or cheek coverts

Bill

Back

Moustache

Scapulars

Throat

Tertials

Breast

Secondaries

Secondary coverts

Primaries

Primary coverts

Belly

Leg or tarsus

Vent

Under tail coverts

Tail

Hind toe

Birds are vertebrates, *just like mammals, reptiles, and amphibians. They share a basic body plan with these animals, but a knowledge of their specific features is a great bonus when watching and identifying birds.*

The bones of a bird's wing *attach to feathers that overlap like tiles on a roof. The shapes and relative sizes of the feathers vary between bird families.*

Part of the upper arm bone

Forearm bones

Thumb

Wrist bones

First finger

Second finger

Attached to the thumb bone is a moveable wedge of feathers, the alula or bastard wing.

Small marginal and median coverts at the front edge of the wing.

The greater coverts lie over the base of the larger flight feathers. Pale tips to the greater coverts may create a distinct "wing bar".

Attached to the upper arm bone are the tertials – the innermost of the larger flight feathers.

Attached to the forearm bones are the secondaries – the large feathers along the trailing edge of the inner wing.

At the wingtip, attached to the digits, are the stiff primary feathers.

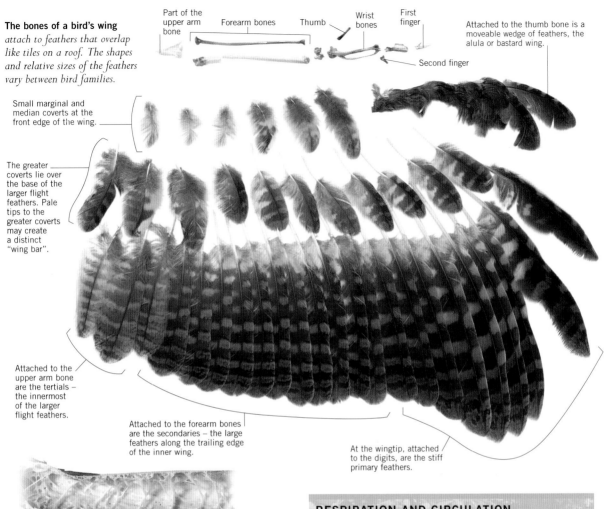

Major bones *in the avian skeleton are hollow, for all-important lightness, with a network of intricate internal supports for added strength and rigidity.*

Design for flight

Birds fly using their modified forelimbs, and taking to the air requires a short, explosive burst of energy. Many birds fly at high speed, incorporating sharp acceleration and deceleration into their flight patterns; others exploit windcurrents and columns of warm, rising air to remain aloft for hours on end. Small songbirds, with rapid, whirring, or flitting wingbeats, fly immense distances – even by human standards – on their annual migrations. Some seabirds and swifts may even remain airborne for two or three years without once coming to land. Their highly efficient circulatory, respiratory, and digestive systems support their high-performance lifestyle.

RESPIRATION AND CIRCULATION
Birds live life at a fast pace and have high metabolic rates. They change food into energy very quickly, and distribute food and oxygen to their muscles with great efficiency. Heartbeats vary from 100 beats per minute in large species to 1,000 in smaller birds. Birds' lungs are far more efficient than those of mammals. They have developed extensions, called air sacs, to maximize uptake of oxygen. There are usually nine of these air sacs, which extend into all parts of the body and even penetrate into some of the bones.

Trachea

Syrinx

Lung

Air sacs

The avian respiratory system

Feather shapes

A bird's basic shape and proportions are largely determined by its internal structures. But superimposed upon these are extra features created entirely by variations in feather shape. These are usually, but not always, related to physical function; the long, "fingered" wingtips of some birds of prey and storks, for example, allow air to slip through slots between the upcurved wingtip feathers. This increases stability by minimizing turbulence and drag at the wingtip – a feature copied by aircraft designers. Long tail feathers improve aerodynamic streamlining and increase the area of control surfaces, improving steering and braking. Similarly, feathers on legs and feet provide insulation for ground birds in cold regions. Other dramatic feather shapes, however, are purely decorative; they are typically seen in males of polygamous species that seek to impress potential mates. They may be combined with striking colours and patterns and are often emphasized in the stylized postures of courtship displays. More rarely, the shape of the bill (such as the Puffin's colourful sheath) and fleshy wattles on the head perform similar functions.

The Magpie's long, narrow tail serves multiple functions. It improves balance and manoeuvrability, but it is also jerked and swayed to communicate with other Magpies.

Tail acts as a counterbalance for the body

The male Black Grouse has a complex tail that is used as a visual signal. The tail is spread and the white under-tail coverts puffed out, making the male visible to females watching from afar.

Lyre-shaped tail impresses females

FORM AND FUNCTION

Europe's birds show great variations in size and shape, and these variations can usually be related to diet and habitat. Tiny, lightweight birds have evolved to eat insects and minute seeds on the thinnest twigs of trees. Short-billed, short-legged finches hop on the ground to search for seeds. Round-bodied, short-billed, short-legged birds, such as the Quail, slip through short, dense vegetation; while rails, which creep through vegetation growing in water, have longer toes and longer bills. Herons have long legs, necks, and bills to catch fish in shallow water while other species swim or dive from the air.

Grey Heron: long, stabbing neck

Quail: short bill, short legs

There are usually 12 tail feathers in six symmetrical pairs. The tail as a whole can be tilted, twisted, and swayed to one side to aid balance on a perch, to help when braking, and to steer a bird in flight.

The tips of the tail feathers are often slightly ragged – the result of being dragged on the ground or knocked against perches or vegetation.

A Woodpigeon's tail is long and wide, but simple in shape. It has obvious physical functions, providing balance and offering a large surface area when spread in flight. The central feathers have little movement, but the others can be spread fanwise, each successive pair sliding beneath their neighbours. From above, the centre feathers are most obvious on the closed tail.

Small feathers on the rump conceal the preen gland and overlie the base of the upper tail coverts.

The upper tail coverts conceal the base of the tail feathers and add extra stiffness and support.

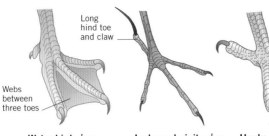

Long hind toe and claw

Reversed outer toe

Webs between three toes

Sharp talons

Water birds *have webbed feet that splay out on the backward stroke and close up on the forward stroke.*

Larks and pipits *that walk through short grass have long toes and a specially long hind claw.*

Hawks and falcons *have strong feet with a muscular grip and sharp, curved claws for killing their prey.*

Woodpeckers *have two toes forward, two back, to give a better grip around branches as they clamber on trees.*

Foot design *varies greatly between species. Birds like this Moorhen have multipurpose feet with long, simple toes for wading, walking on floating vegetation, and clinging to upright stems. The Coot walks less, but swims more, and has broadly lobed toes, like those of a grebe.*

Walking and perching

Most birds have three toes forward, one back, and a tendon behind the "ankle" that naturally tends to close their toes around a perch when they bend their legs. Owls, woodpeckers, and cuckoos have the outer toe turned backwards. Ringed Plovers have just three toes: the hind toe is tiny or absent on birds that walk or run on flat, open ground. Birds of prey use their feet for killing small prey and for holding food as they tear it with their bills. Others, such as Blue Tits, hold food with their feet as they peck it but others, such as Starlings, do not. Only a few, such as Bearded Tits, scratch the ground with their feet to expose food: most ground-feeders, such as Blackbirds, use their bills. While Cormorants are adapted for swimming and have all four toes joined by large webs, they are equally at home perching in trees.

Coming to land *at the nest, a Rough-legged Buzzard flaps its wings forwards, and swings its fanned tail downwards, using it as an airbrake.*

Senses

Birds live perpetually on their wits. They must find and catch food, locate and attract mates, and repel rivals while constantly being alert to danger. They must know where they are, and have a sense of time in order to know when to migrate and build their nests. Evolution has tailored the senses of each species to its environment, often to remarkable effect.

All-round vision
Panoramic, 360° vision lets a Snipe spot potential danger.

Vision

Most birds have reasonably good vision. Typically, their eyes are set wide apart on either side of the head, giving a broad angle of coverage to the front and sides to pick up approaching danger. There is usually only a small zone of "binocular vision" – the area the bird sees with both eyes. Seeing with both eyes allows birds (and people) to perceive depth and pinpoint the position of an object, so it is important for precision tasks, such as feeding. It becomes particularly important for birds that feed on moving prey, and these species tend to have eyes facing the front that allow for a wider area of binocular vision. These birds, including owls and some birds of prey, make up for their restricted view to the side by swivelling their heads to look behind them. Some birds of prey have truly exceptional eyesight; an eagle may see the

The visual world of a bird *is difficult for humans to imagine. This pigeon can see through an angle of over 300° and is also sensitive to wavelengths of light that are invisible to us. This ability helps it pick out seeds on the ground.*

movement of a hare three kilometres (two miles) away, while we may just pick it out at 100m (330ft); a buzzard can see a small grasshopper from a distance of 100m (330ft), while it disappears from our view at 30m (100ft). This acuity of vision comes from the design of the eye. The eye has two types of light-sensitive cells: rods, which pick up shape and movement, and cones, which detect colour and detail. Our eye has 200,000 rods, but a bird of prey may have 2 million rods, enabling it to resolve between three and four times more detail than we can.

Special sight

Specialized eye design equips some birds with "extra" visual senses: owls, for example, are richly endowed with rod receptors on the retina. This means they can see shape and movement with remarkable clarity in twilight (although they cannot see in pitch darkness). Birds such as Kestrels have yet another visual ability: they can detect the urine of their prey as a splash of ultra-violet "colour" – a wavelength of light invisible to most animals.

Falcons such as the Peregrine *have large eyes protected by wide supra-orbital ridges. The eyes are almost fixed, and a hunting Peregrine turns its head from side to side to scan for potential prey.*

ANGLES OF PERCEPTION

Woodcocks have large, bulging eyes set at the widest point of the head so they see behind as well as they do in front. This is valuable when they are at their most vulnerable, when probing for worms. A pigeon has a small blind spot immediately behind it, but its field of view is still very wide. An owl maximizes its area of binocular vision; combined with its sharp hearing, it is able to pinpoint its prey with great accuracy in poor light.

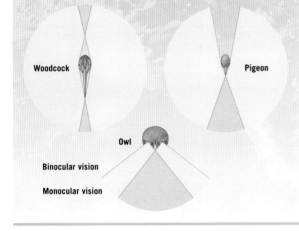

Woodcock

Pigeon

Owl

Binocular vision

Monocular vision

The sense of smell *is usually poorly developed in birds, but a few use it to great effect. Petrels and shearwaters, such as this Manx Shearwater, find their burrows in intense darkness partly by their distinctive smell. Some vultures also detect food by smell.*

The weakest sense: smell

A bird's nasal cavity has a rudimentary organ for detecting smell; indeed, most birds seem to have no sense of smell at all. The shearwaters and petrels are exceptions, having complex nasal passages and "tubular" nostrils at the base of the bill. A sense of smell undoubtedly aids them in locating fishy oils and other offal on the surface of the sea, guiding them to food, as well as helping those species that come to land only at night to locate their nests in the dark. It is also likely that the pressure of the air in these tubular openings helps shearwaters and albatrosses to make maximum use of air currents over the open sea, which they rely on in long-distance flight.

A delicate touch *allows some birds to find their food. The Green Woodpecker can extend its 10cm- (4in-) tongue into the network of tunnels of an ants' nest. Its sticky barbs withdraw ants, pupae, and eggs.*

Hearing

Birds constantly use calls to communicate with one another, and use their good hearing to detect approaching danger. Many species adapt their behaviour to make use of this sense: Woodpigeons, for example, are noisy in flight but they often glide momentarily, probably to listen for possible predators or other pigeons. Some birds also use their ears to detect their prey: Great Grey Owls hear (and catch) voles under deep snow.

Barn Owl skull

Large, high ear opening

Smaller, lower ear opening

A hunting Barn Owl *can fix the position of a sound to within 1° in total darkness. The ears are different sizes and set assymetrically on the head; this makes it easier to pinpoint the location of sound.*

17

Flight

FLIGHT REQUIRES LIFT, FORWARD PROPULSION, and delicate, precise control. Of the 50 muscles involved in moving a bird's wings, three are most important: one provides the downbeat, one adjusts the angle of the leading edge of the wing, and one helps (together with air pressure on the wing and a bird's own weight) to bring the wing back up. The wing can be warped, angled, withdrawn, or extended at will.

Maximum attack
Spread wings and tail give maximum control for landing at the nest.

Taking off

For most birds, getting airborne is the most demanding part of flight. To gain lift, birds must force the wing surface against the air using their muscles, or create a movement of air over the wing by forward motion. Some, such as the Fulmar, simply face into the wind or leap from a cliff ledge and sail away into the breeze. But when taking off in still air or from a level surface, a bird must generate its own lift by springing upwards with its legs and using strong downbeats of its wings. This is no problem for small, lightweight species, which take off from the ground or fly from twig to twig hundreds of times each day. Larger birds, such as the Mute Swan or Great Bustard, however, find it exhausting.

Combining a spring *upwards and forwards with deep strokes of its wings, this Herring Gull takes to the air from a ledge.*

Flight structures

Each of a bird's flight feathers is like a miniature aircraft wing. The feather is assymetrical; its thick shaft is displaced towards the front and its broader vane is at the back, which creates an aerofoil shape. Numerous smaller, contour feathers smooth the body shape to reduce drag and increase the efficiency with which the bird slips through air.

A bird's rigid backbone and ribcage keep its body extended in flight. The main muscles are streamlined and conical in shape, which keeps their weight concentrated near the bird's centre of gravity.

Wing shape varies greatly between species (see right). Long, narrow wings, such as those of swifts and shearwaters, aid prolonged gliding; while fingered wingtips reduce turbulence and improve stability. Gamebirds have short, round wings that beat rapidly, giving fast acceleration; however, they use energy so fast that flight is restricted to short bursts.

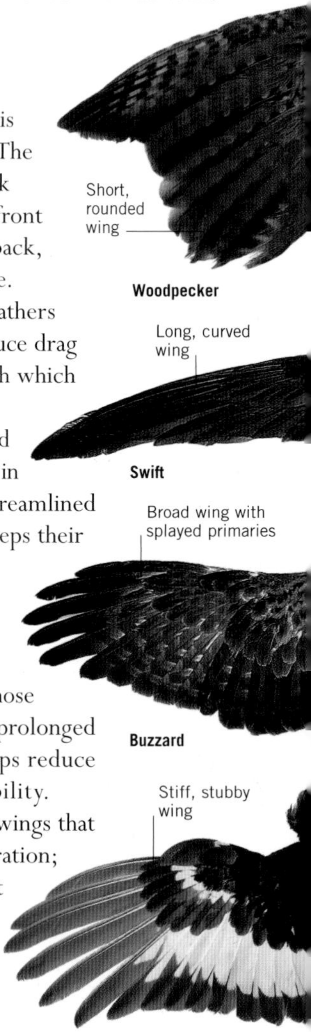

Short, rounded wing

Woodpecker

Long, curved wing

Swift

Broad wing with splayed primaries

Buzzard

Stiff, stubby wing

Black Grouse

Wing shapes *are tailored to flight patterns. The woodpecker's are ideal for manoeuvrability; the swift's for speed and endurance; the buzzard's for soaring; and those of the grouse for quick take-off from the ground.*

Wings raised

Leading wingtip
feathers curve up
and separate

Head slung low

The vulture is *a superb glider. Its wings raise in
a "V" above its heavy, low-slung body, so creating a
natural tendency to correct sideways tilt in the air.
The leading primary tips curve upwards while the
rear ones are pressed down, making a warped
surface that can be twisted for precise control.*

Gliding and flapping

A bird's wing is an aerofoil, which generates lift as it
moves forward. Its top surface is curved and longer than
the underside, so air passing over the top of the wing has
farther to go than air passing beneath the wing. The result
is that air above the wing is "thinned out" compared to the
air below; this creates a difference in pressure that pushes
the wing upwards.

Gliding birds have long, broad wings that generate
plenty of lift, but even so they lose height and must climb
again using wingbeats or soaring (see below). Most birds,
however, have shorter wings that allow only for brief
glides; they must flap their wings – and use much more
energy – to gain height and move forwards. Small birds
on migration take on extra fuel before departure, which
they store as fat. They can lose as much as 50 per cent of
their body weight during their arduous flights.

FEATHER DESIGN

Feathers are made of keratin, just like
human fingernails. A hollow central shaft gives
strength and rigidity. A thin outer web and
a broader inner web extend out on either side
to make up the vane. This consists of a series
of long barbs, "zipped" together by complex
hooks and barbules. Down
feathers close to the body
lack these barbules, and
so have a looser texture.

Shaft

Outer web (cutting
or leading edge)

Inner web (trailing edge)

Barbs and barbules become
unhooked at the tips

Shaft

Soaring birds, *such as these White
Storks (left), use rising air to gain
height without effort (below).
Rising air is found in thermals
over hot cliffs and towns, or where
natural obstacles, such as hills,
force prevailing winds upwards.*

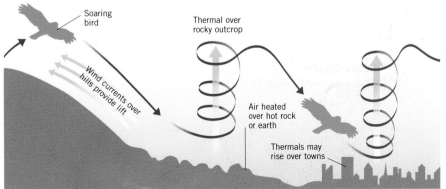

Soaring
bird

Wind currents over
hills provide lift

Thermal over
rocky outcrop

Air heated
over hot rock
or earth

Thermals may
rise over towns

Migration

THE TWICE YEARLY MIGRATION of birds is among the wonders of the natural world. The Swift, for example, can cover more than 800km (500 miles) a day when it undertakes its autumn flight; and it does so without making calculations or conscious judgements of weather conditions. The physiological and behavioural mechanisms underlying bird migration are increasingly well understood; nevertheless the journeys of some species remain magically impressive.

Cuckoo
Juvenile cuckoos migrate to Africa alone; they get no help at all from their unknown parents.

The advantages of migration

Migration describes a regular, seasonal movement from one region to another, and back again. The migration of some bird species are long distance journeys of hundreds or even thousands of kilometres.

Many birds fly long distances between their winter quarters in temperate or tropical areas and their breeding areas in the north. The benefits of migration are clear: birds can exploit the temporarily plentiful food supplies that develop in the long days of the northern summer; they avoid competition from species left behind in "winter" areas; and they reduce mortality from predation

White storks *(above) move south in huge, spectacular flocks of tens of thousands of birds. In some species, not all birds in a population make migratory flights; some Goldcrests (right, above) remain in the UK throughout winter, while others make exhausting flights south and west within Europe. Willow Warblers (right, below) always move south to Africa. Although they face great stress on migration, they survive well in warmer winters.*

Goldcrest

Willow Warbler

SEASONS AND SEASONALITY

Seasons arise because the Earth is tilted on its axis through an angle of 23.5°. In summer, the Earth's inclination tips the North Pole towards the Sun, producing 24-hour daylight; in winter, the Pole is tipped away from the Sun and remains in constant darkness. These effects are most extreme at the poles but at higher latitudes they are apparent as the seasons. At the equator, the effects are barely noticeable, and there are no seasons.

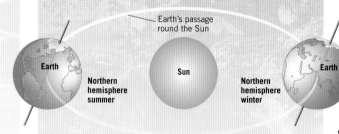

Earth's passage round the Sun

Earth

Northern hemisphere summer

Sun

Earth

Northern hemisphere winter

The Earth circles *the sun once each year and spins around its own axis every 24 hours. The tilted axis relative to the Sun produces the changing seasons, so marked in Europe.*

(because they are exposed to a particular predator for only part of the annual cycle).

Migration is triggered by a mixture of factors, of which day length is perhaps most important. Changes in day length cause shifts in a bird's hormonal balance; the bird eats more, lays down fatty energy reserves, and becomes increasingly restless. Once prepared for migration, favourable weather conditions signal the time for departure.

SELECTED MIGRATION ROUTES

Honey Buzzard

Greenland
Wheatear

House Martins *are part of the
broad and massive front of passerine
migration from Africa to Europe
that takes place in April. In summer,
they are seen in all parts of Europe
except Iceland. They all return to
Africa in the autumn.*

Greenland Wheatears *migrate through
western Europe in May but return direct
to Africa in autumn across the sea.*

Honey Buzzards *and many
other soaring birds cross
the Mediterranean at
the narrowest points, to
avoid long sea crossings.*

House Martin

Seasons and patterns

In general, songbirds migrate at night, pausing to feed and
rest in the day, while larger birds fly by day. Some species
follow the north-south advance and retreat of isotherms –
lines of equal temperature – while others seemingly have
an in-built clock, arriving at their destination on almost
the same day every year.

Birds such as Wheatears, Chiffchaffs, and Sand Martins
move north through Europe as early as March. Swallows,
House Martins, and Willow Warblers move two or three
weeks later, reaching northwest Europe in early April.
Later migrants include Swifts, which reach the UK in
early May, and Spotted Flycatchers, which still move
north as late as June. Waders, such as Dunlins, Knots,
and Bar-tailed Godwits, and wildfowl such as Brent Geese
that breed in the Arctic, delay their northward journey
until the tundra ice melts in May and June. By late July
they are forced back south again.

The migration route taken is consistent within
a species, but there are no general rules within
families; warblers, for example, have many migrant
species as well as many species that remain in Africa.

UNWITTING MIGRANTS

Long-distance migration flights are challenging. Birds must
be physically fit, laden with fat as "fuel", and ready to take
advantage of favourable winds and clear weather. Sometimes,
they fly away in good conditions, but encounter wind, rain,
or fog on their journey, and become disoriented or simply
blown off course. North American birds
migrating south across the west Atlantic
and Gulf of Mexico occasionally get caught
in the weather systems sweeping across
the Atlantic, and turn up as rarities in
Western Europe.

Northern
Parula

Hoopoe

Hoopoes moving north *to
France sometimes "overshoot"
and turn up in small numbers
in the UK. Northern Parulas
are rare strays from North
America in October gales.*

21

Feeding

BIRDS DISPLAY A HUGE RANGE of feeding adaptations. Specializations of anatomy and behaviour allow some species to take fast-flying insects on the wing, while others catch fish at depths of up to 100m (330ft) in the oceans. Some types of food, however, are little used by birds, especially tough vegetable matter that requires prolonged digestion by bulky organs.

Easy pickings
Seabirds exploit waste fish cast aside by trawlers.

The digestive system

To fuel its high-energy lifestyle, a bird must eat well and often – it simply cannot afford to feed on bulky, low-nutrition foods. For this reason, there are few birds that graze on plant leaves and shoots. Birds also have another restriction on their diet – they need to be as light as possible and their weight must be concentrated at the centre of gravity; consequently, in place of heavy teeth and jaws, birds have a food-grinding organ – the gizzard – within the body.

A bird's jaws extend to the bill with its horny sheaths. A fleshy extension of the oesophagus – the crop – can store large amounts of food temporarily, allowing the bird to gorge quickly.

From here, food is passed to the muscular gizzard, which contains grit swallowed by the bird; contraction of the gizzard grinds up food and separates indigestible items, such as fur, feathers, and bones, which are ejected through the mouth in neatly packaged pellets.

The intestines are firmly anchored in place to minimize internal movements in flight. They are longer in herbivorous and fish-eating birds, shorter in birds with a more easily digested diet, such as fruit eaters and carnivorous species. They empty through the cloaca – a common opening for waste and the genital ducts.

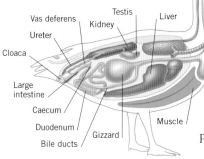

A bird's *digestive system differs markedly from that of mammals. The intestines are less clearly differentiated into distict segments, but they carry out the same role of breaking down food into smaller molecules that can be absorbed into the blood.*

Vas deferens
Testis
Kidney
Liver
Ureter
Cloaca
Large intestine
Caecum
Duodenum
Bile ducts
Gizzard
Muscle
Tongue
Syrinx
Oesophagus
Crop

Both Swallows (left) *and Peregrines (above) catch food in the air. Swallows snatch insects in their mouths and swallow them aloft, while Peregrines catch large prey with their feet and must descend to eat.*

Small waders, *such as this Green Sandpiper, reach invertebrate prey by wading and use their fine bills to pick food from the surface or just below.*

Feeding strategies

Small birds need to feed most frequently: in winter, they must eat almost constantly by day to survive the long, cold nights. Large birds of prey, however, gorge themselves and then fast for several days; similarly, the larger gulls may eat irregularly and then spend many hours inactive. Only a few large vegetarians, such as geese, are able to eat grass in large enough amounts to compensate for its low nutritional content.

Some birds, most notably crows and large gulls, are omnivorous, eating almost anything they can find, from insects and earthworms to dead animals, fruits, and all kinds of rubbish. Others are highly dependent on a narrow diet: Gannets eat only fish, pigeons depend on grain, swallows catch flying insects, Crossbills eat conifer seeds. They are unable to substitute alternatives. Between these generalists and specialists, most species have a mixed diet, although they may be restricted to particular habitats by virtue of their size and shape. Snipe, for example, probe with their long, sensitive bills in soft mud for worms: in dry weather or frost, they are entirely unable to feed. Spoonbills sweep their broad-tipped bills through shallow water to find invertebrates; they cannot feed on dry land.

Some species change diet with the seasons. Blackcaps are insectivorous in summer, but eat berries in autumn; Brent Geese eat eel-grass on estuaries until it is all used up, then move on to fields of grass or wheat in mid winter. Jays eat acorns in autumn and store hundreds of them for later use, even feeding their chicks on sprouting seedlings in spring. Magpies are largely insectivorous, but turn to eggs and nestlings for a time in spring.

SKULLS AND BEAKS

With front limbs completely adapted for flight, most birds – with the exception of birds of prey and parrots – catch and hold their food with their beaks alone. The shape and size of the beak or bill is closely tailored to the type of food eaten. Geese (right), for example, have broad bills for tearing and eating large quantities of grass.

Eye socket

Upper mandible

Upswept bill

Forward-facing eyes

Avocet *The upcurved bill allows a sideways sweep through shallow water, parallel with the surface.*

Hooked tip

Powerful jaws

Capercaillie *The hooked bill tip is excellent for grasping tough conifer leaves from trees and crushing seeds.*

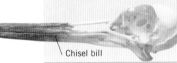

Seed cracking bill

Strong jaws

Finch *The deep, broad bill with sharp cutting edges is good for de-husking seeds; the strong palette crushes them.*

Chisel bill

Oystercatcher *The stout bill is flattened into a blade and is neatly inserted between the valves of a shellfish.*

Delicate tip

Pigeon *This bird's narrow bill tip and forward-facing eyes are ideal for picking small seeds from the ground.*

Soft larvae *and small insects are picked from foliage by the fine bills of warblers, such as this Wood Warbler. Flying insects are snapped up by flycatchers.*

Finches and buntings, *such as this Snow Bunting, as well as larks, gamebirds, and others, eat seeds and manipulate them with their bills and tongues to remove inedible husks.*

The bills of *some seed eaters have special functions. This Linnet's small bill can take small seeds from the ground or plants, but the longer, finer bill of the Goldfinch is more specialized for the latter.*

Courtship

MOST BIRDS KEEP THEIR DISTANCE from one other, even within a flock. To reproduce, they must temporarily break down these barriers and, in most species, work as a team for several weeks to rear their young. To do so, they perform ritualized courtship displays. Males show how fit they are for fatherhood, females select the best mates, and lasting pair bonds are constantly reinforced.

Frequent song
Male Song Thrushes sing to advertize their presence.

Song and display

For most of their lives, small birds are constantly alert to predators and deliberately keep a low profile. This all changes when they need to establish or defend a territory and attract a mate. At these times, the males make themselves more obvious to females by showing off their plumage patterns and singing loud and long – day after day. This showy behaviour is risky, but it carries a valuable prize – that of successful reproduction.

The purpose of courtship displays is to give the birds (usually the female) the chance to select the "fittest" mate, and, by ritualizing the encounter, to reduce the natural animosity between the male and the female. Pair formation is usually closely linked with territorial behaviour. Most male songbirds, as well as most birds of prey, waders, and wildfowl, set up and defend territories – areas over which they have exclusive claim – and many of the signals used to ward off rivals are the same as those used to attract mates. A male Mallard will make preening movements that show off a brightly coloured patch on the wings both when quarrelling and when courting. Territorial and courtship displays are similarly combined in the song flight of a Greenshank, the drumming of Snipe, and the tumbling display flights of Lapwings.

The showiest displays usually take place amongst species that do not form lasting pairs. Male Black Grouse and Ruffs, for example, perform noisy mock battles in a traditional display arena, while females look on.

Goldeneyes perform *complex, repetitive displays. Several males gather around a female and show off their plumage, throwing their heads back, splashing the water with their feet, and calling. The female shows readiness for mating with a low, sleek soliciting posture.*

PAIRED FOR LIFE?

The relationships between male and female birds are highly variable. Some species pair for a single season only; others pair consistently in successive years, but almost as a by-product of returning to the same nest site; others still have a lasting relationship with more than one mate. A few species, such as Mute Swans, maintain genuine life-long partnerships.

Dunnocks *have unusual pairing habits: there can be normal breeding pairs, bigamous males with two or more hens, and even two males attending one female.*

Dunnocks

Mute Swans *pair for life, with only rare cases of "divorce". If one partner dies, the survivor finds a new mate. Courtship displays reinforce the bond.*

Mute Swans

Sexual selection

A female bird judges a potential mate by a variety of parameters – quality of song and display ritual, size, and colour. In general, older males are favoured because they have already proved that they can find food efficiently enough to survive. Once a pair has formed, the male jealously guards his mate to ensure that he alone will fertilize her eggs; a male pigeon, for example, follows his mate so closely that he almost trips over her tail, and if she flies off, he follows wingtip-to-wingtip. In many species, however, both male and female will attempt to mate with other suitable individuals while their "partner's" back is turned.

Gannets perform highly stylized displays that communicate detailed information. This bill scissoring is a greeting ceremony, while a single bird stretching its bill skywards indicates its intention to leave the nest.

PLUMAGE DIFFERENCES

In species with long-lasting pair bonds, such as Mute Swans, males and females are hard to distinguish. But in the ducks, where there is frantic competition for mates, the sexes look very different. There are no set rules for plumage differences, even within families: the Blackbird shows differences between male and females, while the related Song Thrush has none. In birds like Dotterels and Red-necked Phalaropes, the usual courtship behaviours and plumage differences are reversed, with dull males and brightly coloured females.

Dotterel males *are dull in colour. The male incubates the eggs, which the female ignores after she has laid a full clutch.*

Male

Dotterel females *are brightly coloured and take the initiative in courtship, but have little or nothing to do with their chicks.*

Female

Mallard males *are bright in winter, when they form pairs, but become dull in summer when they moult and are unable to fly.*

Male

Mallard females *are dull brown and inconspicuous all year: they are chased relentlessly by males in late winter.*

Female

Male Black Grouse face up to each other at dawn. Each spring, all the males in one area collect together for sham battles. They call loudly, spread their tails and under-tail coverts and leap into the air. This attracts females, which select the "best" male to mate with.

Nesting

A BIRD'S NEST IS NOT A "HOME", but simply a temporary container for its eggs. Some birds make no nest at all, or at best scrape a shallow hollow in sand or soil. Many nests, however, have a longer life, as the young birds remain in them until they can fly. Few are used a second time in one season, but larger, more durable nests, such as those of crows or eagles, are re-used over many years.

Gathering materials
Nests beside water risk flooding, so Coots build high nests of plant stems.

Materials and construction

Nests come in all shapes and sizes. Some are extremely elaborate and can take take two or three weeks to make. Reed Warblers, for example, weave neat baskets around several upright reed stems; these nests are sufficiently elastic to survive the highest winds and deep enough to prevent eggs from rolling out. Long-tailed Tits' nests are made of thousands of feathers, bits of lichen, moss, and other vegetation, and spiders' webs, and will actually stretch to accommodate the rapidly-growing brood.

Larger species, such as Ravens, Grey Herons, and Ospreys, build nests of thick sticks, lined with finer stems, grass, and mud. Rooks are quick to steal sticks from neighbouring nests if they are left unattended. Such bulky nests may last for years and are are strikingly obvious, especially in winter when trees lose their leaves.

Ground nests are simple scrapes edged with pebbles. The birds add pebbles and grass stems with exaggerated head movements – part of a ritual that reinforces their attachment to the site.

Song Thrushes construct *neat cup nests lined with dried mud and dung; other thrushes line the mud layer with fine grasses. Growing chicks leave the nest before they can fly.*

Redstarts nest *inside tree holes or boxes; their protected nests are loose and poorly structured (above). Reed Warblers build their nests on reed "stilts" (right).*

Eggs and egg-laying

Producing eggs is an energy intensive business. A female tit needs to increase her food intake by about 40 per cent, and the male may feed her extra rations during this period. Eggs are usually laid early in the day. Their colours are deposited on to the shell in the female's oviduct and they are usually, but not always, constant within a species. Guillemot's eggs, for example, vary greatly in colour, perhaps to help the birds identify their own eggs on a crowded ledge; other species, such as Red-backed Shrikes, have two or three colour variants. The function of colour is to camouflage the eggs – especially important in ground-nesting birds.

Most birds lay one egg a day, and wait until the last or penultimate egg is laid before they start to incubate, with the result that all the eggs hatch together. Others, such as owls, start to incubate from the very first, so their eggs hatch in sequence. Nest parasites, such as the Cuckoo, have remarkably short incubation periods, so their eggs hatch before the eggs of the host species, which the Cuckoo chick ejects from the nest.

Little Owl　　**Ringed Plover**　　**Blue Tit**　　**Guillemot**

Egg sizes and patterns *are highly variable. Little Owl eggs are typical of hole-nesters – white for visibility, round to fit neatly inside. Ringed Plovers lay eggs with sharp points; these point inwards to fit under the incubating bird. Blue Tits' eggs are typical of songbirds, while Guillemots lay eggs shaped to fit under one wing on a narrow ledge.*

Nest sites

In most cases, it is the female bird that selects the nest site and carries out the building work. Nests are usually hidden to help reduce predation. Wrens nest under overhangs in banks or above streams and Robins build their nests in low vegetation in banksides or hollows within thickets. Merlins nest in deep heather, usually choosing a slope so that they can see at least part of their surroundings. Seabirds come to land only to nest, and they are often very vulnerable to predators because they are slow and cumbersome walkers. For this reason, they nest on sheer cliffs or deep inside burrows, which they visit only at night. Grebes build semi-floating nests, anchored to vegetation or floating weed. They cover their eggs with damp weed when they are off the nest, not relying on camouflaged eggs.

Seabird colonies *may be huge and spectacular, with overwhelming movement, sound, and smell. Kittiwakes choose tiny, isolated ledges, building a small nest of seaweed and grass, while Guillemots choose longer, bare ledges and jostle shoulder to shoulder.*

Ringed Plover *chicks hatch covered with down and ready to feed themselves. The eggs need to be large to accommodate such big chicks. Their speckled pattern gives excellent camouflage.*

Sand Martins *have tiny, weak legs and are practically unable to walk. They need safe nests hidden away deep inside tunnels. They dig these into firm sand or soft sandstone cliffs.*

Grey Herons *nest early in the year, before leaves are on the trees, and their stick nests are eyecatching: camouflage for these big birds is not an option. Even their eggs are strikingly pale blue; an adult Grey Heron remains at the nest at all times to protect eggs and chicks from possible predators.*

Rearing

THE ESSENTIAL GOAL FOR ANY BIRD IS to reproduce – to pass on its genes to future generations – and much everyday bird behaviour is concerned with competition for mates, nest sites, and providing for the young. Birds exhibit a wide range of nesting strategies that let them exploit the best available foods, at the right times of year, to rear the largest number of viable offspring.

Brood parasites
Cuckoos lay eggs in other birds' nests and leave care to the "foster" parents.

How many eggs?

Each set of eggs incubated together in one nest is a clutch, and the chicks that hatch from one clutch are called a brood. Some birds have one clutch each year (single brooded), while others have two or more. Species that feed their chicks on a special food that is only briefly abundant, tend to produce just one large brood; Blue Tit chicks, for example, are fed on a springtime "burst" of nutritious caterpillars. If food is available in smaller quantities all summer long, producing several smaller broods is a better strategy; Blackbirds, for example, have three or four a year. Some owls lay large clutches, but only when food is abundant (when there is a "plague" of voles, for example) do they rear all their young; if food is short, only the bigger chicks survive.

Feeding the young

Songbirds hatch blind, naked, and helpless, and must be fed large amounts of high-protein food to achieve phenomenal rates of growth. Tits, for example, supply their chicks with thousands of caterpillars each day. Finding food is often the main responsibility of the male, and for birds like the male harrier, which feeds several families at once, it is a busy time. Most species continue to feed the young for a few days after they have left the nest. Some divide broods in two, half with each parent; others leave this work to the male while the female lays a new clutch.

Red-legged Partridges *(top) have short lives. They rear 12–15 chicks at a time, and start breeding at just one year old. Fulmars (above), in contrast, live for 30 years and rear one chick a year, which breeds when seven years old.*

Timing of the *breeding season and clutch size are critically important for survival of the next generation. Birds employ a variety of breeding strategies.*

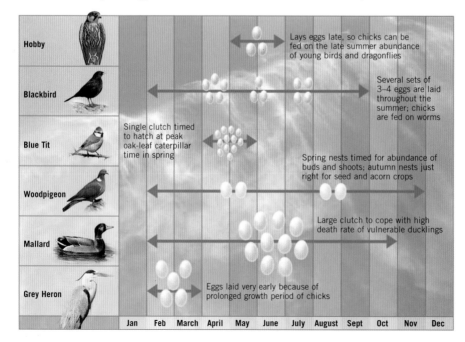

Hobby		Lays eggs late, so chicks can be fed on the late summer abundance of young birds and dragonflies
Blackbird		Several sets of 3–4 eggs are laid throughout the summer; chicks are fed on worms
Blue Tit	Single clutch timed to hatch at peak oak-leaf caterpillar time in spring	
Woodpigeon		Spring nests timed for abundance of buds and shoots; autumn nests just right for seed and acorn crops
Mallard		Large clutch to cope with high death rate of vulnerable ducklings
Grey Heron	Eggs laid very early because of prolonged growth period of chicks	

| Jan | Feb | March | April | May | June | July | August | Sept | Oct | Nov | Dec |

Parent birds find food and instinctively take it to the nest, but they need a strong stimulus to release the food into the mouths of their chicks. The baby birds beg with high-pitched calls and brightly coloured, wide open mouths to trigger release from the parent. Some nestlings have coloured spots inside their mouths to increase the effect.

FENDING FOR THEMSELVES

Blackbird chicks grow rapidly and become very large within two to three weeks of hatching. Their large size makes them highly vulnerable in the small nest, so the chicks leave the nest a few days before they can fly. They take cover on the ground, where they are still fed by their parents – a strategy that increases their chances of survival. Chicks of waders, such as Lapwings, and ducklings hatch wide-eyed and covered in down, and leave the nest within hours. They feed themselves from the start, but are brooded by the parent in cold or wet weather. But Puffin and shearwater chicks leave the nest alone at night, head out to sea, and never see their parents again.

Blackbird fledgling

Survival and recruitment

Each pair of birds only needs to successfully rear two offspring in its lifetime to keep overall numbers stable. Different species employ different strategies in this "numbers game". Slow breeders have just one or two chicks each year over a long lifetime. They invest plenty of time in rearing the young, which tend to remain in the nest for longer. Fast breeders, in contrast, rear large families, with a huge surplus of young. Parental care is less intensive and, in most years, the majority of the offspring will die. The fast breeders are better at colonizing new habitats, because they are able to make rapid use of new resources, whereas species that are slow breeders tend to fare better in habitats where conditions are more stable.

Young Rooks *hatch over several days. The first and largest takes most of the food; the last is least likely to survive to adulthood.*

Getting started

Seeing birds at close range is rarely easy. Good fieldcraft will help you get the best possible view, and the right equipment will put you in the heart of the action, where you can observe and record the fascinating diversity of birds and their behaviour.

Observing with binoculars

An ESSENTIAL PIECE of birdwatching equipment is a good binocular. Top makes can be expensive, but a moderately-priced pair, chosen, used, and maintained with care, will give excellent results. Binoculars don't allow you to see any farther, they just magnify what is already visible, but magnification is not the only factor to bear in mind. Image brightness, build quality, and ease of use are important too, so try out a few pairs before parting with your money.

Comfort zones
Buy binoculars that fit your hands well: these are too large.

EQUIPMENT GUIDE

The best binoculars have lenses made from low-dispersion glass that maintains colour accuracy. Lenses are coated to minimize reflections from the surface and keep the image bright: any good make will be up-to-date with modern technology, but basically you get what you pay for.

Individual eyepiece adjustment

Objective lens

Folding pocket binoculars

Small diameter lenses

Compact models *may fold down to fit into a shirt pocket. Although highly portable, the small objective lens limits the brightness of the image. These are useful as a "second pair" rather than your mainstay.*

Eyepiece

Focus wheel

Rubber armour

Porro prism binoculars *have a simple construction, and are best value for those on a budget. They may be encased in rubber for better grip and reinforcement against knocks. The wide shape gives an excellent 3D image.*

Focus wheel

Solid, sturdy build

Roof prism binoculars *are light and compact and often waterproof and gas-filled. The objective lens is almost in line with the eyepiece. They must be well-engineered, so avoid cheaper models.*

Choosing binoculars

Binoculars come in many shapes and sizes, but their key specifications are given by a pair of numbers – 10x40, for example. The first figure is the magnification, indicating how many times larger an object will appear when viewed. The second is the diameter of the objective lens; the larger this is, the brighter the image will seem. Ranges of 7x35 to 10x50 are ideal.

Do not be tempted by higher magnifications, which have a narrow field of view and are hard to hold steady. Pay attention to comfort – the binoculars should fit well in your hands and be light enough to carry. You may have them around your neck for hours.

Consider how well the eyepiece fits the shape of your face. You may prefer a harder eyepiece that sits tight against your eye socket (reducing shake) or a softer one for comfort; either way, it should not let in too much light from the side. The focus wheel is used constantly when birdwatching: you should be able to turn it effortlessly with a fingertip, without having to move your whole hand. Large binoculars may make this difficult for small hands, so always try before you buy.

Naked eye view   **8x magnification**   **15x magnification**

Binoculars simply magnify *the light that you see with the naked eye and do not enhance the image on a dull or misty day, although a large objective lens may seem to give a slightly brighter image than the naked eye at dusk. Too high a magnification, above 10, means a tiny field of view and too much distortion and shake.*

Using binoculars

Before using binoculars, you'll need to make some simple adjustments. All binoculars have a single eyepiece adjustment, used to compensate for differences between your eyes. This needs a one-off setting, to be remembered and used without further alteration. First, use the central

Before adjustment

wheel to focus on a distant object with a hard edge. Now cover the right lens with your hand and focus sharply on the object, with your left eye relaxed. Now cover the left lens and focus the right eye using only the individual (right) eyepiece setting. Both eyes will now be balanced. Note the setting and check it occasionally to ensure it has not moved. From now on, you will use only the main focus wheel to focus on different distances.

After adjustment

Movable bridge

The distance between *the eyepieces can be set to match the gap between your eyes. Just widen or squeeze the two halves of the body until you get a single, sharp image. You will always see a single circle, never the figure-of-eight you so often see in films.*

The smallest jolt *is magnified by binoculars. Leaning them against a solid object is the simple solution; a thumb against your chin helps. Gyroscopically-stabilized binoculars are available at a high price.*

MAKING A SPECTACLE

Spectacle-wearers using binoculars without their glasses often find that image quality is poor. However, using binoculars while wearing prescription glasses presents its own difficulties because the eye is too far from the eyepiece, and light can enter from the side. A raised finger or thumb helps block out this stray light, but the edges of the image may still appear blurred or dark. To avoid this problem, buy binoculars with eyepieces that are adjustable for spectacle wearers. You can "snap" the eyepiece down, almost level with the lens, which allows the eye to be much closer to the lens, so widening the field of view.

Normal eyesight   **Corrected for spectacles**

Fieldcraft with binoculars

The first sign of a bird's presence is likely to be its call, or the gentle movement of leaves. Get its general bearings first by using your ears, then, facing the area, try to see the bird. Keep your head and body still and swing the binoculars up to your eyes, always keeping the bird fixed in view; don't look down at your binoculars while lifting them up and then swing them around trying to find what you are looking for. Wedge a finger against your forehead, or your thumb against your chin, for extra stability.

Binocular cases are best left at home or on the back seat of the car. Outside, carry your binoculars on a strap around your neck to keep them ready for action at all times; a rain cover for the eyepiece lenses is useful. Clean the eyepieces often – eyelashes leave greasy smudges that blur the image.

When you are having lunch or a drink, get into the habit of swinging your binoculars to one side: there is nothing worse than an eyepiece full of biscuit crumbs or spilt coffee.

EXPERT TIP

■ On a cold day in a warm car, or when leaving a cool room to go out into hot, humid conditions, get your binoculars out of their case a few minutes before you need them. This reduces the likelihood that they will steam up at the exact moment when you might need them ready for action.

Scopes and tripods

WHILE GOOD BINOCULARS ARE an essential piece of kit for the birdwatcher, telescopes are an optional extra. They are a real boon when observing at long range over lakes and estuaries, and provide stunning close-up detail of birds in more closed environments. However, they have significant drawbacks. They are expensive, and they need to be used on a stable platform – usually a tripod – that adds awkward baggage to a day out.

Fixed focus
A good scope on a tripod will enhance enjoyment of birds.

Choosing a telescope

With optical equipment, price is usually a good indicator of quality. Top of the range telescopes can cost more than a family holiday, so it is vital to try before you buy. Field testing is best, because you cannot assess equipment in the confines of a shop; visit a birdwatching fair, where many manufacturers will have their equipment set up in "real life" conditions, and talk to other enthusiasts about their experiences.

Line up *your scope by looking along its casing (left), then bring your eye to the eyepiece and focus on the bird (below).*

These binoculars *can be converted economically into a short scope by the addition of an optional eyepiece.*

Scopes provide a magnification of about 30x or more. Some have a fixed focal length, but it is worth considering models fitted with "zoom" lenses, which provide more flexibility. In the past, a long focal length was achieved through long physical length, and telescopes had to be made of several extendable sections for portability. Such designs are still available today, but many modern scopes use internal prisms to reduce length; some are very compact indeed. As with binoculars (see pages 32–33), the brightness of the image depends, in part, on the diameter of the lens, so you will have to balance light intake with bulk. Special lenses, designated fluorite or ED, increase image brightness, but add to weight and cost.

Eyepiece attachment

Tripod

Tilt control

Scopes may be fitted with straight or angled eyepieces; the former are easier and more intuitive to "aim" at a distant bird. Angled scopes offer other advantages: they are far more comfortable to use when mounted on a tripod, especially when keeping low to the ground; and a view of a bird is easier to share between people of different heights.

EXPERT TIP

■ Fast responses will help you spot elusive or quick birds, so get familiar with the action of the focus wheel on your scope. A simple mnemonic like "up close, down there" will help you remember that the wheel rolls "upwards" to focus on nearby objects and "downwards" to focus on distant objects.

Using your scope

The extremely long focal length of a telescope means that every tiny shake and judder of the hand is magnified and the image wobbles unacceptably. Hand-holding a scope is impractical, and some kind of support is essential: most people favour a sturdy tripod, but clamps and beanbags are more portable alternatives. A screw bush on the barrel of the scope allows for secure attachment to a tripod, and most tripods can be fitted with a strap, allowing you to carry the whole, rather cumbersome, ensemble over your shoulder.

Always keep your eye directly in line with the eyepiece; if it is off-centre, the image you see will be vignetted or in soft focus. (This is harder than it sounds, especially if using a straight scope fixed to a tripod.) Also, try viewing through your scope keeping both eyes open; this will ease eye strain and you will be aware of other birds as they enter your peripheral field of vision.

Keeping the scope *steady is essential. Look for sturdy supports, such as walls and branches, when out in the field. A beanbag will mould to the barrel of the scope, cushioning it and preventing abrasion.*

Clamps that *screw into a scope's tripod bush are highly portable. They are particularly useful in a cramped hide, where they can be fixed to the viewing slot. Special window clamps can be fixed to a car window.*

A good tripod *will provide stability in any situation. Choose one with a combined control for the pan/tilt head — it is faster to use. Teamed with an angled scope, it can easily be used when seated.*

EQUIPMENT GUIDE

A compact scope with an angled eyepiece is favoured by most birdwatchers because it allows for great flexibility in viewing position, is relatively light in weight, and usually comes with great optics. It does, however, take time to get used to not looking straight at the bird.

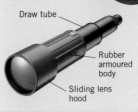

Focus wheel

Body can swivel inside fixed ring for awkward angles

Tripod bush

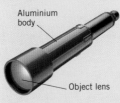

Draw tube

Rubber armoured body

Sliding lens hood

Straight scopes *with telescoping tubes are long and require more practice for quick use in the field. The focus is adjusted with the movable draw tube; a smaller, end tube adjusts the magnification.*

Aluminium body

Object lens

A simple scope *with a fixed focal length provides an inexpensive entry into long-distance birdwatching. Some models are very small, even collapsing down to fit into a pocket.*

Rubber eyecup

Focus grip

Eyepieces *can be changed to add extra magnification, or to change from a fixed magnification to a zoom. The quality of the eyepiece affects the quality of the image; good ones are expensive.*

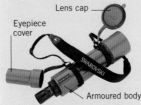

Lens cap

Eyepiece cover

Armoured body

Carrying straps *and lens caps attached to the body of the scope allow for quick use. A rubber-clad body and seals at the junctions of moving parts prevent the penetration of dust and water.*

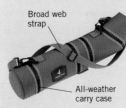

Broad web strap

All-weather carry case

A carrying case *provides protection but can be pricey. A cheaper alternative is to cover your scope with a plastic bag and carry it with the eyepiece tucked up under your coat.*

Photography

Bird photography is as much science as art. It calls for technical aptitude and excellent fieldcraft as well as an "eye" for a picture, but it can be immensely exciting and rewarding. For professional results, it calls for considerable investment in time and equipment, but good results can be achieved with a modest outlay, especially given the quality of digital cameras.

Close view
Long lenses are bulky and need to be fixed on a tripod.

EQUIPMENT GUIDE

A compact digital with interchangeable lenses allows the flexibility of a 35mm single lens reflex, but is much cheaper using a memory card and computer without the cost of film. A zoom lens, as good as you can afford, will get you close to your subject.

45–150mm lens

Autofocus technology *is available in even the simplest cameras, but you must investigate the capabilities of a camera/lens combination before you buy. Otherwise, you risk being disappointed if your kit can't lock on to and maintain focus on a flying bird.*

Camera body

Shutter release

Autofocus lens

Pan and tilt head

Telescopic legs

A tripod *is essential for preventing "camera shake" when using a long lens. Buy the heaviest and most sturdy that you can bear to carry.*

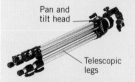

Gadget bag

Sturdy bags *protect valuable equipment in the rough and tumble out of doors. Rubberized canvas bags are hard wearing, but synthetic ones are lighter.*

Buying the kit

You can take excellent pictures of bird habitats and favourite sites with a compact "point and shoot" camera. Such cameras, with their all-purpose zoom lenses, take reasonable pictures of bird flocks and even close-up garden birds, but you need something much better to get the stunning, frame-filling shots of birds that you can see throughout this book.

Compact digital cameras with interchangeable lenses offer portability, affordability, quality, and economy. Buy a good lens with a focal length equivalent to a 300 or 500mm in traditional 35mm terms (a 45–90 zoom would be a good start but you will soon want a longer lens to get you up close). Get a good skylight/ultraviolet (UV) filter (for protecting the lens as well as clarity of image) and a "lens pen" for thorough cleaning.

Approaching birds

A typical lens with a 50mm focal length gives an angle of view of about 40° – roughly the same as that seen with a naked eye. Telephoto lenses used by bird photographers have a focal length equivalent of 300 or 500mm, or more, giving a much narrower angle of view, which effectively means a greater magnification. As well as magnifying the subject, they amplify every movement of the hand and need to be supported on a tripod and used with the fastest possible shutter speed to avoid camera "shake".

Armed with a good telephoto lens, you will still need to get within a few metres of a pigeon-

EXPERT TIP

■ Modern cameras automatically adjust exposure and focus, but you need to learn more about photographic techniques to get the best results. Read the camera booklet thoroughly and start to experiment with different shutter speeds, apertures, and other options.

Fix your camera *to a tripod and wait for birds to appear in front of you: a drinking pool in a wood or park is an ideal place.*

Birds will approach *a fixed hide quite boldly. Supporting the lens on a bean bag lets you react fast to new arrivals.*

Movable tent-like hides *can be positioned in just the right spot, concealing photographer and tripod.*

Window clamps *can transform your car into a mobile hide. Cold or damp weather may cause condensation problems.*

The garden *is a good place to practise your photographic skills. Keep still and wait for birds to approach a feeder.*

Stalking birds *takes practice and patience. You'll need to use a tripod in all but the brightest conditions.*

sized bird to get a frame-filling image. This will tax your field skills far more than everyday birdwatching. As you approach the bird, keep low and below the skyline, using whatever cover is available – bushes or hollows behind rising ground. Avoid sideways movement, which seems to disturb birds more than a direct approach, and move slowly, a step at a time, taking advantage of any moment that the bird may be looking away or busy preening. Camouflage clothing, of less value for normal birdwatching, may help in your photographic endeavours.

Exposure effects

A camera records an image when light, focused through the lens, falls onto a digital image sensor. Pictures are stored on a memory card and then downloaded onto a computer, where they can be adjusted using systems on the computer or bought with the camera, or via some independent

NIGHT PHOTOGRAPHY

Low light levels need not be a barrier to bird photography. It is possible to get good images of birds, such as owls and nightjars, using a portable flash gun. A more exotic (and expensive) alternative is to use an image intensifier. This device fits on to your camera lens via an adapter. It amplifies incoming light and displays the enhanced image on an internal screen. The camera records the image from the screen.

Camera with intensifier

Image intensifiers *produce monochrome images with a strong green cast. They are useful when recording behaviour of nocturnal birds.*

Setting the shutter speed *adjusts the amount of light reaching the image sensor. A fast speed "freezes" movement; a slow speed means that moving birds are blurred.*

Setting the aperture *changes the amount of light passing through the lens and affects the depth of field: a wide aperture give a shallow zone of sharp focus.*

Flash can be used *to light birds in deep shade, or to create more pleasing effects when used to "fill in" shadows in addition to natural light.*

software. The amount of light reaching the sensor must be carefully controlled to achieve the correct exposure; too much light (overexposure) results in pale, washed out pictures; too little light (underexposure) produces dark, muddy images. The camera allows you to control exposure by changing the diameter of the aperture through which light passes; and by changing the length of the exposure by adjusting the shutter speed. Various combinations of shutter speed and aperture can achieve the same correct exposure, but the resulting pictures will look very different. For example, setting shutter

speed at 1/1000 second and aperture to f5.6 will achieve the same exposure as settings of 1/60 at f22. Using a fast shutter speed, such as 1/1000 second, will "freeze" a moving bird, while at the slower shutter speed of 1/60 second, a moving bird may appear blurred, and the picture will probably suffer from camera shake, especially if a long telephoto lens is used.

Also, using a large aperture (with a smaller number, such as f2.8 or f5.6) gives a shallow depth of field. This may mean some of the bird is out of focus, but it could isolate an in-focus bird from an out-of-focus background. An aperture of f22 can keep the whole bird in focus but the background will be sharper, too, creating a more cluttered effect. You can experiment to get the best effects: either for the "perfect portrait" of the bird, or the most artistic or impressionistic picture.

Many people are content to set their camera to "automatic" and allow its onboard computer to sort out exposure and focus. In most situations this produces acceptable results, but understanding and exploiting the effects of different settings and options on your camera will help you make more creative images — and stand out from the crowd.

Stalking with *a long lens and a tripod is the simplest way to get good pictures of common birds.*

Cliff environments *provide easy pickings for the photographer. Cliff-nesting birds cluster together in high concentrations and are not easily scared off by approaching humans.*

Light and lighting

Most photographs of birds are taken in natural daylight, but the quality of the light can vary considerably. Diffuse sunlight filtered through thin cloud or patchy leaves is ideal for capturing a naturalistic portrait of a bird. Morning and evening light illuminates a bird from the side, adding interest (and a slight warmer colour cast) to your pictures, while overhead light in the middle of the day tends to be less flattering.

Direct sunlight produces dense shadows that can appear as ugly "black holes" in a photograph. A ring or a flashgun set to low power, or a disc of reflective foil around the lens, can help "fill in" these shadows to produce a more balanced image. Flash can also be used to "freeze" a bird in motion because the duration of the burst of light is as little as one ten-thousandth of a second. Be warned, however, that pictures taken with a flash can look horribly "artificial", because the light comes from a single, intense point source, creating unnatural highlights and deep shadows beyond.

Pan your camera *keeping the running or flying bird in the centre of the frame. The bird will be sharper, but the background will blur.*

Blur adds atmosphere *to an otherwise ordinary image. Use a slow shutter speed and allow the bird's movement to "paint" the film.*

Flash photography *freezes the fastest action and allows every feather to be seen pin sharp. It does, however, create unreal highlights in the bird's eye.*

Using a long lens *is not the only way to get close to the action. Position your camera near a nest or display site, take cover, and trigger the shutter remotely using a long cable release. This accessory is readily available from all good photographic suppliers.*

Shallow depth of field *created by using a wide aperture can isolate a bird against a fussy background by restricting the zone of sharp focus.*

Notes and sketches

A GOOD FIELD GUIDE is an indispensable companion, but try not to rely too heavily on its seductive images and pat descriptions of birds. Only by making your own notes and sketches will you learn about the infinite variety of form, plumage, and movement in the birds you see. Making notes is a discipline you should adopt because it forces you to really look at birds and fix their characteristics in your mind.

Portrait sitting
Sketching records detail in the Olive-backed Pipit.

Sketching and painting

Not everyone can be an accomplished artist. Creating beautiful images of birds is a rare skill, but aesthetic excellence is not the goal of a field sketch. Such a drawing aims to capture essential information about a bird; it is visual shorthand that only you need to be able to understand, and if it looks good too, consider it a bonus. Birds cannot be persuaded to pose, so you will need to work fast. Start by laying down the basic shape of the body, head, legs, wings and tail. Try to get the outline right: only then will the patterns of eyestripes, cheek patches, wingbars, and so on fit together in the right proportions.

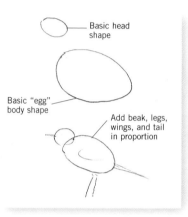

Basic head shape

Basic "egg" body shape

Add beak, legs, wings, and tail in proportion

❶ **Begin your sketch** *by recording the bird's general shape. Draw oval or egg shapes for the head and body. Pay close attention, keeping the elements in proportion.*

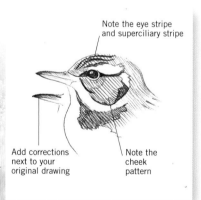

Note the eye stripe and superciliary stripe

Add corrections next to your original drawing

Note the cheek pattern

❺ **Look closely** *at the bird's head. Record the plumage and details of the bill. Concentrate on recording the relative size of each feature.*

Believe your eyes

Always draw what you see. If a bird appears podgy, then draw it as such, even if your field guide describes it as "slim". Start by drawing details that stand out most to you – try to remember the important features for the relevant group of birds. Be patient. Proficiency in drawing birds will come with practice; first, try sketching garden birds to learn about feather patterns, before sketching in the field.

Sketches can *record a bird's movements and flight patterns – characteristics lost in a photograph.*

Throat may puff in and out, changing the bird's profile

The tail swings up and down in typical bobbing movement

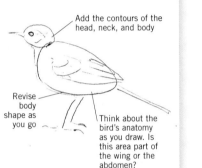

Add the contours of the head, neck, and body

Revise body shape as you go

Think about the bird's anatomy as you draw. Is this area part of the wing or the abdomen?

❷ **Start filling in** *details of the bird's "feather map". As you build up the sketch, you will almost certainly need to revise the bird's proportions.*

Keep building detail for as long as the bird is in view

Important or eyecatching features can be drawn first

❸ **Your sketch** *is now taking shape. Look more closely at the bird and try to pick out the different feather tracts. Make notes on plumage colour and posture.*

Note the shape and colour of the primaries, secondaries, and tertials

Add notes to your sketch

Rump and tail coverts may only be glimpsed: add details before you forget

❹ **If time allows,** *make separate sketches of different parts of the bird, such as the head and the proportions of the wing and tail. You can assemble them into one image later.*

Note tail details

What shape are the "spots"?

Use notes to correct errors on your sketch, such as "not so angular", for example

❻ **Make a separate sketch** *of the chest. It may appear "spotted", but what shape are the spots – oval, round, or diamond shaped? Do they run together into stripes?*

Does the stripe touch the bill or fall short?

Does the dark eyestripe underline the superciliary or cut through it?

Is the back heavily streaked or softly marked?

Have I drawn in the closed secondaries? (they are easily overlooked)

Do the spots on the chest merge into one another?

The final result

Back at home, *refer to your sketches to produce a final, colour image. Even now, keep asking yourself questions to achieve the most accurate depiction.*

What to record

Taking notes is a personal matter, with no set rules. The simplest record takes the form of a diary full of bird lists, numbers, notes and sketches, and observations about habitats and viewing conditions. Use a hardback book if you prefer, but most notes are now kept on a computer. Sketches can be pasted into the diary, or scanned and added in to the computer file: don't neglect a notebook in the field just because you use a laptop at home. Looking through old notebooks helps you relive the day and reminds you what to expect at particular places at certain times of year.

Reviewing your records from a paper-based system, however, does become time-consuming, especially after

Ringing studies *throw light on bird movements and lifespans. A metal ring with a unique number can only be read in the hand; coloured rings can be seen on more distant birds.*

FIELD NOTES

There is an established system of record keeping in the UK and most of Europe, with local "bird recorders" co-ordinating reports. The notes that you make of species, numbers, and places will help to build up the annual picture in each region. Before publication in a county bird report, rare birds are assessed by an expert committee, who will expect detailed notes and sketches as "evidence". In the case of extremely rare birds, these will go to a national rarities committee for assessment.

Field notebook

Bird diary

Transfer your field notes
to a bird diary (above) to keep clear records of your sightings. Data can also be uploaded to birdwatching websites (right).

you have been watching for a few years. Imagine, for example, trying to find how many times you have seen a Firecrest, or the earliest sighting of a Whitethroat in spring. A more organized system on your computer – even with a simple "word search" – allows you to find and arrange your records more easily.

Getting involved

The first simple step is to send records to your local recorder. Recorders form a national network, each having responsibilities for an area or region, maintaining a lasting, published record of the status and occurrences of wild birds. Many areas have local clubs and these mostly have good websites. On these, you can both learn what other people have seen and report your own sightings: these are then automatically sent on to the recorder. A great way to report birds wherever you are, even when on holiday abroad, is to use BirdTrack, a web-based system of recording birds that helps to monitor their status, range, and movements.

There are many surveys that welcome new participants, from general nation-wide breeding and wintering bird surveys to counts of estuary and wetland species. You can become involved in regular weekly or one-off annual counts of garden birds, too. The important thing is to make your most useful and interesting data and observations available to others, especially "official" local monitoring systems and organizers of the national surveys. This can give your own enjoyment more

Two skills are needed *when taking part in a bird census — identification and counting. It is easy enough to count a few starlings on a lawn, but estimating huge numbers of waders flying to a roost is considerably more challenging.*

BIRD SOUNDS

All field guides transcribe bird sounds into words, but the assorted *tiks*, *taks*, *chicks*, *chaks*, and *tchuks* tend to be of most use only after you have heard them. Nevertheless, the difference between a *tik* and a *tchuk* can be critically important in identification.
Prepare yourself by listening to bird songs and calls on CD, and try transcribing what you hear in the field.

shrr-ooo
schrree-een!
chshree-ip

Creative writing *helps make sense of sounds: use bold, italic, and capital letters for emphasis and rising, falling, or tapering lines to show pitch and volume.*

purpose and really help conservation efforts. For example, in Britain, the Breeding Bird Survey (BBS) is a vital means of monitoring the health of bird populations. It requires volunteers to survey a selected site for a few hours, three times a year, and new surveyors are always needed.

Hand counters *help you to accurately keep a tally. You can count one species in your head, another on the counter.*

You could also get involved in ringing birds. You will need to have proper training before you can take part in this type of survey, but marking birds with individually numbered metal rings allows scientists to follow many aspects of their lives, and calculate such things as survival rates and population trends as well as following migration routes. For more information on how to take part in ringing studies, contact the British Trust for Ornithology or BTO (in the UK), or your local bird organization (see page 216 for details). You can also report any ringed bird that you find to these organizations.

Bringing birds to you

THERE IS NOTHING QUITE LIKE seeing birds at close range, or even tempting them to feed from your hand. The trust they show, combined with the chance to examine every feather in detail, creates a special experience, well worth a little effort. The obvious place to get close to birds is in the garden, where you can use food and other temptations to win their confidence.

Fruit feast
Birds such as Starlings feed on windfalls from fruit trees.

Food in the garden

Birds are highly active animals but carry few fat reserves to sustain them in lean periods. Their need for a regular intake of energy-rich foods will tempt them into your garden, especially if "natural" foods are in short supply, so putting out a variety of foods in a range of feeders is guaranteed to bring a shifting population of birds into your garden. Traditionally, people put food out for birds in the winter months, but studies have shown that supplementary food is just as useful in the breeding season, from February to September.

No special equipment or proprietary food is required to attract ground-feeding birds. Simply put grated stale cheese on the ground beside shrubs (for cover) to tempt shy Dunnocks, or scatter kitchen scraps and unwanted fruit at the edge of the lawn for Blackbirds and Song Thrushes. Place the food in "clumps" a few metres apart to allow several birds to feed without aggression.

Erecting a bird table makes observation easier, because the birds feed at head height, and is also more hygienic than distributing food on the ground. Bird tables should be placed about 2–3m from a tree or bush – far enough to deny access to squirrels, but close enough to afford an easy escape route should a sparrowhawk or other predator be sighted.

Feeders and bird tables
attract a variety of species, from Blackbirds on open tables, to Coal and Marsh Tits, Nuthatches, and woodpeckers on hanging feeders and baskets.

Avoid putting out *more food than the birds can eat: you will encourage disease as well as unwanted visitors, such as rats and town pigeons.*

Seed mix

Stout
metal
cage

Suckers for
attachment

Smooth
baffle

Ceramic
bell

Loose baffle

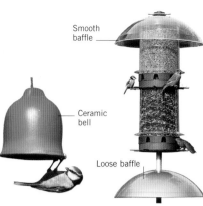

Caged feeders *allow
access by small birds, but
deter larger species and
full-grown squirrels.*

Multi-port *plastic feeders
are robust and allow the
use of smaller seeds and
specialist seed mixes.*

A lightweight tray
*fixed to a window with
suckers allows super-
close-up viewing.*

Blue Tits *hang from
ceramic or plastic "bells"
filled with a mix of suet
and nuts.*

Swinging plastic baffles
*below and above a
hanging feeder help
to fend off squirrels.*

Hanging feeders

Some bird species, such as Blue and
Great Tits and Nuthatches, naturally
feed acrobatically, hanging from
twigs and branches. They benefit
from hanging feeders, which range
in sophistication from a simple, fresh half
coconut suspended from a hook, to plastic
tubes filled with seed or nuts (see above). Feeders can be
suspended from branches, mounted on poles, or even
attached to windows, so that birds can be viewed at close
quarters. Using several feeders of different designs will
allow you to put out a mixture of seed types to increase
the range of birds that visit the garden.

Birds such as Treecreepers and Goldcrests are unlikely
to use hanging feeders or even venture on to a bird table,
but it is still possible to create feeding opportunities for
them in the garden. Try suet and cheese smeared into
cracks in bark, or nuts and dried fruit squeezed into
holes drilled in a log.

Cleanliness and hygiene

Keeping bird feeders clean is a matter of common sense.
Move feeders and tables from time to time to prevent
a build up of droppings beneath; clean them occasionally,
using a weak solution of domestic bleach and a brush
dedicated to the purpose. Always wear rubber gloves
when handling feeders – some bird diseases can be
transmitted to people – and keep the feeders out of
reach of children and pets. Buy seed and nuts only from
reputable companies; low grade feed may be affected by
aflatoxins – poisons produced by microscopic fungi that
are lethal to birds.

FOOD TYPES

Birds need high quality, high energy foods. Peanuts are the
traditional favourite, but carefully selected seed mixes are far
closer to a bird's natural diet.

Rolled oats *can be used on an open table or
scattered on the ground, to attract a number
of seed and cereal eaters.*

Peanuts *are ideal for tits, Nuthatches, and
woodpeckers, but are prone to contamination
with aflatoxin, a poisonous mould.*

Hemp and niger seed *is perfect for
Goldfinches which find it irresistible, even in
gardens where they have not appeared before.*

Sunflower seeds *appeal to many birds,
especially Greenfinches, which split off the
husks and take the sunflower hearts.*

Proprietary seed mixes *maximize food value
while minimizing waste; the seed is already
husked and 100% edible.*

Seedcake *made from suet, oatmeal, and seeds
is a high energy food specially formulated for
finches and other table feeders.*

Mealworms *can be bought dried or live and
neatly packed so you need not handle them,
although they are ideal for hand-taming Robins.*

A standard nest box *for Blue Tits is ideal for a small garden. A hinged roof allows for easy winter cleaning.*

Rugged boxes *blend inconspicuously into a wildlife garden. Try to put the box on the "dry" side of the trunk.*

A rot-proof *"woodcrete" box will last a lifetime and resists the onslaught of woodpeckers and garden predators.*

A deep, open front *allows an excellent view for the sitting bird, appreciated by nesting Spotted Flycatchers and Pied Wagtails.*

Swift boxes *may fit along the eaves, but those set into the wall often prove more successful.*

Nest boxes

Few gardens contain the old trees and dense hedges that birds favour as natural nest sites, so after wintering in your garden, many birds simply leave to rear their young. Thoughtfully sited nest boxes will encourage them to stay throughout the summer, and treat you to fascinating displays of courtship, territorialism, and feeding. Nest boxes can be bought off the shelf or simply constructed at home; if buying a ready-built nest box, always use a reputable manufacturer because badly designed boxes may

injure birds or leave them open to attack from predators. The overall dimensions of the box, the size of the entry hole, and its location in the garden will determine the species that will make use of it, although some birds will never be tempted into these artifical nest sites. Match the size of the entry hole with the species you wish to attract: a 25mm (1in) diameter is ideal for Blue Tits, 28mm (1⅛in) for Great Tits, and 32mm (1¼in) for sparrows.

Siting a nest box

There are a few general rules about where boxes should be placed, but much depends on the size and layout of your garden. They should be 2–3m (7–10ft) above ground (perhaps more in a tall tree), inaccessible to cats, and hidden from prying eyes. Open boxes for Robins or Spotted Flycatchers should be placed in a dense creeper on a wall, while boxes for Pied Wagtails can be wedged just off the ground in a woodpile or similar spot. Big boxes for Tawny Owls or Jackdaws need tall, dense trees (evergreen oaks are ideal) and Starlings prefer to be up high on a tree or the gable end of a house.

Blue Tits *squeeze a nest of moss and feathers into a box. They may have as many as 12 chicks, but garden-nesting birds usually have smaller broods.*

A tall tree *is an ideal place for a nest box. Choose a tree away from feeders in the garden, to avoid conflict. Position the box so that the entrance faces away from early morning or midday sun.*

Bathing helps *a bird keep its plumage in top condition. Birds raise and lower their feathers when in a bath to allow water to reach the skin.*

Water for drinking and bathing

Birds welcome a shallow bird bath, both for drinking and for bathing. Water is needed both in the dry summer months and in the winter, when frost seals off natural supplies. A simple dish with gently sloping sides is ideal, but make sure the sides are not shiny or slippery. The dish should be set into the ground for extra stability and insulation from the frost; adding a simple perch or stick gives smaller birds a chance to reach the water, while deeper sides give bigger species enough depth for a proper bath. Keep the water clear of fallen leaves and clean out droppings as often as you can, always leaving the water clean and fresh: don't risk contamination with bleach or any other cleaning or anti-freeze solutions. Position the dish so that it is visible from a window; the presence of water attracts many species, and you could even see a bathing woodpecker or Sparrowhawk, especially early in the morning.

If space allows, a pond will greatly enhance the appeal of your garden to birds. Wagtails and others will come to forage for insects and worms, and larger expanses of water will attract ducks, herons, and even kingfishers. When establishing a new pond, add a few buckets of water from an established one; this will give a kick start to populations of aquatic invertebrates upon which birds feed.

Garden visitors

Any well-planned bird garden will attract good numbers of everyday birds, such as Blue and Great Tits, Blackbirds, Robins, House Sparrows, and Starlings, but other visitors depend on the location of the garden. If it is near a wood, for example, you could expect Nuthatches and perhaps Long-tailed Tits, Goldcrests, and Bullfinches in spring (if you have fruit trees). In autumn, warblers such as Blackcaps and Lesser Whitethroats, come into gardens to feed on soft berries, and migrant Chiffchaffs often sing in August and September as they pass through. You may not realize they are in your garden until you hear the song. In winter, Redwings and Fieldfares are possible and the most desirable garden bird of all, the Waxwing, could appear on a cotoneaster bush or apple tree.

CREATING NESTING OPPORTUNITIES

Safe nest sites are essential for small birds. If your garden is new, you can give nature a helping hand by creating an artificial thicket. Gather a few sticks and tie them together into a loose mass with garden twine; gently tease out the sticks to form a rough cup shape. Fix the bundle to a tree trunk, and train ivy or another creeper over the "nest" to provide cover. Plant gorse or another spiny plant around the foot of the tree; this will help to deter cats, which are responsible for the majority of garden bird kills. You could also invest in a humane, electronic deterrent that emits high pitched bleeps whenever a cat enters your garden.

Cover with ivy or another creeper

Make a "nest" shape from bundled twigs

Creating bird habitats

GARDENS ARE VITAL FRAGMENTS of wildlife habitat. They provide feeding and nesting opportunities for many bird species at a time when development and agricultural intensification are putting pressure on "wild" places. With a little imagination, it is possible to maximize the wildlife potential of your garden and attract many and varied species.

Kingfishers
These birds may visit garden ponds early, before people are about.

Garden features

A typical garden, with a lawn, flowerbeds, hedge, and one or two ornamental trees, is already a good bird habitat. However, its wildlife value can easily and inexpensively be enhanced without radically changing its character or adding to maintenance time.

An extensive lawn is a rather sterile environment for birds, but patches of lawn in a mixed garden are valuable, attracting Blackbirds and Song Thrushes. A larger, rougher lawn attracts feeding Starlings. Pied Wagtails like large grassy areas, but are less likely to visit a small, enclosed lawn. Try to design a lawn with irregular shapes; this will create more "edge" (where grass and flowerbeds join) that is favoured by birds.

Flowerbeds are good, so long as they are not sprayed extensively with pesticides. They provide cover, and freshly turned or weeded earth is ideal for ground feeders, such as Robins and Dunnocks.

Native shrubs and berry-bearing plants are better than exotics, but small conifers are useful in early spring when they offer secure cover for nests. Hedges are perfect for nesting birds; a big yew hedge offers not only nest sites, but food too.

Leave logpiles *in your garden. They are good for insects and spiders — just the place for a feeding Wren.*

Use natural foods *and kitchen scraps as well as commercial feeders and special seed mixes: thrushes love such foods.*

Berry-bearing plants *attract many birds, especially in autumn when they are fattening up to gain "fuel" for long migratory journeys.*

Steep, landscaped banks *on wilder pools may even tempt Kingfishers to nest: a perch will help them fish.*

The importance of water

All birds need water, all year round. Although many species take in sufficient fluids from their juicy food or from dew on leaves, they all need deeper water in which to bathe. In really dry weather, and again in cold winter conditions, even the smallest bird bath or dish of water is invaluable. In winter, keep standing water free of ice by putting a floating tennis ball in a birdbath or pond. On no account should you add any kind of chemical anti-freeze agent to the water.

Always keep water as fresh and clean as possible: if a bird bath is used by a flocks of Starlings, they may empty it in an hour or two and also soil the bowl, so it is worth sweeping it out and refilling it whenever you can.

Planting for birds

Many shrubs produce a good crop of berries, which are a vital source of food in autumn. Consider planting snowberry, cotoneaster, holly, pyracantha, hawthorn, honeysuckle, or yew, all of which are also very attractive plants in their own right. Elder is another excellent shrub, its sweetly scented flowers and sugary berries appealing to birds from spring to early winter; however it quickly forms tall thickets and needs to be tightly controlled.

Plants such as St John's wort, clematis, Michaelmas daisy, sedum, and buddleia are magnets to insects, which are, in turn, taken by birds. Don't rush to dig out clumps of nettles because their hairy leaves are often covered in caterpillars. Dwarf conifers are good too, tempting Wrens and Dunnocks to search for grubs and spiders in the deep shade that they cast; they are also ideal for winter roost and early nest sites. Creepers, such as Clematis, passion flower, Boston ivy, climbing hydrangea, Virginia creeper, and others, produce perfect cover for roosting and nesting House Sparrows and are ideal places for putting up boxes for Spotted Flycatchers and Robins.

Creating a wetland is ambitious but it can be done if a brook passes through your garden.

Bird baths provide essential water for drinking and bathing; they should be topped up and cleaned as often as possible.

GARDEN PLANTS

Variety is the key to a successful wildlife garden. Within the constraints of garden size, aspect, soil type, and location, choose a selection of plants that will attract birds throughout the year. Plant a mixture of herbs, grasses, shrubs, and climbers to provide cover at a variety of levels – especially in areas next to bird feeders. If space allows, plant a fastigiate (columnar) tree, which will add still more to bird diversity.

Teazels are large and elegant plants that need space. Their stiff, spiny seedheads will bring in small groups of Goldfinches in late summer.

Yarrow is a low-growing, scented herb that draws in many pollinating insects in summer. Its seeds are eaten by House Sparrows, tits, and finches,

Wild rose produces fleshy hips that ripen in September, and which remain until the end of winter, attracting birds, such as thrushes, Waxwings, and Serins.

Ivy is a superb wildlife plant, giving thick winter cover, an abundance of berries, and a remarkable flush of late flowers, bringing in abundant insects.

Hazel is appealing in late winter with waves of yellow catkins. It produces a crop of small, hard nuts that are eaten by woodpeckers and Nuthatches.

Alder is a medium-sized, highly attractive waterside tree; its plentiful winter cones supply seeds to foraging flocks of Siskins, Redpolls, and Goldfinches.

Holly is used as a secure roost and nest site for Robins, Blackbirds, and Song Thrushes, but also has a fine berry crop for Mistle Thrushes in winter.

In the field

Birds have evolved to exploit almost every environment on our planet, and the rich variety of habitats in Europe gives the birdwatcher the chance to see a dazzling range of species. Each type of environment has its own challenges and brings its own rewards.

COMMON SIGHTINGS

Purple Sandpiper
A wader that prefers rocks to mud. It favours barnacle-encrusted seaweedy pools.

Red-breasted Merganser
A showy bird of sheltered water around rocky headlands as well as quiet sandy bays.

Black Guillemot
A classic year-round seabird on and around small rocky islands in the north.

Eider
Large flocks like big sandy bays and mussel beds, but families feed in small inlets on rocky shores.

RACING THE TIDES

A rocky headland will often protrude into a narrow channel at the head of a bay or estuary. Many birds are attracted by the churning tides around the exposed rocks. Shags swim and dive in surging swell right against the rocks, surviving miraculously as they search out fish in tangled beds of seaweed. Gulls pick up fish, shellfish, jellyfish, and starfish that have been stranded on the rocks, or they settle on the water, looking for anything edible. Common and Arctic Terns dive headlong into the fast currents and Gannets search out shoals of silvery mackerel, diving for them in a short-lived feeding frenzy. Eiders, Red-breasted Mergansers, grebes, and divers keep to quieter waters a little offshore, although when the tide is slack, the Eiders potter about in seaweedy pools right at the edge of the beach, often allowing remarkably close views.

A hide fixed *near a wader roost will give you memorable views, but you must stay inside until after the birds have dispersed.*

COMMON SIGHTINGS

Ringed Plover
At home on firm sand as well as mud, nesting on an open sand or shingle beach.

Herring Gull
Drops shellfish on to rocks to crack them open, and searches the tideline for food.

Rock Pipit
Nests in nearby rocks, feeds on grassy places in summer, but a great beachcomber in the winter months.

Oystercatcher
Nests on shingle beaches and uses its strong bill to open shellfish on rocks.

THE SHINGLE SHORE

The bare stones of a pebbly beach offer little food to waders and shorebirds, but strandlines of drying seaweed are full of invertebrates, attracting Rock Pipits and perhaps Starlings, Chaffinches, and other land birds. One wader, the Turnstone, is a specialist in this habitat, finding food beneath lumps of weed and debris.

There is often a cliff above a shingle beach, which will have Jackdaws and pigeons – probably "town pigeons" gone wild, but look for Stock Doves, too. Peregrines nest in such places and may be seen soaring, waiting for a chance to catch a pigeon. In southern Europe, eroded cliffs with small cavities may have Crag Martins, Swifts, or breeding Pallid Swifts.

There is little point *being too clever with camouflaged clothes on an open beach: birds will see you anyway. Sit still for a while, instead.*

Rocky, sandy, and shingle shores

Sandwich Tern
Flighty and quick to desert their nests, breeding terns should be given a wide berth.

BEACHES ARE EXPOSED, difficult habitats, but they have benefits for some birds. Rocky islets and headlands are secure nesting places for gulls and terns. They are also good places to see birds at any time of year. A rocky shore offers limited opportunities for long-billed probing birds, but others forage in the tangled seaweed and rock pools. Sand and shingle beaches are far less productive than estuaries: nevertheless, a strandline left at high tide may attract a surprising variety of species.

Keeping a distance

Shoreline habitats have little or no cover, and it is hard to keep out of sight even with camouflaged clothing. Often the best option is to watch from a distance using a good scope on a sturdy tripod. However, some birds are remarkably tame: Purple Sandpipers and Turnstones, for example, will happily feed close by if you keep still and quiet.

Cautious steps

If you walk along the water's edge, birds on the beach will probably fly off ahead of you. This unsettles the birds and makes for a frustrating day out for you. Take a detour to the top of the beach to get round the other side of the birds, and observe from the cover of dunes or bushes just inland. In summer, breeding gulls and terns may dive noisily at your head when you approach. If this happens, turn round and walk away openly, so that they can see you have gone and feel able to return to their eggs. Birds feeding on the shoreline leave clear footprints and mark the sand with their bills as they probe for food. Watch a feeding Shelduck or Oystercatcher, then check the marks in the sand. You'll soon become familiar with these telltale signs.

Little Terns *nest in a shallow scoop on a sand or shingle beach. The two or three eggs in the nest are well camouflaged, so be careful where you tread.*

EXPERT TIP

■ A sand bar across a shallow channel or an isolated stony beach may be an interesting place to explore, but be aware of dangerous tides and currents that can cut you off with little warning. Study local tide tables and take advice from wardens and seasoned birders on site.

ROCKY BEACH, NORWAY

SHINGLE BEACH, PUGLIA, ITALY

Open seas and cliffs

CLEAN, COLD, NORTHERN SEAS are rich in fish and attract a wide range of birds. These seagoing specialists are usually weak and clumsy on land, but must return to lay their eggs and rear their young. Most find a cliff with ledges, safe from predators and right at the edge of the sea, so they can glide down to their natural element in a moment. The huge seabird cities on coastal cliffs – many of which are accessible by land – are among the most exciting and dramatic places in the world to watch wildlife.

Puffin
Seabirds are busy commuters once their chicks have hatched.

Colony visits

Seabird colonies offer excellent opportunities for viewing, especially in the nesting season between March and late July. Clambering over cliffs can be hazardous, however, so seek out cliffs with specially-built platforms and safe watchpoints. Out of the nesting season, seabirds are often far from land, swept far and wide by gales. But in spring and autumn, when many species migrate, they pass close by headlands – great spots for watching seabirds pass by offshore, or "seawatching". This requires practice, as birds go by once and rarely come back. Check weather reports too – prolonged, onshore winds drive birds inshore, making it possible to observe the dramatic movements of tired birds at close range from viewpoints on the coast.

> **EXPERT TIP**
>
> ▪ If travelling by ferry, find a sheltered spot on deck where engine vibration is minimal. Using binoculars, scan the sea in the middle distance – don't try to look out too far. Keep glancing forward to get advance warning of approaching birds.

Watching from boats

There are "seabird specials" that take you close in under a cliff colony, a great experience if you can stand the motion of a bobbing boat. Other special trips take you farther out to sea specially to see migrants, and may even use "chum", a foul mixture of oily fish waste, thrown overboard to attract petrels and shearwaters. If you have a strong stomach, you may enjoy brilliant views of seabirds at sea. A long-distance ferry usually gives the best chance to see seabirds far offshore. The birds fly fast and there is no chance for a second look; practice with your binoculars until you can keep a moving bird in focus.

Trawlers catch *thousands of undersized fish, which are thrown back into the sea, even though they are dying. Seabirds take advantage of this generous handout.*

WATCHING SEABIRDS AT SEA

Observing birds from a boat can be great fun – but watch out for your binoculars. Even in fine, sunny conditions, sea spray will soon coat their lenses and cloud your vision, and salt in the water will corrode mechanics. Keep some soft, dry cotton handkerchiefs in a warm pocket and carefully dry the lenses every so often. A rain guard on the eyepieces is a good idea: and when not using your binoculars, keep them tucked inside the front of your coat. When back at base, wipe metal casings with a soft cloth lightly dampened with clean water. Waterproof binoculars, usually filled with nitrogen to eliminate internal fogging, are invaluable but expensive.

Keep warm: a tight-fitting hat and gloves are essential because it can be cold on the sea even in the height of summer. Don't forget to take notes as it is easy to forget what you have seen – a pencil will smudge less than a pen.

Open boats *operate close to the shore in summer, giving good views of birds such as Shags, terns, and Kittiwakes.*

COMMON SIGHTINGS

Guillemot
Abundant at big colonies, it stands upright like a penguin, and swims in flocks offshore.

Lesser Black-backed Gull
Commonest on flatter, heathy ground on top of larger islands; follows ships.

Arctic Skua
Breeds in the north: great to watch chasing terns from a headland in autumn.

Gannet
This bird's stark white colour helps attract other Gannets to good fishing areas.

CLIFF PATROL

Observing cliff-nesting birds, such as these Kittiwakes, requires a little planning. You may be restricted to a couple of points or platforms, so time your visit to whenever the cliffs are most clearly illuminated by the sun. Safety should be your priority. Grassy slopes above cliffs are lethal, and you should never clamber over fences for a better look, or leave well-marked footpaths. Give yourself plenty of time: seeing that elusive first Puffin might be tricky, and you might find it hard to drag yourself away from a splendid cliff full of Kittiwakes and Guillemots. If you can, visit a Gannet colony – perhaps the most dramatic and exciting sight of all. Take a telescope if you have one: seabirds are fantastic in giant close-up.

Creature comforts *are essential when watching migrating seabirds for hours at a time: find a natural easy chair.*

COMMON SIGHTINGS

Fulmar
Unable to stand on land, but a master at sea, using the wind to glide efficiently.

Rock Dove
Colonies untainted by interbreeding with domestic pigeons are restricted to the north.

Jackdaw
A great acrobat around coastal cliffs, using the upcurrents and wind to great effect as it swoops in and out.

Razorbill
Nesting in cavities, it is often less obvious than the Guillemots on their open ledges.

COMMON SIGHTINGS

Dunlin
A benchmark small wader: get to know it well in all its seasonal variations.

Common Gull
A medium-sized gull, elegant, white-headed in summer, with a dusky streaked hood in winter.

Knot
Medium size, medium bill, medium leg length, but with a character all its own.

Brent Goose
Most in Europe are this dark-bellied type, but in Ireland "pale-bellied" Brents have almost white undersides.

WATCHING ESTUARY BIRDS

Light, shade, and reflections from water and wet mud make birds hard to identify, but the sheer abundance of birds is more than enough compensation. Watch from a spot at the head of an estuary as the tide rises; you'll see grebes, divers, ducks, and maybe even a Razorbill or two drifting in with the current. At the same time, watch the flocks of waders pushed off the mud by rising water and trying to locate their roosting places. You can go there next time, and settle down an hour or two before high tide to watch them arrive and sort out their favoured places: each species will occupy the same spot week after week, year after year.

Estuaries are often considered winter birdwatching areas, but they have an abundance of birds all year round: waders can be watched from late summer to late spring.

Thousands of waders *pack into a thin strip of land as they roost at high tide. Consult tide tables to time your visits: huge spring tides are the most rewarding.*

COMMON SIGHTINGS

Curlew
Pale brown with streaks close-up, but dark from a distance.

Redshank
Looks dark and dumpy at long range, but its flight pattern is highly distinctive.

Wigeon
Common on grassier marshes, where it grazes on drier ground in large, concentrated flocks.

Shelduck
A striking bird of open mudflats, nesting in nearby dunes.

OUT ON THE MARSH

Salt-marshes can be tough, dangerous habitats. The sticky, oozy creeks of a deeply eroded marsh can fill with frightening speed as the tide flows in, cutting off your retreat. Don't stray into these areas; instead look for marshes with raised edges, sea walls, or footpaths that provide safer vantage points.

A good strategy is to find a sheltered spot below the skyline or against a bank, sit down, and let the birds come to you. Salt-marshes have an abundance of specialized, salt-tolerant plants that attract insects, and so are full of food for birds. Redshanks, Black-headed Gulls, ducks, pipits, terns, and larks nest here in the summer. But don't be just a fair weather visitor: a long walk in winter can be exhilarating, bringing you good views of visitors from across northern Europe and Asia and even Arctic Canada.

Mudflats and estuaries *can be bleak and windswept in winter, but many are close to roads so you can turn your car into a cosy hide. Invest in a window clamp for your scope for vibration-free viewing.*

ESTUARY, SOUTH WALES

SALT-MARSH, ESSEX, ENGLAND

Estuaries, mudflats, and salt-marshes

Hen Harrier
This hunter is seen over short salt-marsh vegetation.

Twice daily, incoming tides enter estuaries and inundate the mudflats and salt-marshes at their edge, enriching them with food. Twice daily, the mud is exposed to the sun and open air. It is a tough environment, but countless invertebrates thrive within the sediment. These creatures, in turn, attract scores of wading birds looking for an easy meal. Waders spread out over vast areas at low tide and concentrate into flocks at undisturbed roosts at high tide, when the ducks and seabirds take their turn to find food.

Stealth and concealment

Estuaries are incredibly productive habitats – better than the most fertile farmland. Their rich harvest of invertebrates is divided up between numerous bird species, which have bill shapes tailored to exploit different prey animals. Plovers, for example, have short, sturdy bills to deal with molluscs and crustaceans, while godwits use their long, fine-tipped bills to probe deep in the mud for marine worms. Getting good views of these birds calls for sound fieldcraft and good local knowledge. Wearing sombre or camouflaged clothing will help you melt away into the background of marsh and dunes. The open beach at low tide, however, offers little cover. It is best to wait until the tide rises, and watch with a good telescope from a safe vantage point, such as a fixed hide.

Long-range watching

Birds in these environments are typically distant and often backlit by silvery mud. You will need to learn to identify them more by shape and motion than by small details of colour and pattern. Even the most comprehensive field guides offer limited help in these habitats – there is no alternative to experience.

A fixed watchpoint *overlooking a high tide roost has the advantage of being in the right place for the birds to come close, while causing minimum disturbance.*

EXPERT TIP

■ Compare roosting waders at a distance: Curlews are big, bulky, and dark; Bar-tailed Godwits are smaller and paler; Grey Plovers and tightly-bunched Redshanks are smaller still and dark; Knots carpet the ground in grey flocks; winter Dunlins are small, anonymous, and white-bellied.

57

Rivers and marshes

Cattle Egret
Often feeding in drier spots, Cattle Egrets fly to roost near water.

WATER ADDS ENCHANTMENT and variety to any birdwatching trip. Land, water, and waterside birds can all be seen beside a marsh or river, with the edge of the habitat providing the best spots for observation. Ducks and waders paddle in the shallows, terns dip for insects and fish, and wagtails and pipits look for food washed up along the shore by the water and wind. Almost anything may stop by to bathe or drink.

Look both ways

For a birdwatcher, approaching a river, lake, or marsh is always exciting. The transitional habitat – where water meets land – attracts a great variety of birds, and you can never predict what rarity might be visiting. Your success in these habitats requires stealth, because sudden movement will send Moorhens and Water Rails scuttling into reeds, put ducks and waders to flight, and flush that longed-for Kingfisher even before you see it. Go carefully, and stop and look along the water's edge as soon as you arrive. Look both ways along a stream or even a ditch, and move quietly and slowly.

EXPERT TIP

▪ If a potentially interesting bird dives into deep cover, it is often better to walk away and return later than to wait in the hope that it will reappear. When you return, be prepared. Approach with great care, binoculars raised and focused to search a promising spot.

Patience rewarded

Once at the water's edge, keep quiet and sit still. Most marsh birds are elusive rather than shy, and will begin to emerge from the surrounding vegetation within a few minutes, often affording very close views. Surrounded by dense cover, wetland habitats reward the birdwatcher with a good ear for calls. Waders usually call as they fly in or fly off; Kingfishers almost invariably call in flight; and wagtails arriving to feed will usually call too. In summer, Reed and Sedge Warblers call repeatedly, even if they are not singing. Their chorus is at its best at dawn in early summer, when the voices of Reed Buntings and Cuckoos add to the cacophony. It is worth spending time with a good CD recording of birdsong to acquaint yourself with wetland sounds.

Flood meadows *are amongst the richest of all bird habitats. A good pair of waders will let you make use of the natural cover provided by trees and hedgerows.*

MARSHES, SOUTHERN FRANCE

RIVER, SCOTTISH HIGHLANDS

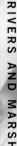

WETLAND GEMS

Freshwater marshes are precious places that are simply alive with good birds. Much depends on the location: in Poland, for example, the specialities might include Great Snipes and Aquatic Warblers, while in Spain, there could be Purple Gallinules, in Greece, Glossy Ibises, and in Sweden, Cranes. Most marshes will have a small list of breeding birds greatly expanded by migrants in spring and autumn. These will include waders and terns, but also wagtails, pipits, swallows and martins, and buntings, all of which feed over or beside water at times. In winter, shallow water attracts an abundance and variety of waterfowl, especially the surface-feeding ducks.

Being so scarce and well-defined in most European countries, wetlands are often protected as nature reserves. Many are equipped with good hides and observation towers.

COMMON SIGHTINGS

Grey Heron
Able to find fish in all kinds of water, from still marshes to the rocky edges of fast-flowing streams.

Whiskered Tern
A southern wetland specialist, nesting on reedy islets and floating vegetation.

Mallard
Common and familiar almost everywhere; a big, handsome duck.

Shoveler
Prefers still water where it can use its specialist filter-feeding technique.

GO WITH THE FLOW

A healthy, unpolluted river is home to a huge cast of bird characters. The cast changes as the river transforms from a fast-flowing young stream in the hills to a hard-working, silt-laden ribbon near the sea. Fast water excludes many species, such as the Snipe and Mute Swan, but appeals to Grey Wagtails, Dippers, and Common Sandpipers. Middle reaches, with overhanging trees, have Moorhens, Little Grebes, Kingfishers, and perhaps Sand Martins if there are earth cliffs. Wider stretches may develop marshy edges or flood meadows if the floodplain is not buried under development or constrained by artificial embankments: these are amongst the best wetland habitats of all with rare breeding waders, such as Ruffs and Black-tailed Godwits, Bewick's Swans and Wigeon in winter, and a variety of birds in riverside woodland.

A boat trip *through a large wetland allows an intimate view of its birds. Some of Europe's great bird areas, such as the Danube Delta, are best seen by boat.*

COMMON SIGHTINGS

Grey Wagtail
Loves rushing streams with plenty of riverside trees and rocks to perch upon.

Dipper
A unique songbird that wades, swims, and dives expertly in cold, clear, fast-flowing rivers.

Kingfisher
Heard more often than seen, it may one day suddenly appear on a branch almost close enough to touch, a magical moment.

Common Sandpiper
A summer bird of stony riversides and shingly beaches.

Lakes, reservoirs, and gravel pits

OPEN AREAS OF FRESH WATER are often found together with marshes and rivers, and divisions between their birds tend to blur. Natural lakes are rather few in most countries, but are supplemented by reservoirs. These can be almost natural in character except for the face of a dam, or almost enclosed in concrete. Other areas of water are increasingly provided by worked-out gravel and sand quarries that have been allowed to flood. They tend to have steep sides and naturally gravelly shores, but can be excellent for birds.

Black Tern
A typical "here today, gone tomorrow" migrant at inland lakes.

Long days, short walks

To a committed birdwatcher, a local reservoir or lake usually becomes a prime spot, much loved and regularly surveyed. Repeat visits to this one location provide a temporal dimension to observations of birds — a real sense of the shifting populations throughout the year. A small lake or pond lends itself to a quick look at lunchtime every day, or a morning walk at the weekend, but watching bigger reservoirs can be a whole day affair. Bodies of water, whatever their size, attract birds on the move, migrants that drop in for a day or two and then move on. Good birds do not always drop by on Sunday mornings, so it is best to go as often as you can, whenever you get the chance.

Getting started

Much depends on the season: find out what your local lake lends itself to. If the water level falls in late summer, go there and look at the mud for migrant waders between July and October. If the water rises and floods a summer growth of vegetation, look for ducks feeding on floating seeds in the autumn. In spring, grassy places by the water can be good for migrant Wheatears and Meadow Pipits or wagtail flocks. The open water itself may attract migrating terns.

In Eastern Europe, *dramatic birds such as White Pelicans may be seen on large lakes: a boat might be the best way to get to them, but disturbance must be minimized.*

EXPERT TIP

■ Look well ahead when walking along a reservoir shore: there is nothing more frustrating than seeing an interesting wader fly off and cross to the other side. It is worth following it to get a better view – chances are it will be common, but one day you may find something really rare.

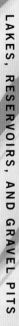

WATERBIRDS AT HOME AND AWAY

Many of Europe's choicest bird sites are associated with water, and visits to the best lakes and reservoirs can be an engaging part of a holiday. If you are planning a trip, timing is everything: unmissable bird spectacles may be restricted to special sites and last only a few days. In Sweden, for example, watching the spring arrival of Cranes is immensely popular, drawing thousands of people to visitor centres. When you arrive at a lake, do some groundwork to plan your full day's watching and so get the most out of your visit: if a well-placed hide faces east, for example, it might be better to visit in the afternoon, with the sun behind you, rather than first thing in the morning.

Back at home, get to know your local lake, reservoir, or gravel pit complex, with all its associated habitats, at all seasons of the year. You will learn what to expect and what is unusual. That way, even a common bird can be especially interesting if it is the first you have seen there.

A concrete basin *may not have the magic of a lake full of Cranes, but it can still attract good birds and may be well worth watching regularly. Watch for migrant terns resting on buoys.*

Gravel pits *have steep, coarse banks, excellent for nesting Sand Martins. The best sites are often the least "landscaped": neat, tidy, grass-covered banks can be almost sterile.*

COMMON SIGHTINGS

Lapwing
Flocks form after breeding as early as June, and are seen flying in lines, "V"s, or irregular masses.

Sand Martin
In late summer and autumn, large flocks concentrate to roost each night in reeds beside lakes and reservoirs.

Ruff
One of the more common waders in late summer and autumn on muddy reservoir shores, often confusing beginners.

Pochard
Usually feeds at night and forms sleepy single-sex flocks by day.

Tufted Duck
Common and widespread, often diving down to feed.

Goldeneye
In winter, likes open, bleak lakes where it spends most of its time diving under to feed.

Great Crested Grebe
From reedy pools in summer it often moves to larger, open lakes in winter to avoid ice.

Mute Swan
Tame in NW Europe, but a dramatic sight in large, wild flocks in the east.

61

Heath and moorland

THESE EXPOSED, IMPOVERISHED HABITATS are typically based on poor soils. They are kept open by grazing animals and periodic fires, and attract birds that thrive in short, thick vegetation. Pools provide habitats for breeding waders, while bushy areas support birds including Reed Buntings and Whinchats on moors, and Dartford Warblers and Nightingales on heaths. Moorland merges into mountain and should be treated with similar respect, but heaths are easy places to watch birds.

Nightjar
Look out for this nocturnal heathland bird at dusk from May to August.

A moorland walk

The most captivating walks through this dramatic habitat take you from low to high altitude, allowing you to appreciate the gradual change from farmland birds in the valley bottoms to moorland, cliff, and scree birds higher up. Walking a level contour around the valleys and hollows is a less arduous alternative. Always pay particular attention to crags and skylines for birds of prey, and any eminences, such as rocks, posts, or hummocks, on which birds are likely to perch.

The moorland *pictured here is a patchwork of different habitats: the heather itself, the pine trees, and the shallow river, which attracts Dippers and Common Sandpipers.*

Heathland delights

True heaths are precious habitats in Europe. The dry, sandy soil, colourful heather, and thickets of birch or gorse have a special community of birds, including Nightjars, Whitethroats, Dartford Warblers, Stonechats, and Yellowhammers in summer. In northern and central Europe, there are still a few places with Black Grouse. Many of the generalist species prefer bushes and thickets, but most heathland specialities are likely to be feeding on the ground (pipits, Linnets, and Woodlarks) or flying overhead (Hobbies).

Look out for special song flights: Tree Pipits "parachute" down to bush or tree tops while singing, while Woodlarks sing while circling, no more than dots in the sky. Low-lying valleys are moist, and here you may find Curlews, Snipes, Redshanks, and Grasshopper Warblers nesting.

EXPERT TIP

■ Walk to the head of a high valley and sit somewhere comfortable in a bed of deep heather. Watch what happens for an hour or so. You might be lucky and see a hunting Hen Harrier, a displaying Merlin, or a Cuckoo looking for Meadow Pipit nests in which to lay its eggs.

HEATHLAND, SOUTHERN ENGLAND

PEAT BOG ON MOORLAND, NORTH WALES

OPEN HEATHS

You'll need to rely on your ears in this environment: Dartford Warblers call a lot but are hard to see unless you first locate one by sound and then sit to wait for it to appear. Grassy spots with sandy soil are favoured by feeding Woodlarks: they are hard to spot on the ground, but usually don't go far if they fly away. Listen for their distinctive *to loooi* calls. Most heaths have gravel paths: it pays to step off them periodically to listen for bird calls without obscuring them by crunching footfalls. Hunting Hobbies, Sparrowhawks, and Buzzards may circle above the heath in warm summer weather. Calling crows may draw attention to circling raptors.

Low-lying heath can be bleak and brown in winter, with fewer birds to be seen. Rare winter birds include Great Grey Shrikes – look for them on bush tops at a distance, then work your way closer for a better view. Redpolls feed in the birches, while thrushes and crows come to the bushy areas to roost at dusk.

Heathland birds *are usually seen at fairly close quarters. A telescope and tripod are an unnecessary encumbrance, but good binoculars are essential.*

COMMON SIGHTINGS

Stonechat
A bird of both heaths and moors, with a liking for prominent bush- or gorse-top perches.

Dartford Warbler
Perky and long-tailed, but almost always remarkably secretive: listen for low, buzzy, churring calls.

Linnet
Nests in small, loose colonies around heaths and moorland, where there are plentiful seeds.

Hobby
Nests in trees, but drifts out over open heath and low moors to catch moths, dragonflies, and small birds on the wing.

THE MOORLAND TAPESTRY

Wide open moors lend themselves to a long hike: take a good map and wear stout boots. Avoid peat bogs and patches of vivid green, which usually indicate soggy, wet places where you might sink in quite deeply.

Regular patches of differently-coloured heather indicate management for grouse. Avoid such areas after August when there will be shooting and you will be unwelcome. In spring, the taller patches are best for singing Whinchats and calling male Red Grouse, which set up territories in the old "leggy" heather and feed in the shorter patches. Pools on the moors with peaty edges and rushy tussocks will often have a pair or two of nesting Black-headed Gulls.

Weather in the hills *is notoriously fickle: you should be prepared for sudden rain and cold or fog. You lose a lot of heat from your head: a warm hat is a good idea.*

COMMON SIGHTINGS

Hen Harrier
The pale grey male and brown female hunt low over a moor, wings raised in a "V".

Snipe
In spring, listen for a vibrant, humming overhead — it may be a drumming Snipe.

Wheatear
Likes grassy spots, but needs a tumble of rocks or a stone wall in which to nest. Its white rump shows as it flies ahead.

Buzzard
Flies up from the valleys below to hunt on open moors, but prefers to be near trees.

Mediterranean scrub

THE CHARACTER OF THE Mediterranean region is largely determined by its vegetation and the way it is used by people. Large parts of the region were once forest. Clearance for cultivation, burning, and heavy grazing by sheep and goats, followed by erosion of the soil, has transformed the landscape. There are a few patches of true desert (in southern Spain), but more often the environment is semi-arid, encouraging a community of short, aromatic herbs and dense, thorny shrubs.

Bee-eater
A classic bird of open space and bushy scrub.

Heat and sun

This is a tough, hot, and dry environment for wildlife and people alike. Nevertheless, in summer it is alive with small birds, and an abundance of butterflies and wild flowers adds to the enjoyment of a wonderful walk. Warblers take tiny insects from foliage, shrikes catch larger insects on the ground, while pipits, larks, finches, and buntings eat a variety of insects, fruit, and seeds. These are best seen early in the day or in the evening, when it is cooler: in the heat of the day, they tend to "go to ground", seeking shade or hiding away inside the bushes. Watch for birds of prey overhead: they feed on the smaller birds, and on big beetles, lizards, and even snakes, which are the Short-toed Eagle's specialist food.

Bright sun can *reflect from your binocular eyepieces and cause glare; block the space next to your eyes with your hands to eliminate stray light.*

Protect yourself

Make sure to wear a hat, use plenty of sun cream, and drink sufficient liquid when spending a day out in this habitat. You must also be careful to look where you are walking: stand still to scan the skies. The scrub is typically made up of spiny and thorny plants that can penetrate flimsy footwear, and sharp limestone rocks are waiting to trip you up. Wear sturdy boots with a good grip: you often have to scramble up or down steep, shaly banks in eroded areas and it is easy to slip. Similarly, spiny grass seeds have a habit of clinging to shoelaces and being very painful when you next tie them up – watch out.

EXPERT TIP

■ Warblers typically skulk deep inside bushes, especially in late summer and autumn. Locate the birds by their calls, stand back, and wait for them to emerge. If you try to flush them out into view they almost always manage to creep out unseen, leaving you disappointed.

VEGETATION TYPES

Where forest has been removed, the resultant growth may be grassy steppe, garrigue, or maquis. Maquis consists mostly of evergreen bushes, heathers, and broom about 2–3m (6–9ft) high, with a lower layer of aromatic herbs, such as sage and rosemary, and many colourful flowers. Where sheep and goats overgraze this tough-looking habitat, taller herbs are eliminated and thorny bushes take over, creating isolated, tight clumps of dense thorn in a sea of low, close-cropped grass and thyme. This is garrigue. Between them, maquis and garrigue cover vast areas of warm, undulating, more or less rocky areas around the Mediterranean; the two are often found interspersed. In the east, tall cypresses add an extra element to the landscape. These are classic areas for the numerous Mediterranean warblers.

Maquis frequently intergrades with more wooded country, where deciduous and evergreen oaks and several species of pine are dominant. Here, look out for Bonelli's and Orphean Warblers, Firecrests, and Red Kites. Woodland on sandier tracts in southern Spain also has Azure-winged Magpies, Red-necked Nightjars, and Great Spotted Cuckoos.

A shallow gully *is usually a good spot from which to observe, particularly if there is water in the bottom. Don't forget to scan the sky for passing birds of prey.*

Hides on scaffolds *are used by photographers. It is best to enter with a companion who then leaves; the birds will return if they think the hide is unoccupied.*

COMMON SIGHTINGS

Short-toed Eagle
Found in open hill country with bushes and patches of forest; hovers over warm slopes.

Thekla Lark
Like the Crested Lark, but commoner in bushy and stony places, and in less cultivated landscapes away from villages.

Woodlark
Flies high in wide circles over bushy areas with patches of bare, sandy ground, and short grass.

Red Kite
Extremely elegant in the air as it searches for scraps, small birds, and mammals over bushy places and riversides.

Stonechat
Typically nervy and noisy when approached, perching on tops of bushes or on overhead wires, calling in irritation and alarm.

Cirl Bunting
Listen for its metallic rattle, given all day long in summer from bushy slopes and trees.

Subalpine Warbler

Dives out of sight into thick, thorny scrub, but may reveal itself in spring during its short, jerky song flights.

Dartford Warbler

Its low, nasal, buzzy churr is distinctive once known, but this is a real skulker in low heather or gorse, often hard to see well or for long.

Farmland

MOST OF EUROPE IS under some form of cultivation. The birds of the farmed countryside are often overlooked, but are fairly easy to observe. The character of farmed land – and its birds – varies hugely. Moorland, heaths, and even estuary marshes are often grazed, but most land is either arable (tilled and planted with crops, and often intensively managed) or pasture for dairy or beef cattle or sheep. Much of southern Europe is under orchards, olives, walnuts, almonds, fruit trees, or vineyards.

Lesser Black-backed Gull
Gulls are commonly seen in the fields from autumn to late winter.

Footpath networks

Arable farms, enclosed meadows, and pastures are private property, and their boundaries must be respected. You should stick to established footpaths or fringing lanes and be sure to shut gates behind you. What you see in farmland depends on season and agricultural practices; if a field is full of autumn-sown cereals and has few hedges, it will most likely support little bird life. Look instead for mixed farmland with fields of grass, stubble, ploughed earth, hedges, and the odd pond. In general, the variety of birds in summer is proportional to the variety of available nest sites; in winter, it depends more on the amount of food available.

Footpaths and lanes *often run alongside a hedgerow or line of taller grasses, giving you something to hide behind, as well as additional bird habitats.*

EXPERT TIP

■ Get a good map and work out a circular route to take in a variety of topography and habitat. If the farmland borders a wood or a lake, so much the better – habitat boundaries are often the most productive. Don't neglect villages – they have their own distinctive birds.

Winter flocks

Many birds from northern and eastern Europe move west in winter, seeking milder weather. Redwings and Fieldfares roam the hedgerows, eating berries, then move to open fields to search for worms. Lapwings and Golden Plovers, often accompanied by gulls, also seek worms. Bramblings and Chaffinches prefer seeds, feeding under clumps of trees, especially beeches in good beech mast years. A mixed flock in winter stubble is now hard to find, but could include Yellowhammers, Reed and Corn Buntings, and finches. Typical year-round farmland birds include Rooks, Jackdaws, Stock Doves, and Woodpigeons. Carrion Crows and Common Gulls flock to fields where animal slurry has been sprayed.

FARMLAND, ENGLAND

BIRDS AND FARMING PRACTICES

Agricultural intensification has robbed many bird species of their traditional habitats. Autumn sowing of cereal crops means that, by spring, many arable crops are simply too dense for ground-nesting birds. Planting huge, uninterrupted monocultures of grain crops has turned large swathes of the countryside into a desert for wildlife. Look out for "conservation headlands" – often strips of land on field margins which are left unmown and untreated with insecticides. You may find patches of local land managed more sympathetically for wildlife, like damp, tussocky pastures or organic farmland, and here you'll get a glimpse of the real potential of this environment as a bird habitat. Keep a pair of binoculars in your car and watch out for feeding flocks or a hunting Barn Owl as you are driving, to take advantage of unexpected viewing opportunities.

Mediterranean olive groves *and orchards provide habitat for diverse warblers, including Subalpine and Orphean Warblers, as well as Serins and Cirl Buntings.*

Mixed farmland *with old hedgerows and varied elevation can look beautiful, but the amount of wildlife still largely depends on the farming practices employed.*

COMMON SIGHTINGS

Little Owl
Usually hunts after dusk; its presence is often betrayed by the alarm calls of small birds.

Yellowhammer
Prefers wide open spaces and low hedgerows in summer; in winter, it joins mixed finch and bunting flocks.

Crested Lark
Commonly seen on roadsides, especially in dry, sandy areas of southern Europe.

Magpie
Abundant in southern Europe and a common farmland bird in the northwest.

Serin
A lively, colourful little finch around olives, vineyards, and orchards.

Corn Bunting
Sits on clumps of earth, posts, and wires, singing its "rattled bunch of keys" song all summer long.

Kestrel
A widespread but declining farmland bird of prey: hovers as if suspended on a string.

Rook
The common, gregarious, farmland crow has a glossy, black body and a white face.

Mountains

DIVERSE BIRD HABITATS characterize the mountain environment. Each level provides its own opportunities for feeding and nesting, attracting both mountain specialists and lowland generalists. Harsh, unpredictable, and sometimes dangerous conditions make watching these birds a real challenge and just keeping up may be a real problem: flocks of eagles and Alpine Choughs sweep quickly from slope to slope or from peak to peak, leaving us struggling far behind.

Lammergeier
A supreme glider and one of Europe's most spectacular birds.

Challenging environment

Mountains are tough places for birds, subject to winds, cold, sudden rain, snow, and fog. Most species that thrive at high altitude are specialists, and seeing them demands patience and dedication. You can see mountain birds simply by walking through the environment, but much of your attention will be taken up with negotiating the rough terrain; make a point of regularly pausing, being still, and looking around. Alternatively, ascend by road or cable car and then look from a vantage point: looking down on birds in flight is particularly exhilarating and interesting.

Climbers and soarers

Some birds cling to the face of cliffs and rocks, where they feed on insects. Scanning steep rock faces in the summer months using a telescope or binoculars can help pick out the movement of species such as Rock Thrushes and Wallcreepers. Thrushes migrate south in autumn and even the hardy Wallcreepers must come down to lower levels in winter. Setting up your scope near south-facing rock outcrops is often rewarding; birds of prey, such as Golden Eagles and Griffon Vultures, circle on their broad wings, getting lift from the air currents rising above sun-warmed slopes. On cold days, they rely on wind being deflected from steep slopes to get essential lift. Smaller birds of prey, such as Peregrines and Kestrels, are lighter and use their own muscle power to move around.

When walking in the mountains *plan your day carefully, and tell someone about your route and itinerary.*

EXPERT TIP

■ Weather conditions in mountains can – and will – change quickly. Whatever the conditions when you set out, always take a map, tough footwear, and warm, weatherproof clothing – even if you only plan to walk a short distance from the road or ski lift.

WATCHING FROM PEAKS AND RIDGES

Even though mountain ranges are vastly expansive places, birds can be easier to see than you might imagine. Rather than looking up into clear sky, keep an eye on the horizon, where peaks and ridges meet the sky. This will give you a reference point from which to begin focusing your eyes, binoculars, or scope when you see a distant dot. Judging size is difficult because there are relatively few human-scale landmarks for comparison. It can also be hard to use plumage as an identifier because birds are often distant or silhouetted. Concentrate instead on the general shape of the bird in flight and on its flight pattern.

Keep your scope mounted on a tripod, trained and focused on a prominent point where you might expect to see birds. This way, you'll be ready for quick action should something appear, however fleetingly.

A good seat *and a scope with an angled eyepiece will pay dividends during a long spell of raptor watching.*

COMMON SIGHTINGS

Alpine Chough
Often in large, swirling flocks, Alpine Choughs move fast over open slopes.

Golden Eagle
Uptilted wings and powerful flight give this eagle great presence at a distance.

Citril Finch
Found close to the tree line, feeding on the ground, this is a speciality of the Alps and Pyrenees.

Ptarmigan
Don't look into the distance for this bird: it is more likely to be under your feet.

WATCHING FROM BELOW

Don't despair if you cannot get to the top of a hill – looking up from below can also be rewarding. To avoid straining your upper back and neck, lie down on your back and watch through binoculars. Most field guide books picture birds from below – ideal for this situation.

The higher slopes of mountains are home to many of the most characteristic mountain birds. Alpine Choughs, Alpine Accentors, and Snowfinches – often remarkably tame – can be seen around ski lifts. In summer, keep listening for the song of otherwise elusive birds, such as Wheatears, Black Redstarts, and Water Pipits. Their songs carry over long distances and echo around the cliffs.

Patience is rewarded *in open mountain habitats. Although it is tempting to keep on the move, it is better to sit and watch.*

COMMON SIGHTINGS

Griffon Vulture
This long-winged bird is often seen soaring in circling groups high overhead.

Chough
Acrobatic and seemingly enjoying life, this bird is an expert flier. Its ringing calls are striking.

Rock Thrush
Found on cliff faces and high pastures in summer, this thrush migrates to Africa in autumn.

Peregrine
You will hear the raucous calls of this falcon if you chance to be near a nest.

COMMON SIGHTINGS

Crossbill
Feeds by prising seeds from pine and spruce cones, so requires mature conifers.

Coal Tit
Happy in conifers and even in a mixed wood; usually spotted in the vicinity of a pine tree. One of Europe's smallest birds.

Firecrest
This elusive bird tests your ability to hear high-pitched sound; listen for its song.

Black Woodpecker
The biggest of all woodpeckers; needs mature trees, often of pine or beech, in which to excavate a nest hole.

NORTHERN FORESTS

The coniferous forests of Scandinavia and Scotland are amongst the most spectacular and unspoilt woodlands that Europe has to offer. Stands of ancient pines, often covering steep slopes, have a rich understorey and support a great diversity of bird life. Undisturbed primary forest is richest, but older plantations are worth a visit too, especially where patch felling or windfall has created more variety in the habitat.

True conifer specialists, such as Capercaillies, Hazel Grouse, and owls are scarce and hard to see. Crossbills and Siskins favour the forest edge or clearings around big clumps of trees, while elusive Goshawks can be watched from a clearing or hilltop in early spring, when they fly up from the trees to display overhead. Crested and Coal Tits, Goldcrests, Firecrests, Nutcrackers, and Chaffinches, although not exclusively conifer birds, still characterize such woods.

Larger birds of *dense woodland, such as this Siberian Jay, may sometimes be seen from a viewpoint in a clearing or at the woodland edge.*

COMMON SIGHTINGS

Nuthatch
Loud whistles and trills give away the presence of this bird in mature woodland.

Blue Tit
A common and familiar component of wandering autumn and winter flocks.

Chaffinch
Territorial in spring, males sing loudly and attract attention. They are often tame and come for crumbs.

Great Spotted Woodpecker
The most common woodpecker through most of Europe.

BENEATH THE CANOPY

Oakwoods typically have large openings in the canopy. Sunlight is allowed to stream in, promoting rich growth of herbaceous plants in the understorey. As a result, the woods are full of insects, berries, and fruits, which provide food for numerous Chiffchaffs, Blackcaps, Chaffinches, Robins, Wrens, and Dunnocks. Coppicing – cutting trees to promote dense growth from the stumps – is ideal for Nightingales which like a thicket at ground level. Woods composed predominantly of beech, however, block out much of the sunlight. There is comparatively little undergrowth, but the open space created is ideal for Wood Warblers and Pied Flycatchers.

Open space *beneath the trees is favoured by Redstarts, Wood Warblers, and Pied Flycatchers.*

BOREAL FOREST, FINLAND

MIXED FOREST, GERMANY

Woodlands

WOODLANDS FALL INTO two obvious groups – coniferous and deciduous – but there are many other factors that determine which birds will visit. Exposure to wind and salt spray, altitude, latitude, and the nature of the soil beneath all play their part. Limestone, for example, encourages ash woods, while deeper soils support oaks, usually mixed with cherry, holly, and hawthorn. Each type of woodland has its own character and attracts its own distinctive birds.

Buzzard
The common, large predator of woodland clearings.

A walk in the woods

Woodlands are naturally thought of as good places for birds. Seeing the birds can, however, be a challenge. Light is poor and cover dense, and crackling footfalls on fallen leaves and branches will scare many species. Wear soft shoes or trainers so that

Leaf fall *makes it easier for you to see birds – and for them to see you. Sombre colours and stealth are called for; wear soft clothes that don't rustle, and stop chatting.*

EXPERT TIP

▪ Not all woods – or patches within woods – are the same. Look out for areas with native trees of mixed age, and uncleared fallen logs. They will harbour a far greater variety of birds than uniform stands of introduced species. Coppices attract a different range of birds again.

you can "feel" the ground beneath your feet, pause regularly and for long periods, and keep quiet. Birds in dense woods are often best seen from just outside, looking in from a clearing or the woodland edge.

Much depends on the season: early spring is perhaps the best time to visit a rich wood; migrant birds join the residents, singing all day as they set up territories and attract mates. The dawn chorus is at its height and worth an early rise to hear. Spring in a deciduous wood is also best for visibility before the leaves are too dense.

Summer and autumn are quieter, and birds remain well hidden. Some, such as Pied Flycatchers, almost disappear in late summer; others, such as Robins, are in moult, and keep a low profile.

Winter possibilities

By winter, most birds have left. The remaining species tend to roam in nomadic flocks in search of food. If you find a flock on a winter walk, you may have a few hectic minutes with birds of many kinds all around you, but the rest of your walk may be almost birdless.

Parks and gardens

FOR MANY PEOPLE, THE GARDEN is the first point of contact with wildlife. For experienced birdwatchers, it is an ideal place to hone identification skills and study behaviour. The variety of birds in gardens and urban parks is surprisingly high; indeed these habitats have become far more important with intensification of farmland. In larger town parks, many species that are shy in the countryside can be observed at extremely close quarters.

Peregrine
This large falcon is increasing as a bird about town.

The urban environment

Town parks, especially those with trees, shrubberies, and lakes, are great places for birds. Woodpigeons and Jays, wild and unapproachable in the country, are tame here; Grey Herons visit lakes and ponds to fish; and Coots, gulls, and ducks add variety. Many birds not only tolerate,

Position bird feeders *carefully in the garden. They should be near natural cover, such as a bush or tree, but not so close that they can be accessed by squirrels and rats.*

EXPERT TIP

■ A tame Robin is great fun, especially for children. Start by tossing a mealworm (bought by post from birdfood dealers) towards the bird. Keep still. Gradually bring the Robin closer. After a few days, the Robin will approach closer and perhaps even perch on your hand.

but positively exploit town settings: town pigeons, and (in continental Europe) Black Redstarts find buildings as good as natural cliffs for nesting; Pied Wagtails like to feed on tarmac and concrete paths; Tawny Owls roost in town parks and catch rats in the streets at night; while Kestrels nest on ledges. Look out for nests on tall buildings – their presence is often betrayed by guano.

Backyard birds

The richest gardens are those at the edge of town, where country and woodland birds spill over in search of food. Even the smallest urban gardens have Blackbirds, Blue Tits, Robins, and Collared Doves. Setting up inexpensive bird feeders filled with a variety of foods will attract a wide range of species: niger seed brings in Goldfinches, for example, and sunflower hearts appeal to Greenfinches (see pages 44–47).

Many people feed birds only in winter, but birds need supplements year-round and benefit from a boost in spring before nesting. Don't forget to put out bowls of water too. Keep them free of ice in winter with a floating tennis ball.

SUBURBAN GARDEN, SOUTHERN ENGLAND

URBAN PARK, LONDON, ENGLAND

USING THE GARDEN

The garden is a good place to test your skill in stalking birds, to try out a new hide, or to test new photographic or other optical equipment before venturing into the countryside.

Taking thorough notes adds another dimension to garden observation. You might enjoy making year-round records of species, numbers, and nest sites in your garden (but take care not to disturb nesting birds). Note down what the birds feed on, record interesting aspects of behaviour through the seasons, and practise sketching, which is the best way to get familiar with a bird's features. The data you collect are valuable – they could form part of a local or national bird survey. Such surveys are important indicators of changes in bird populations.

Getting close to birds is easy in the garden. Nest-box cameras give you stunning high-quality close-ups, allowing detailed examination of a bird's plumage or behaviour.

COMMON SIGHTINGS

Greenfinch
Favours gardens and parks with tall yew trees, old hedges, cotoneaster berries, and peanut feeders.

Great Spotted Woodpecker
The commonest woodpecker in gardens, often on feeders with nuts or fat.

Great Tit
A common garden bird, dominant at bird feeders; strident two-note song familiar in spring.

Kestrel
Rare in gardens, but often seen in towns, catching mice; hovers as if suspended on a string.

WATERY HABITATS

It is worth seeking out a local park that has its own pond or lake. Willows around the water attract Chiffchaffs in early spring, and Kingfishers fish from overhanging branches early in the day before they are disturbed. Grey Herons may nest on wooded islands. Mallards are frequent, but often mix with farmyard ducks and ornamental or escaped species, so expect a few hybrids and odd colours among them. Observe the similarities in lifestyles between the water birds and learn the differences between Coots and Moorhens, and Little Grebes and Tufted Ducks. When familiar with common birds, keep a keen eye out for oddities that turn up in town parks.

A Lapwing roost on a roundabout *on the edge of town shows how well many birds have adapted to an urban way of life.*

COMMON SIGHTINGS

Blue Tit
A common and popular garden bird, frequent on feeders; also uses nest boxes more than any other species.

Chaffinch
One of the earliest singers in spring in the park or garden; quite common visitor to the bird table.

Song Thrush
Its strident, repetitive song is one of the features of spring. Eats snails, smashing the shells against paving slabs or kerbstones.

Blackbird
Common in wooded parks and gardens, often on lawns; has a beautifully rich, melodious song.

How to identify

The enjoyment and study of birds begins with the ability to tell species apart. Identification is a skill that has to be learned. There are no short cuts and no substitutes for hours spent in the field, but learning itself is a worthwhile and fulfilling goal.

Size and shape

A BIRD'S SIZE AND SHAPE ARE excellent clues to identification, but they need to be interpreted cautiously. Size may vary with age and sex, and it is always difficult to judge accurately in the absence of objects to provide a sense of scale. Shape is trickier still. A bird can move its wings, spread its tail, fluff or sleek its feathers, or extend its neck. Shape also depends on point of view, which is rarely a textbook side-on angle.

Goldcrest
Europe's smallest bird can look slim or dumpy as it tightens or raises its feathers.

Judging sizes

Birds have inconvenient forms that make descriptions of size rather difficult: is a Blackbird the size of a shoe, for example, or a Mallard the size of a rugby ball? They also suddenly look much bigger when they spread their wings. It is more useful to try to compare sizes with other familiar birds – a Blue Tit, Chaffinch, Blackbird,

The Dalmatian Pelican *is one of the world's largest flying birds. With a wingspan exceeding 3m (10ft), there is little chance of misjudging this bird's size.*

Woodpigeon, Mallard, and Canada Goose give a good scale of ascending size. Of course, it is first necessary to fix the sizes of your chosen "reference" birds in mind under a wide variety of observing conditions. Distance, heat haze, mist, rain, and snow all affect our perception of size. Remember that the birdwatcher's tools – telescopes, binoculars, and telephoto lenses – all have a foreshortening effect, reducing the apparent distance between near and distant objects.

Difficulties in judging size are compounded if the bird is in flight. Usually the speed of its movement across the sky, and the speed of its wingbeats give useful clues to its distance (and thus size). Shape can be described more objectively than size, and a simple sketch helps record vital detail, but there are pitfalls. To call a bird "slim" or "dumpy" can be misleading, for example: a wagtail can look sleek in hot weather or as round as a tennis ball when bathing or in the cold (see over).

Size comparisons *should be made between birds of the same type. Waders, for example, with their long bills and legs, are hard to compare with other land birds. Try to fix sizes of a few "reference species" in mind.*

RELATIVE WADER SIZES

| Little Stint | Dunlin | Redshank | Bar-tailed Godwit | Curlew | cm |

Black-winged Stilt

Family Recurvirostridae

Species *Himantopus himantopus*

Length 33–36cm (13–14in)

Wingspan 70–75cm (27–29in)

Distribution Breeds locally in S, W, and E Europe, mostly around the coasts; few in winter.

This is a black-backed, white-bodied bird with a very fine, black bill and almost grotesquely long, vivid pink legs. The head pattern varies individually with more or less black on the nape. In flight, the long legs trail well beyond the short tail. It is noisy, with nasal, metallic calls and alarm notes near the nest, but quiet elsewhere.

Stone-curlew

Family Burhinidae **Species** *Burhinus oedicnemus*

Length 40–45cm (16–18in)

Wingspan 77–85cm (30–33in)

Distribution Breeds locally on sandy heaths and fields in the UK, most of France, Iberia, across S Europe, patchily in E Europe; a summer visitor.

A terrestrial bird of open heath and flinty fields, the Stone-curlew stands tall on long, yellow legs. It is pale brown with a pale area at the base of the bill and on the face, and a pale band across the closed wing. In flight, its wings look long and pointed, with bold, white bars and a patch near the tip. It makes loud, eerie calls at dusk.

Ringed Plover

Family Charadriidae **Species** *Charadrius hiaticula*

Length 17–19cm (6½–7½in)

Wingspan 48–57cm (19–22in)

Distribution Breeds mostly on coasts in N and NW Europe and Mediterranean; widespread on migration and in winter on coasts and inland.

Small and strikingly patterned, this plover has a short, orange-and-black bill, orange legs, and bold, black-and-white bands on the head and breast. In flight, it has a long, white wingbar. Juveniles are duller with little black, but have dark brown breast patches, a white mark behind the eye, and a black bill. It forms flocks outside the breeding season. Its call is a mellow, fluty *too-ip*.

Little Ringed Plover

Family Charadriidae **Species** *Charadrius dubius*

Length 14–15cm (5½–6in)

Wingspan 42–48cm (16–19in)

Distribution Breeds widely by fresh water in Europe, except in far N; a summer visitor and widespread in early spring. An autumn migrant.

This small, slender plover is slimmer than the Ringed, with narrower black bands. It has white between the cap and forehead bar, and a yellow eyering. In flight, it has plain, brown wings with a faint bar. The black bill has a yellow mark at the base, and the legs are dull. Juveniles look similar, but have less black. It calls with a short *pew*.

Kentish Plover

Family Charadriidae

Species *Charadrius alexandrinus*

Length 15–17cm (6–6½in)

Wingspan 45–50cm (18–20in)

Distribution Breeds locally around the coasts of Europe; a rare migrant elsewhere.

This small plover can look slim or rather dumpy and short. Unlike other "ringed" plovers, its bill and legs are black. Males have black on the forecrown and sides of the breast, and a rusty cap; females have dark brown in place of the black breast sides. In flight, white wingbars are visible. Its calls include a short, sharp note and a short whistle.

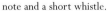

Grey Plover

Family Charadriidae **Species** *Pluvialis squatarola*

Length 27–30cm (11–12in)

Wingspan 71–83cm (28–32in)

Distribution Breeds in the Arctic; a widespread migrant on all coasts and a winter visitor in NW and W Europe, mostly on the coast.

In spring, this is a handsome bird, with black-and-silver-grey spangling above, black below, and a broad white band on the side of the neck and breast. In winter, it loses all the black and the upperparts are duller grey with dark specks. In flight, it reveals a white rump and wingbar and, at all times, unique, black "wingpits". Its call is a triple whistle, *tlee-u-ee*.

Golden Plover

Family Charadriidae **Species** *Pluvialis apricaria*

Length 26–29cm (11–12in)

Wingspan 67–76cm (26–30in)

Distribution Breeds on moors in N Europe, including the northern UK; moves lower and is widespread in S and W from autumn to spring.

A medium-sized, short-billed wader, often found on dry ground, the Golden Plover is spangled buff, black and yellow above and black below in summer. Northern birds have a blacker face and a stronger, white border to the black underparts than southern ones. In winter, it looks warm yellow-brown above (speckled at close range) and yellow-white below. In flight, it has a dark rump and white wingbar. Its call is a high, plaintive whistle — *peoow*.

Winter

Lapwing

Family Charadriidae **Species** *Vanellus vanellus*

Length 28–31cm (11–12in) **Wingspan** 70–76cm (27–30in)

Distribution A summer visitor to moors and pastures of N and NE Europe, resident in the west, mostly a winter visitor in the south; absent from Iceland.

A rather long-bodied, short-legged wading bird of dry ground and marshes, the Lapwing is distinctively dark-backed and black-and-white below, including a bold, white underwing patch contrasted with black flight feathers. In flight, it has a striking, flickering appearance, especially in large, irregular flocks. At close range, it is dark green above, shot with purple-blue on the shoulders. Males have blacker faces and long, wispy crests in summer; females have mottled faces and shorter crests. Juveniles have only a slight crest and are barred with orange-buff above. The song flight is an ecstatic tumbling, rolling, and diving performance with a nasal, slurred song; calls include a nasal *pee-wit* and various *weee* and *wit-wit* notes.

Broad, rounded wings

Knot

Family Scolopacidae **Species** *Calidris canutus*

Length 23–27cm (9–11in)

Wingspan 47–54cm (18–21in)

Distribution Breeds in the Canadian Arctic and Siberia; a regular migrant on most European coasts, common in winter on western estuaries.

This medium to small, chunky wader has a rather short bill and legs. In summer, it is orange-red on the body, mottled black and rufous above. In winter, it is a dull, grey bird, pale close-up but looking dark at long range on mud; in flight, it has a dull, pale grey rump and thin wingbar. Juveniles are scaly above, washed with peachy-buff below.

Winter

Sanderling

Family Scolopacidae **Species** *Calidris alba*

Length 20–21cm (8in)

Wingspan 36–39cm (14–15in)

Distribution Breeds in the Arctic; a regular coastal migrant and frequent on N and W coasts from late summer to spring, on sandy beaches.

A small, fast-moving wader, the Sanderling is stockier than a Dunlin, with a straight bill, jet black legs, a wide, white wingbar, and a clear white underside. In spring, the back and breast are mottled rufous-brown, in winter pale grey; autumn juveniles are spotted with black above. The dark shoulder is often obvious. In flight, it calls a short, hard *tchik* or *tik*.

Winter

Curlew Sandpiper

Family Scolopacidae **Species** *Calidris ferruginea*

Length 18–23cm (7–9in)

Wingspan 38–41cm (15–16in)

Distribution Breeds in the Arctic; a common migrant in spring in SE Europe; in late summer and autumn more widespread in W Europe.

A little larger, more elegant, longer-legged, and longer-billed than a Dunlin, with a wide, white patch above the tail. Summer adults are dark red below; in late summer, they are patchy red and grey. Juveniles in autumn have clean, scaly upperparts and pale underparts, with an almost unstreaked, bright buff breast. Legs and bill are black. The call is a soft, chirruping *churr-rip*.

Juvenile (autumn)

Little Stint

Family Scolopacidae **Species** *Calidris minuta*

Length 12–14cm (4½–5½in)

Wingspan 34–37cm (13–14in)

Distribution Breeds in the Arctic; a spring migrant in the Mediterranean, but more common in autumn in NW Europe. Rare in winter.

This is the smallest common wader; a short-billed, black-legged, active bird. Adults are dark-spotted, red-brown above, white below. Juveniles have a neat, streaked cap, a pale stripe over the eye, a streaked patch at the side of the breast, and mottled, rusty upperparts with cream "V"-shaped lines. Its call is *tit* or *ti-titit*.

Juvenile (autumn)

Purple Sandpiper

Family Scolopacidae **Species** *Calidris maritima*

Length 20–22cm (8–9in)

Wingspan 40–45cm (16–18in)

Distribution Breeds locally in Scandinavia and Iceland; widespread on rocky NW coasts from late summer to spring.

This small but thick-set wader of rocky sea shores has a dark bill, pale yellow at the base, and dull orange-yellow legs. Summer adults and juveniles have rusty spots and streaks above; winter birds are dull grey-brown with scaly, whitish feather edges above, and a plain head except for a white eyering and throat. A wide, black rump and white wingstripe are visible in flight. Its calls are high, thin notes.

Wood Sandpiper

Family Scolopacidae **Species** *Tringa glareola*

Length 19–21cm (7½–8in)

Wingspan 36–40cm (14–16in)

Distribution Breeds in N and NE Europe; a sparse migrant in spring in W Europe, commoner in autumn; commoner in S Europe on passage.

Larger than a Common Sandpiper, and slighter, browner, and longer-legged than a Green Sandpiper, this wader is brown above and white below, with buff chequering on the back and wings. In flight, a dull, pale grey-brown underwing, square, white rump, and extensively barred tail are seen. Calls with a high, sharp *chiff-iff-iff* in fast flight.

Dunlin

Family Scolopacidae **Species** *Calidris alpina*

Length 16–20cm (6–8in) **Wingspan** 35–40cm (14–16in)

Distribution Breeds in the northern UK, Scandinavia, Iceland, and locally around the Baltic; common from late summer to late spring on all coasts.

Thin white wingbar

Usually the commonest of the small waders and a benchmark for the identification of others, the Dunlin is a social bird of shores and waterside habitats of all kinds. In summer, it is easily told by its rectangular black belly. It is bright buff to rusty-brown above with blackish streaks; its breast is grey-buff, with fine, darker streaks. Winter adults are grey-brown above, white below, with a dull, greyish breast. Juveniles are bright buff-brown above with long, pale creamy lines and white below, with obvious blackish smudges and streaks along the flanks. The bill is usually slightly downcurved; the legs are black. In flight, it has a white wingbar and a dark rump bordered by white sides. It calls a vibrant, thin, high but weak *trreee*.

Juvenile moulting to winter

Dunlins plod lethargically when walking.

Green Sandpiper

Family Scolopacidae **Species** *Tringa ochropus*

Length 21–24cm (8–9in)

Wingspan 41–46cm (16–18in)

Distribution Breeds in N and NE Europe; a widespread migrant from mid summer to spring elsewhere; local in W and S Europe in winter.

This is a medium-sized wader, dark brown and white, but usually looking almost black and white, especially in flight. It is identified by its dark upperside with very large, square, white rump and black-tipped white tail, white belly, blackish underwings, and dull legs. Its call is a loud, fluted, almost yodelling *tlu-wee, wee-wee*.

Common Sandpiper

Family Scolopacidae **Species** *Actitis hypoleucos*

Length 19–21cm (7½–8in)

Wingspan 32–35cm (12–14in)

Distribution Summer visitor to most of Europe except Iceland, beside lakes and rivers; a common migrant, but rare in S and W in winter.

Slim and long-tailed, with a characteristic up–down swing of the rear body, this bird is mid-brown above and bright white below. It has a white crescent in front of the wing, a long, white wingstripe, and a dusky breast with a paler centre; the legs are greenish to yellowish. It flies with stiffly bowed wings and calls *tswee-wee-wee*.

Redshank

Family Scolopacidae **Species** *Tringa totanus*

Length 27–29cm (11in)

Wingspan 45–52cm (18–20in)

Distribution Breeds widely in marshy places in NW, N, and E Europe, locally elsewhere; widespread as a migrant and in winter.

A medium-sized wader with rather long legs and medium-long bill, the Redshank is noisy and obvious in the shoreline. It looks dark brown, with a whiter belly. Its legs and the base of its bill are red (but paler and yellower in juveniles). In flight, it shows a bold pattern with a white rump, broad, white bands on the backs of the wings, and white underwings. Its calls are a fast, nervous *tyew-yu-yu* and variations.

Greenshank

Family Scolopacidae **Species** *Tringa nebularia*

Length 30–35cm (12–14in)

Wingspan 53–60cm (21–23in)

Distribution Breeds locally on moors in Scotland and N Europe. Widespread migrant; in winter, a few are seen in W and S European estuaries.

This beautiful wader is a little larger and longer-legged than a Redshank. It looks pale grey and white, mottled darker above in summer, and often whitish around the head in winter. Its bill is quite thick and slightly upcurved, its legs pale grey or yellow-green. In flight, it shows dark wings with no white, but a long "V" of white on the back. Its calls are more even, less hysterical than a Redshank's, a rich, triple *tyu-tyu-tyu*. It is easily located by its loud, ringing voice.

Turnstone

Family Scolopacidae **Species** *Arenaria interpres*

Length 21–24cm (8–9in)

Wingspan 44–49cm (17–19in)

Distribution Breeds locally in Scandinavia and Iceland; widespread on North Sea, Baltic, and Atlantic coasts, local in Mediterranean in winter.

A small, stocky, short-legged wader of rocks and shingle, with a short, stout, uptilted bill. It has short, orange legs and a dark breastband. In summer, it is piebald on the head, rufous and black above; in winter, the head is duller, the back black and dark brown. In flight, it has striking, white wingbars and a white rump. Its calls include a short, hard *tchik* and *tuk-a-tuk-a-tuk*.

Spotted Redshank

Family Scolopacidae **Species** *Tringa erythropus*

Length 29–32cm (11–12in) **Wingspan** 48–52cm (19–20in)

Distribution Breeds in northern Scandinavia and Siberia. A widespread migrant, especially in autumn; a few in winter on W European estuaries.

Slim-billed and long-legged, but quite round-bodied, the Spotted Redshank is a little larger than a Redshank and more active in its feeding, even swimming and diving at times. In summer, it is smoky-black, with very dark red or blackish legs. In winter, it is pale grey, white below, with a dark eyestripe below a white line. Its legs are bright red. Juveniles in autumn are browner. All have plain wings and a white oval on the back in flight, and call a clear, sharp *chyew-it*.

Winter

Long, black, red-based bill

Black-tailed Godwit

Family Scolopacidae **Species** *Limosa limosa*

Length 36–44cm (14–17in)

Wingspan 62–70cm (24–27in)

Distribution Breeds in Iceland, rare in UK, more common in Low Countries and E Europe; common migrant and winter visitor in S and W.

This is a large, long-legged wader with a long, straight bill. Summer males are brick-red with blacker bars on the flanks and a white belly, females paler. Juveniles are similar but with scaly, rufous feather edges above. In winter, the Black-tailed Godwit is very plain grey-brown. In flight, it reveals a bold, white rump, black tail, and long, broad, white wingbars.

Bar-tailed Godwit

Family Scolopacidae **Species** *Limosa lapponica*

Length 32–42cm (12–16in)

Wingspan 61–68cm (24–27in)

Distribution Breeds in Siberia and extreme N Europe; in winter, widespread on coasts, especially estuaries of NW Europe.

In summer, this godwit is more coppery-red than the Black-tailed; in winter, it is streaked above and like a Curlew in pattern, with a brighter buff breast. In flight, it shows plain wings, a pale, barred tail, and a white rump, and is less eyecatching than the Black-tailed. It has a slightly upcurved bill and rather short legs.

Juvenile

Whimbrel

Family Scolopacidae

Species *Numenius phaeopus*

Length 40–46cm (16–18in)

Wingspan 71–81cm (28–32in)

Distribution Breeds on barren moors in Iceland, Scotland, and Scandinavia; a migrant in W Europe.

Like a small Curlew or a larger, darker Bar-tailed Godwit, the Whimbrel has a thick, downcurved or "bent" bill and a more strongly striped head. In flight, it looks chunkier, darker, and quicker than a Curlew, but it is best identified by its call: a fast, high, even trill *ti-ti-ti-ti-ti-ti-ti-ti*. It has dark outer wings and a white rump, revealed when flying.

Curlew

Family Scolopacidae **Species** *Numenius arquata*

Length 50–60cm (20–23in) **Wingspan** 80–100cm (31–39in)

Distribution Breeds on moors and meadows in most of N Europe, local in S and W; widespread in winter and as migrant in spring and autumn.

Gull-like shape

The Curlew is a big, brown wader of moors and heaths in summer, estuaries and marshes in winter. It is mottled and streaked brown, pale at close range but looking dark at a distance on pale mudflats, where it feeds in isolation but roosts in long lines or groups. The long, downcurved bill is distinctive. In flight, it has no white wingbar but the outer wing looks rather darker than the inner half; the rump and lower back are white. Its flight is strong, regular, and gull-like. Calls include a fluty *cur-lee*, a hoarse *whaup*, and a lyrical, bubbling, beautiful song.

Curlews at a high-tide roost.

Ruff

Family Scolopacidae

Species *Philomachus pugnax*

Length 20–32cm (8–12in)

Wingspan 46–58cm (18–23in)

Distribution Breeds locally in N and NW Europe; regular migrant throughout.

Male Ruffs are larger than Redshanks, females smaller. Spring males are multi-coloured with crests and extravagant ruffs; in winter, they have dull whitish heads. Females are brown and boldly blotched above; autumn juveniles have bright buff feather edges above and are ochre-buff below with yellow-olive legs. They have thin wingbars and a white patch each side of the rump. It rarely calls.

Juvenile

Snipe

Family Scolopacidae **Species** *Gallinago gallinago*

Length 25–28cm (10–11in)

Wingspan 37–43cm (14–17in)

Distribution Breeds widely but very locally on wet meadows, moors, and heaths; NE birds move south and west in winter, when widespread.

The Snipe is a small, richly-patterned, short-legged wader with a long, straight bill. It has long cream stripes on the back, a striped head, and a white trailing edge to the wing. In spring, it perches on poles, calling *chip-per chip-per;* otherwise it is secretive in wet marshes, flushed at close range with a short, harsh *scaaap* call.

Jack Snipe

Family Scolopacidae

Species *Lymnocryptes minimus*

Length 17–19cm (6½–7½in)

Wingspan 30–36cm (12–14in)

Distribution Breeds in N and NE Europe; widespread but very local in winter.

A tiny bird, with a shorter bill than the Snipe, and a darker back, longer, broader cream stripes above, and a dark central crown (the Snipe has a pale line along the centre). In flight, it is weaker and less dashing (the Snipe flies up high in a fast zigzag; the Jack Snipe flies up underfoot, goes in half circle, then settles again). It usually feeds in dense, wet vegetation, so is hard to spot. Its shorter bill is usually obvious. It rarely calls in winter.

Woodcock

Family Scolopacidae **Species** *Scolopax rusticola*

Length 33–38cm (13–15in)

Wingspan 55–65cm (21–25in)

Distribution Breeds in woods over much of N and NE Europe and locally in C and SE Europe; found widely in S and W in winter, in woods.

Similar to the Snipe, but rarely seen in the same habitat, the Woodcock is a bird of woods and boggy clearings. It is usually seen at dusk in spring and summer, flying over the forest, calling with croaks and sharp whistles. It has a peaked head, with dark, crosswise bars and a long bill; the underside is closely barred. Difficult to find and observe on the ground, it flies up fast from underfoot with noisy wings.

Skuas, gulls, terns, and auks

Skuas are maritime birds, dark with pale wing flashes; some have several colour forms. Gulls vary from small to very large. They are black or grey above and white below, and are hooded or white-headed in summer. Terns are slimmer, with angular wings and dark caps. Auks are penguin-like seabirds that only come to land to breed.

Great Skua

Family Stercorariidae **Species** *Stercorarius skua*

Length 50–58cm (20–23in) **Wingspan** 125–140cm (49–55in)

Distribution Breeds very locally on moors and islands in Scotland, Iceland, and Scandinavia; widespread at sea in spring and autumn, rare in winter.

The biggest skua, the Great Skua is like a heavy, dark, young gull or a big bird of prey. It is streaked dark brown, with a big white patch on the outer wing. The head is often paler, streaked, and with a hint of a dark cap, and it has a thick, hook-tipped, black bill. It flies low and steadily over the sea but chases other seabirds, up to the size of a Gannet, with speed and agility.

Arctic Skua

Family Stercorariidae

Species *Stercorarius parasiticus*

Length 37–44cm (14–17in)

Wingspan 97–115cm (38–45in)

Distribution Breeds in Iceland, Scandinavia, and Scotland; widespread offshore on migration.

An elegant skua, similar in size to the Common Gull. It has long wings and a wedge-shaped tail with a central spike. It is dark above and pale below, with a black cap and dusky breastband, or all-dark; the wings have a flash of white on the leading edge towards the tip. Juveniles are more gingery-brown or greyish, barred with grey-buff or rufous, and they lack the tail spike.

Black-headed Gull

Family Laridae **Species** *Larus ridibundus*

Length 34–37cm (13–14in) **Wingspan** 100–110cm (39–43in)

Distribution Breeds widely across Europe; E and N European breeders move south and west in winter, when common and widespread by sea and fresh water.

Dark ear spot

This small, active, noisy gull is very pale, with an obvious, white flash along the leading edge of the wing and a dusky patch beneath, giving a marked flickering effect in flight. In summer, it has a dark brown hood, a thin, dark, plum-red bill, and dark red legs. The non-breeding adult has a white head with dark ear spot, and a bright red bill and legs. Juveniles are tawny-brown on the head and neck at first, but soon become whiter; the wings have a brown band and trailing edge, and a white flash partly obscured by black-brown. The bill is pale buff with a black tip, the legs orange-buff. In summer, immatures gain a partial brown hood and the wing pattern fades. Calls include sharp notes, a short *kik*, *keeya*, and the longer *kyowww*.

Winter

Summer

Common Gull

Family Laridae **Species** *Larus canus*

Length 38–44cm (15–17in)

Wingspan 105–125cm (41–49in)

Distribution Breeds locally in NW Europe, including the UK and Ireland, and more widely in NE Europe; widespread but local in winter.

A medium to small gull, elegant in flight. The Common Gull is mid-grey above, with grey- to yellow-green legs, a slim bill, and black eyes. The long, narrow wings have a large, black area and big white spots at the tip. The immature has a black outer wing and hindwing bar, brown forewing, and a white tail with a sharp, black band at the tip.

Winter

Herring Gull

Family Laridae **Species** *Larus argentatus*

Length 55–67cm (21–26in)

Wingspan 130–160cm (51–62in)

Distribution Breeds commonly on coasts of NW and N Europe; northern birds move S in winter around North Sea and UK; common inland.

A large, heavy gull with a thick bill. The adult is silver-grey and white, with a streaked head in winter. Its bill is yellow with a red spot, the eyes pale, the legs pale to dusky pink, and the wingtips black with white spots. Immatures are streaky brown but gain pale grey above with age. It makes loud, wailing calls.

Yellow-legged Gull

Family Laridae **Species** *Larus michahellis*

Length 55–65cm (21–25in)

Wingspan 130–150cm (51–59in)

Distribution Breeds locally in C Europe, more widely in the Mediterranean and Iberia; a late summer to winter visitor to UK.

Very like the Herring Gull, the Yellow-legged Gull is slightly darker than southern Herrings (Scandinavian ones are more similar), with a much whiter head in winter. In autumn, the legs are rich yellow and the head dusky, with blacker wingtips and a brighter bill. Juveniles are more rusty-brown, the rump and tail whiter with a clearer black band.

Lesser Black-backed Gull

Family Laridae **Species** *Larus fuscus*

Length 52–67cm (20–26in)

Wingspan 128–148cm (50–58in)

Distribution Breeds on cliffs and moors in N and NW Europe; mostly a summer visitor in the N but remains in winter in UK and SW Europe.

Like a dark-backed Herring Gull, this gull is slaty-grey or darker above, blending evenly into black wingtips with less white than the Herring; the legs are bright yellow (dull in winter). Its head and breast are heavily streaked in winter. Immatures have darker wings than Herrings of the same age, and gain dark grey on their backs with age.

Winter

Kittiwake

Family Laridae **Species** *Larus tridactyla*

Length 38–40cm (15–16in) **Wingspan** 95–110cm (37–43in)

Distribution Breeds on cliffs (and buildings) on the coasts of the UK and Ireland, Iceland, Scandinavia, western France, and Iberia; widespread at sea in winter.

Blue-grey back

A medium to small maritime gull, rare inland, the Kittiwake has a large, rounded head. It has very short legs and walks poorly on land. In summer, its head, neck, body, and tail are striking white against the silver-grey wings and back; the outer wings are paler, with neat black tips. It has a yellow bill and black legs and eyes. In winter, the rear head and neck are smoky-grey, and it has a sooty ear spot. The juvenile has a black bill, black collar, a black diagonal across the inner wing, and a black outer wing, creating a bold, zigzag pattern in flight; in summer, the black fades, especially on the inner wing; immatures look paler and washed-out and the outer wings become brownish. Loud calls at colony include a ringing *kit-i-ya-wake* and high, mewing notes.

Juvenile birds sit on beaches or flat rocky platforms.

Great Black-backed Gull

Family Laridae **Species** *Larus marinus*

Length 64–78cm (25–30in)

Wingspan 150–170cm (59–66in)

Distribution Breeds locally on sea cliffs in UK and Ireland, Iceland, and Scandinavian coasts; more widespread in NW Europe in winter.

This is the biggest, heaviest gull with the largest bill. In summer, it is black above with a white head and body; in winter, the head remains mostly white. Its legs are pale pink to whitish. The juvenile is boldly chequered above, its heavy bill mostly black at first, gaining a pale tip. The back gets blacker with age.

Winter

Little Gull

Family Laridae **Species** *Larus minutus*

Length 25–27cm (10–11in)

Wingspan 70–77cm (27–30in)

Distribution Breeds very locally in E and NE Europe, rare in W; widespread migrant in W Europe and Mediterranean areas.

The smallest gull, the Little Gull is tern-like in buoyant flight. In summer, it is pearly-grey with a jet black hood, dark bill, and red legs. In winter, it loses the hood. The underwing is black with a broad, white rear edge and tip. Juveniles are brown-black above, with a dark smudge on the side of the breast; the back becomes grey, then grey and white with a black "W" across the upperwing and a white underwing.

Winter

Little Tern

Family Sternidae **Species** *Sterna albifrons*

Length 22–24cm (9in)

Wingspan 48–55cm (19–21in)

Distribution Breeds widely but very locally on sand and shingle beaches. Mostly very scarce around the coasts of Europe; absent in winter.

The tiny Little Tern is fast-flying with deep, whirring wingbeats. It is pale grey and white with a white forehead, black hood, blackish outer wing, orange legs, and yellow bill (blacker in winter). The juvenile is browner on the head and back, dusky along the fore-edge of the wing, and its bill and legs are dark. The bird is best identified by its small size. It calls with a high, quick, chattering *kurr-i-eek* and a short *ay-ik*.

Sandwich Tern

Family Sternidae **Species** *Sterna sandvicensis*

Length 36–41cm (14–16in)

Wingspan 95–105cm (37–41in)

Distribution Breeds very locally but widely on sandy coasts of NW Europe. A widespread migrant, but very rare in winter.

This large, long-winged, pale tern is strikingly white below and silvery-grey above even at great range. It has a rather long head and bill, and a short tail. The adult has a black bill with a pale yellow tip, black legs, and a bushy nape; the cap is black in spring, but the forehead becomes speckled white by mid summer. Juveniles have brown bars above and a dark tail tip. Its call is a distinctive harsh, rhythmic *kierr-ink*.

Common Tern

Family Sternidae **Species** *Sterna hirundo*

Length 31–35cm (12–14in)

Wingspan 70–80cm (27–31in)

Distribution Summer visitor to much of Europe, breeding inland and on coasts, most commonly in N and NE; a widespread migrant.

A slim tern, grey above and paler below, with a black cap in summer. It has red legs and a red bill with a black tip. In flight, it shows a dusky mark towards the wingtip on top (wingtip blacker in autumn), dusky tips to the outer wings below, and a translucent patch behind the bend of the wing. Juveniles have a similar underwing; the upperwing has a grey trailing edge and pale midwing panel, and the bill is pale at the base.

Gull-billed Tern

Family Sternidae **Species** *Sterna nilotica*

Length 35–42cm (14–16in)

Wingspan 76–86cm (30–34in)

Distribution Breeds locally in the Mediterranean area and NW Europe; a rare migrant away from these areas, and absent in winter.

A medium to large tern, the Gull-billed is like a greyer Sandwich Tern, but with a stouter black bill and longer legs; its rump and tail are very pale grey. In winter, it is very pale with a black eye patch. It shows a dark trailing edge towards the wingtips in flight. Juveniles have a black mask and stubby dark bill. It feeds over marshes as well as water, sometimes on the coast, and migrates over the sea. Its calls include a hard, deep *chu-vik*.

Black Tern

Family Sternidae **Species** *Chlidonias niger*

Length 22–24cm (9in)

Wingspan 63–68cm (25–27in)

Distribution Breeds commonly on marshes in NE and E Europe, rare and local in W Europe; widespread as a migrant, especially in autumn.

A small tern that feeds by dipping to the water surface (not diving). In summer, the adult is sooty-black with a white patch under the grey tail. In winter, it is dusky grey above (the juvenile browner), grey on the tail, with a white underside and a black hood extending below the eye and on to the nape. It has a dusky patch on the side of the chest, and dark legs and bill; the juvenile has a paler midwing panel.

Arctic Tern

Family Sternidae **Species** *Sterna paradisaea*

Length 32–35cm (12–14in) **Wingspan** 80–95cm (31–37in)

Distribution Breeds commonly in N and NW Europe, mostly along coasts; a widespread migrant in W Europe in spring and autumn.

Clean, pale wing

The Arctic Tern is very like the Common Tern, but is greyer below, with shorter legs, a rounder head, a short neck but a longer tail (so is shorter at the front but longer behind than Common in flight). It has a spiky, all-red bill. The upperwing is paler towards the tip without the dark wedge, the underwing whiter with a fine, tapered trailing edge to the tip (Common's is broader and blunt-ended), and more extensively translucent. The adult Common has a white forehead in autumn, while the Arctic retains the black cap longer. The juvenile has a short, blacker bill (base is pale on the Common), a blackish forewing, scaly midwing, and a white area on the hindwing (Common has a grey bar).

Whiskered Tern

Family Sternidae **Species** *Chlidonias hybridus*

Length 24–28cm (9–11in)

Wingspan 57–63cm (22–25in)

Distribution Breeds locally in S Europe. A rare spring and autumn migrant or vagrant farther north; absent in winter.

The Whiskered Tern is larger than a Black Tern but its behaviour is similar. In summer, it has white cheeks and throat, a black cap, a grey upperside, and a blackish belly; in winter, it is much whiter, paler than the Black above, with a dark eyepatch, streaky crown, no dark breast patches, and a whiter rump. The juvenile has brown bars on its back, quickly becoming greyer with age, and a whitish rump and grey tail.

Puffin

Family Alcidae **Species** *Fratercula arctica*

Length 26–29cm (10–11in)

Wingspan 47–63cm (18–25in)

Distribution Breeds on coasts and islands around northern France, the UK, Ireland, Iceland, and Scandinavia; at sea in winter.

This small, stumpy, small-winged auk has a triangular bill, grey facial disk, and all-black upperwings. In summer, adults have orange legs and a bright red, yellow, and blue-grey bill; in winter, this becomes smaller and darker. Juveniles have a small, dusky-grey bill and a smoky-grey face, blacker around the eyes. Flight is low and whirring, showing the bright white belly and grey underwings.

Guillemot

Family Alcidae **Species** *Uria aalge*

Length 38–46cm (15–18in)

Wingspan 64–73cm (25–28in)

Distribution Breeds locally on sea cliffs from W Iberia to Scandinavia and Iceland; widespread at sea outside the breeding season.

An upstanding, sharp-billed auk with a brown to black head and upperparts (blacker in the north), white underparts, and a white trailing edge to the wing. Some have a white "spectacle". In winter, its head is white with a black cap and eyestripe. The tail is short and square, held low on the water. It calls with loud, growling, rolling notes at colony, but is silent at sea.

Razorbill

Family Alcidae **Species** *Alca torda*

Length 37–39cm (14–15in)

Wingspan 63–67cm (25–26in)

Distribution Breeds on cliffs in N and NW Europe including Iceland, where it is locally abundant. Widespread at sea in winter, scarce in estuaries.

A thick-set auk, the Razorbill is very black on the head and upperparts except for a white line on the hindwing and a white streak in front of the eye; the bill is deep, flattened, and crossed by a white line. In winter, the head is white below, with a deep black cap reaching below eye level. On water, its pointed tail is often raised. In flight, its narrow, black rump with white sides is obvious.

Pigeons and doves

There is no strict difference between pigeons and doves. They are soft-feathered, sleek, small-headed birds with long tails and broad wings; the bill is small, weak, and has a small fleshy patch (the cere) at the base. They are mostly silent in flight but may clap their wings in display or alarm, and have distinctive, repetitive songs.

Woodpigeon

Family Columbidae **Species** *Columba palumbus*

Length 40–42cm (16in) **Wingspan** 75–80cm (29–31in)

Distribution Breeds in most of Europe except the extreme north. Birds from the north and east move south and west in winter.

The largest pigeon, the Woodpigeon is marked by a striking white patch that runs from front to back across the open wing, and shows as a line on the bend of the closed wing. The adult has a white neck patch, absent on the juvenile. It is grey above and pink on the breast; the pale tail has a broad, dark tip. Its song is a soothing *coo-cooo-cooo, coo-coo, cuk*.

Rock Dove

Family Columbidae **Species** *Columba livia*

Length 31–35cm (12–14in)

Wingspan 63–70cm (25–27in)v

Distribution Breeds locally on coasts of NW Europe and mountains of S Europe; widespread as town pigeon – domesticated birds gone wild.

This neat, handsome pigeon has a broad, white rump patch and two wide, black bars across each wing. It is pale grey above, with a white underwing and dark head and breast. Town pigeons (derived from domesticated Rock Doves) are often similar in plumage, but with a larger white spot on the bill. Its song is a deep, rolling *coo*.

Stock Dove

Family Columbidae **Species** *Columba oenas*

Length 32–34cm (12–13in)

Wingspan 63–69cm (25–27in)

Distribution Breeds over most of Europe except far N in parks, farmland, and mountainous areas; eastern birds move west in winter.

Smaller, rounder, and shorter-necked than the Woodpigeon, the Stock Dove glides on angled wings. It has no white on the wings or neck, but is blue-grey with a dark tail tip, very short bars on the hindwing, a grey underwing, and a large, pale panel on the upperwing. It looks rounder-headed and shorter-necked than homing pigeons. Its song is a deep, mechanical, almost booming *orr-woo orr-woo*.

Collared Dove

Family Columbidae

Species *Streptopelia decaocto*

Length 31–33cm (12–13in)

Wingspan 47–55cm (18–21in)

Distribution A widespread resident in Europe, following rapid expansion to the west.

A small dove with a neat, round head and a long tail. The Collared Dove is plain greyish- or sandy-brown with a pinker breast, a subtle pale blue area on the upperwing, a bluish-grey underwing, and a thin, black collar. Its tail is dark above with a white tip when fanned; below, the basal third is blackish, the rest dull white. It calls in flight with a loud, sneering, nasal *zweeer*; its song is a monotonous, deep *cu-coo-cuk* or *coo-rrooo-coo*.

Turtle Dove

Family Columbidae **Species** *Streptopelia turtur*

Length 26–28cm (10–11in)

Wingspan 47–53cm (18–21in)

Distribution A summer visitor, breeding across most of S and C Europe, but absent from the northern UK, Ireland, Iceland, and Scandinavia.

The smallest European dove, with a wedge-shaped tail and narrow, angled wings. It is pale and warm brown, pinker below, with bold, dark chequering on the back, and a striped, black-and-grey neck patch. Its tail is dark with a narrow white "V"-shaped tip above, broken in the centre; below is a broader, white area. Its flight is quick, rolling from side to side with flicked wings, its song a purring *torr toorrrr*.

Owls and nightjars

These are two unrelated groups, both mainly nocturnal. Owls vary from tiny to very large; they have forward-facing eyes, hooked bills largely hidden in facial feathers, and sharp, hooked claws. Nightjars are long-winged and long-tailed, with small feet and tiny bills, but wide mouths; they catch insects in the air at dawn and dusk.

Tawny Owl

Family Strigidae **Species** *Strix aluco*

Length 37–39cm (14–15in) **Wingspan** 94–104cm (37–41in)

Distribution A widespread resident in all kinds of woods; absent from Ireland, Iceland, and northern Scandinavia.

A large, thick-set, big-headed owl, the Tawny Owl has a rounded shape at rest, but is often thinner and more upright if alarmed or discovered at a daytime roost. It is strictly nocturnal. Mottled rufous to grey-brown, it has paler underparts, a wide, round, pale facial disk, big, black eyes, and a diagonal row of pale spots on each side of the back. In flight, it looks heavy, big-headed, and broad-winged, and is very short-tailed. Its call is a loud, nasal, repeated *kew-ick* or *k'week*; its song is a hollow, wavering, breathy hoot, *hooo, hu, hu-hooooooooo*.

Scops Owl

Family Strigidae **Species** *Otus scops*

Length 19–21cm (7½–8in)

Wingspan 47–54cm (18–21in)

Distribution A summer visitor to S and E Europe; a few remain in winter in extreme S. A very rare vagrant north of its usual range.

A small, slim owl with an angular head. Its ear tufts are raised in alarm or display but are usually lowered, giving a flat-topped head shape. It is grey with rufous patches above and close dark bars and streaks. Its yellow eyes are hard to see. Usually detected by its call after dark, it may be seen in street lights or torch beams. Its song is a loud, fluty, melancholy *pew* or *kiew*, repeated every 2–3 seconds.

Barn Owl

Family Tytonidae **Species** *Tyto alba*

Length 33–39cm (13–15in) **Wingspan** 85–93cm (33–36in)

Distribution Breeds in the UK, SW, W, and C Europe on farmland, moors, and marshes; a few wander in winter but are rare outside the usual range.

 A medium-sized owl, the Barn Owl looks very pale, with a white, heart-shaped facial disk, and small, black eyes bordered by a little orange-buff. In the UK, France, Spain, and Italy, it is very white on the face and underparts. Elsewhere, the underparts are deep orange-buff with darker spots. Its upperparts are pale yellow to sandy-buff with grey areas and pepper-and-salt speckling. In flight, it looks large-headed, short-tailed, with rather short, rounded wings, and often hovers. Calls include a vibrant shriek.

The Barn Owl appears top-heavy on its perch.

Little Owl

Family Strigidae **Species** *Athene noctua*

Length 21–23cm (8–9in)

Wingspan 50–56cm (20–22in)

Distribution A widespread resident on farmland in the south of Europe; absent from the northern UK, Ireland, Iceland, and Scandinavia.

 This is a dumpy, large-headed owl, with a broad, flattish head and low, frowning brows. It has copious pale spots on its liver-brown back, small, pale dots on its dark forehead, whitish eyebrows, and clear, bright yellow eyes. It stands upright, or very rounded, often on open perches, and its flight is quick and undulating like a woodpecker. It has fluty calls, like *keee-ah*.

Short-eared Owl

Family Strigidae **Species** *Asio flammeus*

Length 34–42cm (13–16in)

Wingspan 90–105cm (35–41in)

Distribution Breeds on moors in N and NE Europe, locally in W; a widespread migrant or winter visitor, often dependent on vole numbers.

 This large, pale owl is often seen by day. It has beautifully mottled sandy-brown plumage, streaked on the creamy breast, whiter below, with large, pale spots above. In flight, it reveals long wings with a dark "wrist patch" and a big orange-buff area near the wingtip, and glides gracefully like a small harrier. Its bold, yellow eyes, set in black, are often visible at quite long range.

Long-eared Owl

Family Strigidae **Species** *Asio otus*

Length 35–37cm (14in)

Wingspan 84–95cm (33–37in)

Distribution Breeds in woods, except in Iceland and extreme N Europe; birds from N and NE move south in winter, when more widespread.

A large, brown, strictly nocturnal owl. Slimmer than the Short-eared, it has darker, more extensively streaked underparts, bright orange eyes, and longer ear tufts, often erect. In flight, it may look very similar to the Short-eared Owl, but the outer wing patch is more orange, the inner wing more evenly barred, and the tail more narrowly barred. Its song is a simple, deep, moaning or a cooing hoot.

Nightjar

Family Caprimulgidae

Species *Caprimulgus europaeus*

Length 26–28cm (10–11in)

Wingspan 54–60cm (21–23in)

Distribution A summer visitor over most of Europe but very localized on bushy heaths.

This strange bird sits tight by day, and is usually seen at dusk. It has a complex grey, buff, and brown pattern on its long body, long wings, a broad, square tail, and a tiny bill and legs. Males have white corners to the tail and spots on the outer wing, obvious even at dusk. Its call is a low, nasal *goo-ik*, the song at dusk a prolonged, hollow, wooden trill, varying abruptly in pitch, and often followed by several wing claps as the bird flies off.

Kingfishers, swifts, and cuckoos

This is a mixed group of small to medium-sized birds. Kingfishers have very short legs with fused toes, long, dagger bills, and upright, heavy bodies. Swifts are slender, fork-tailed, short-headed, aerial birds, with long, scythe-like, stiff wings. Cuckoos have small heads, wide bodies, broad-based but tapered wings, and long, broad tails.

Kingfisher

Family Alcedinidae **Species** *Alcedo atthis*

Length 16–17cm (6–6½in) **Wingspan** 24–26cm (9–10in)

Distribution Breeds by fresh water across Europe except far north; a summer visitor in the far N and E of its range.

The Kingfisher is a small, stocky, short-tailed bird of watersides, with a large head and thick, dagger-like bill. Despite its blue-green upperside and orange underside, it is often difficult to see in light and shade above rippling water. It may be heard first as it calls while flying away, or glimpsed as a small shape diving head first into water with a loud "plop". It flies low, fast, and direct, with its back and rump shining bright, electric blue. The male's bill is black, the female's red at the base. Its call is quite loud, sharp, and penetrating; a high, whistled *keee* or *ch'k-keeee*.

Bee-eater

Family Meropidae **Species** *Merops apiaster*

Length 27–29cm (11in)

Wingspan 36–40cm (14–16in)

Distribution A summer visitor to sandy areas and riversides in S Europe, and locally in France; a rare migrant and sporadic breeder farther north.

A long-winged bird with a long body that tapers into an elongated tail with a central spike. Its bill is thick, black, and slightly downcurved to a point. Its plumage is blue-green below with a black-bordered yellow bib, and mostly warm brown above with golden shoulders. In flight, the underwing is a pale, shiny coppery colour, fading to silvery near the tip, with a broad, black trailing edge. Its call is a loud, rolling, throaty *prrup prrup*.

Swift

Family Apodidae **Species** *Apus apus*

Length 16–17cm (6–6½in)

Wingspan 42–48cm (16–19in)

Distribution A summer visitor, absent from Iceland and the extreme N of Europe; commonest in S Europe from April to August.

A strictly aerial bird, coming to land only at the nest and almost never seen perched. It looks all-dark except in good light, when a whitish throat is visible, the upperwing is browner, and the underwing has a pale, shiny effect. Its tail is deeply notched and its wings are stiff, hardly flexed, and held in a smoothly-curved scythe shape. Its call is a loud, high-pitched, vibrant screech.

Alpine Swift

Family Apodidae **Species** *Apus melba*

Length 20–23cm (8–9in)

Wingspan 51–58cm (20–23in)

Distribution Breeds in the mountains and gorges of S Europe, north to the Alps; a rare migrant elsewhere. Migrates to Africa in winter.

This large swift has the same basic shape as the smaller species, with a narrow, pointed head, notched tail, elongated body, and long, smoothly-curved, stiff wings. Its flight is more powerful and with slower beats than the Swift. It is paler brown above, with a brown breastband, a pale throat, and an extensive, white belly obvious even at height, flashing as the bird tilts sideways. Its call is a loud, chattering *chit-it-it-it-it-it* or *chet-er-et-er-et-er-et*.

Cuckoo

Family Cuculidae **Species** *Cuculus canorus*

Length 32–34cm (12–13in)

Wingspan 55–65cm (21–25in)

Distribution A widespread summer visitor to moors and fields, except in Iceland; a common migrant in early autumn in coastal areas.

A long-bodied, short-billed bird, with long wings, often drooped below a raised tail. It has a pale grey head, back, and throat, and is whiter below with even, grey bars. In flight, the broad-based wings taper to a point, with wingbeats below body level; its long tail is blackish with white spots. Juveniles are brown and barred, with a white nape spot. Its call is a loud *cuck-cooo*.

Hoopoe

Family Upupidae **Species** *Upupa epops*

Length 26–28cm (10–11in) **Wingspan** 44–48cm (17–19in)

Distribution A summer visitor to SW, C, SE, and E Europe, in open areas, bushy woodland, and farmland. A rare migrant in the UK; a few are seen in winter in the extreme S of Europe and Mediterranean islands.

Unique in Europe, the Hoopoe is long-billed and long-bodied, with a fan-like crest. The crest is often folded flat but may be raised in a broad, black-tipped fan, even in flight. This bird is surprisingly hard to see on the ground in light and shade. Its back and wings are boldly barred black-and-white and it is pink-buff to sandy on the head and body.

In flight, the Hoopoe recalls a spotted woodpecker momentarily, but is much broader-winged and longer-tailed, with a white rump and tailband; its flight is springy, less undulating than a woodpecker's, with a quick, quite bounding, erratic action. It walks slowly on the ground, probing with its bill. The song is a far-carrying, quick, mellow, piping or fluted *poo-poo-poo* on one note.

Dazzling pattern in flight

Roller

Family Coraciidae **Species** *Coracias garrulus*

Length 30–32cm (12in)

Wingspan 52–57cm (20–22in)

Distribution A summer visitor in wooded areas of SW Europe, more common in E Europe. A very rare vagrant in NW Europe in summer.

Jackdaw-like in size and shape, but larger-headed, with a thick bill, the Roller is pale blue-green on the head and body, and brown on the back. In summer, it becomes a brighter, deeper turquoise-blue, but in autumn, pale buff feather edges obscure much of the colour. In the air, it reveals wings of deep purple, blue, and black, especially in its tumbling display flights.

Woodpeckers

Small to quite large woodland birds, woodpeckers have strong feet with two forward- and two rearward-facing toes, stout, chisel-like bills, and stiff tails, which support them as they cling upright to tree trunks or branches. Some species feed on the ground. They have a deeply undulating flight with short bursts of wingbeats, and loud calls.

Great Spotted Woodpecker

Family Picidae **Species** *Dendrocopos major*

Length 22–23cm (9in) **Wingspan** 34–39cm (13–15in)

Distribution Breeds across Europe from the UK eastwards, absent from Ireland, Iceland, and northern Scandinavia; some move west in winter.

A medium-sized, strikingly-patterned woodpecker, with a vivid red patch under the tail. It is glossy black above with a large, long, white shoulder patch, pale to deep buff below. Males have a red patch on the nape and juveniles have red caps. It is found in all kinds of woods. In spring, it drums with its bill against a branch, making a short, abrupt, rapid burst; its call is a loud, short, slightly squeaky *tchik!*

Lesser Spotted Woodpecker

Family Picidae **Species** *Dendrocopos minor*

Length 14–15cm (5½–6in)

Wingspan 25–27cm (10–11in)

Distribution Resident in woods over most of Europe, except the northern UK, Ireland, Iceland, parts of Iberia, and northern Scandinavia.

A tiny, sparrow-sized woodpecker of treetops and spindly bushes, the Lesser Spotted is closely barred with white across its black back (the bars often merge into a central white patch, but there is no white shoulder patch). The male has a red crown. There is no hint of red under the tail. Its flight is weak, hesitant, and deeply bounding. The main call is a quick, nasal, high but loud *pee-pee-pee-pee-pee-pee-pee*.

Green Woodpecker

Family Picidae **Species** *Picus viridis*

Length 30–33cm (12–13in)

Wingspan 40–42cm (16in)

Distribution A widespread resident in heathy and wooded areas, absent from Ireland, Iceland, and extreme N and E Europe.

 A large, long-bodied woodpecker, with a bright greenish yellow rump. The head is pale with a black eye patch, a black moustache (with a red flash in the male), and a red cap; juveniles have grey spots on the cap and dark bars on the sides of the neck and underparts. The back is apple-green, the wings browner, and the underside a pale greenish yellow. It feeds mostly on the ground. Its typical call is a strident, laughing outburst, *klew-kew-kew-kew-kew.*

Black Woodpecker

Family Picidae **Species** *Dryocopus martius*

Length 40–46cm (16–18in)

Wingspan 67–73cm (26–28in)

Distribution A widespread but local resident in mature woods. Seen in northern Spain, and across most of C and N Europe.

 The biggest of the woodpeckers, but slim and rangy with a slender neck, the Black Woodpecker is all dull or glossy black except for a red crown (on the male) or red nape (on the female). The whitish bill may stand out and the whitish eye is visible at close range. When in flight, it seems large, long-winged, and less undulating than other woodpeckers. Its calls are far-carrying: a rapid, ringing *krri-krri-krri-krri* and a mournful, piping *pyeee*; its drum is very loud.

Wryneck

Family Picidae **Species** *Jynx torquilla*

Length 16–17cm (6–6½in)

Wingspan 25–27cm (10–11in)

Distribution A summer visitor to woods in most of continental Europe; a regular but scarce migrant in the UK.

 This unusual migrant woodpecker is closely mottled and streaked with brown, golden-buff, grey, and black, with a long, black line on the lower neck and back, and a dark mask. It is rather inconspicuous and usually detected by its call – a nasal, quite loud *pwee-pwee-pwee-pwee-pwee-pwee.* In flight, it can recall a large warbler or small thrush more than a woodpecker.

Larks

Larks are small, mostly terrestrial birds, walking when on the ground, and basically pale brown with streaks of dark brown and buff above. They include some superb songsters. Their songs, habitats, flight patterns, and precise patterns of streaking on the underside are helpful identification guides, but some species are difficult to tell apart.

Skylark

Family Alaudidae **Species** *Alauda arvensis*

Length 18–19cm (7–7½in) **Wingspan** 30–36cm (12–14in)

Distribution A widespread breeder on moors, heaths, and farmland, except in Iceland; many from N and E Europe move south and west in winter.

 A rather large, richly-coloured lark, the Skylark has a short, blunt crest, usually held flat, a stout bill, and a gorget of fine streaks above a white underside. In flight, its angular wings show a distinctive, pale line along the trailing edge and the outer tail feathers are white. The call is a *chirrup* or a high, thin *see*, the song a magnificent outpouring of throaty, rapid warbling (higher and silvery from a distance) in a high, hovering song flight.

Crested Lark

Family Alaudidae **Species** *Galerida cristata*

Length 17–19cm (6½–7½in)

Wingspan 30–35cm (12–14in)

Distribution Resident in farmland and sandy areas in W, S, C, and E Europe, very rarely straying beyond this regular range.

 A pale lark, often looking rather sandy-orange or warm sandy-brown in good light, with a sharp, usually upstanding crest. In flight, it reveals broad, plain wings without any white, a very short tail with pale, sandy outer feathers, and pale underwings tinged buffy-orange. Its call is a fluty, whistled *teeu-too-dee-u* or *du-ee*, its song a variation on this theme in flight.

Woodlark

Family Alaudidae **Species** *Lullula arborea*

Length 15cm (6in)

Wingspan 27–30cm (11–12in)

Distribution Breeds on bushy heaths in most of Europe, except for the far north; mostly a summer visitor in E Europe.

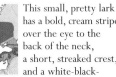

This small, pretty lark has a bold, cream stripe over the eye to the back of the neck, a short, streaked crest, and a white-black-white patch on the edge of the wing. In flight, it reveals broad, round wings with no pale trailing edge, and a short, round tail with white corners. It has a wonderful rich song, its call a fluty *t'l-oo-ee*.

Short-toed Lark

Family Alaudidae

Species *Calandrella brachydactyla*

Length 14–16cm (5½–6in)

Wingspan 30cm (12in)

Distribution A summer visitor to S and E Europe; a rare migrant in NW Europe, mostly in autumn.

A small, pale lark, the Short-toed has a creamy underside with only a few streaks at the sides of the breast; the dark neck patch is usually hard to see except when the head is stretched upwards. It usually has a dark cap and a long, pale stripe over the eye. A darker midwing panel is edged paler; in flight, the wings show two pale bars and the tail has white sides. Its calls are sparrowy chirrups.

Calandra Lark

Family Alaudidae

Species *Melanocorypha calandra*

Length 17–20cm (6½–8in)

Wingspan 35–40cm (14–16in)

Distribution Resident, locally common, in SW, S, and SE Europe; a very rare vagrant elsewhere.

A large lark, forming big flocks when not breeding, it is characterized by its thick, pale bill, broad, pale line over the eye and under the cheek, and a variable, but usually conspicuous, black neck patch. In flight, it has long, broad, bright brown wings with a wide, white trailing edge; from below, the wings are black with a bold, white edge, contrasting with the clean, white underside. It sings in flight with Skylark-like song.

Martins and swallows

These are aerial feeders, with long or triangular wings that are much less scythe-like than the swifts', and forked tails, some with long outer streamers. They have short, weak legs and hardly walk, but often perch on wires, trees, the ground, or on cliffs. They are social, especially in autumn when they form large roosts and migrating flocks.

Swallow

Family Hirundinidae **Species** *Hirundo rustica*

Length 17–19cm (6½–7½in) **Wingspan** 32–35cm (12–14in)

Distribution A summer visitor to villages and farmland in almost all of Europe except extreme N and Iceland; rare in winter.

A widespread and familiar swallow with a long, deeply-forked tail (the streamers longest on older males), the Swallow is glossy blue above and whitish to deep pink-buff below. It has a dark red throat and blue-black breastband. In flight, it shows white spots across the base of the spread tail. It has a flexible, fluid flight with wings angled back, much less stiff than any swift. It usually flies low with a swooping, twisting action when feeding, but is more direct on migration. Its calls are slurred, its song trilling.

Long wings sweep back

Red-rumped Swallow

Family Hirundinidae **Species** *Hirundo daurica*

Length 14–19cm (5½–7½in)

Wingspan 30–35cm (12–14in)

Distribution A summer visitor to S Europe, especially Spain, Portugal, and the Balkans; a rare migrant or vagrant farther north.

This handsome swallow has a slightly chunkier body, squatter shape, and stiffer, straighter wings than the Swallow, and glides more like a House Martin but with a long, deeply-forked tail. It has a dark cap above a rufous face and rusty collar, a blue-black back, duller wings, a pale to deep rufous-buff rump, and a black tail with no white spots. From below, the pale throat and a black patch under the tail are good clues.

Sand Martin

Family Hirundinidae **Species** *Riparia riparia*

Length 12cm (4½in)

Wingspan 26–29cm (10–11in)

Distribution A summer visitor to waterside areas, from early March, across most of Europe except Iceland; migrates to Africa in winter.

A small, lightweight martin with rather broad-based wings that are angled back and flicked or fluttered in flight. It is brown above with no trace of blue or white, and dull white below with a brown breastband. It is often seen near or over water, especially lakes and reservoirs, and nests in colonies, in tunnels in sandy cliffs. Its calls are weak, dry, twittering sounds.

House Martin

Family Hirundinidae **Species** *Delichon urbica*

Length 12cm (4½in)

Wingspan 26–29cm (10–11in)

Distribution A summer visitor from April to October over most of Europe except Iceland, from sea level to mountainous areas.

This small martin is easily identified by its bold, white rump and typical mud nest under the eaves of a building. It is blue-black above, browner on the wings, and white below including the feathered feet; juveniles and soiled adults may show duller, brownish white rumps. It flies quite stiffly, its flight weaker and less fluent than a Swallow's, and usually at a greater height.

Crag Martin

Family Hirundinidae

Species *Ptynoprogne rupestris*

Length 14–15cm (5½–6in)

Wingspan 32cm (12in)

Distribution Mostly resident in S Europe; a very rare migrant elsewhere.

A quite large, thick-set martin, grey-brown in spring, browner in summer, with a dusky underside and paler breast. Its notched tail has a row of square, white spots across the middle, best seen from below as it fans its tail in a quick turn. The underwing is pale greyish with a prominent, blacker wedge from the base. Its flight is elegant and powerful, sweeping gracefully across cliff faces or over water. Its calls are insignificant, short, chattering notes.

Pipits and wagtails

Pipits are subtly beautiful but mostly streaky brown, while wagtails are more boldly patterned with grey, white, black, and yellow according to the species. They are all quite slender birds with long or very long tails, slim bills, and long, spindly legs. They feed on the ground but some species settle freely in trees; pipits sing in special display flights.

Tawny Pipit

Family Motacillidae **Species** *Anthus campestris*

Length 15–18cm (6–7in) **Wingspan** 28–30cm (11–12in)

Distribution A summer visitor, breeding across the southern half of Europe; a rare migrant or vagrant farther north.

 Wagtail-like in flight

A large, wagtail-like pipit, the Tawny is quite long-bodied but well-built, with a long tail and long, pinkish legs. Adults are pale, sandy-brown, sometimes greyer or more buffy, with a pale stripe over the eye, a thin, dark moustache, a blacker tail with wide, white sides, and a row of dark spots across the wing coverts. Juveniles are more streaked in late summer. Its song is a loud *chu-vee, chu-vee*, its call a slightly grating *schweep* and shorter *tchup*.

Rock Pipit

Family Motacillidae **Species** *Anthus petrosus*

Length 16–17cm (6–6½in)

Wingspan 23–28cm (9–11in)

Distribution Breeds around coasts of Scandinavia, the UK, and Ireland; seen on coasts farther south in winter.

The Rock Pipit is a stocky pipit with distinctive dark legs. In summer, Scandinavian birds have a pale stripe over the eye and, sometimes, a greyer head and pinker breast; UK birds are duller, grey-brown above, more yellow-buff below with more blurred, dark streaks. The outer tail feathers are pale grey. Its call is a full, simple *fist* or *feest*.

133

Meadow Pipit

Family Motacillidae **Species** *Anthus pratensis*

Length 14–15cm (5½–6in)

Wingspan 22–25cm (9–10in)

Distribution Resident and a winter visitor in NW Europe, a summer visitor in the N and NE; a migrant and winter visitor elsewhere.

This small pipit of heaths and moors is rather nervy in its behaviour. Streaked brown above, some are greyer or more yellow-buff; it is creamy below with fine, black streaks. It has pale legs and white tail sides. It sings in a "parachute" flight from and back to the ground and has sharp, repeated, *seep-seep-seep* or short *ptip* calls in flight.

Tree Pipit

Family Motacillidae **Species** *Anthus trivialis*

Length 15cm (6in)

Wingspan 25–27cm (10–11in)

Distribution A summer visitor and widespread migrant, breeding in woodland clearings and on bushy heaths with trees.

Small and sleek, the Tree Pipit is like the Meadow but is a little more solidly built and more yellow-buff below, with streaks on the breast, and flanks almost unmarked. Close up, pinker legs and a short hind claw can be seen. It sings in "parachute" flight from and back to a treetop, with a rich song ending in *swee-swee-sweeee*. Its call is a hissy or buzzy *teeess*.

Yellow Wagtail

Family Motacillidae **Species** *Motacilla flava*

Length 17cm (6½in)

Wingspan 23–27cm (9–11in)

Distribution A summer visitor, except in the far NW, to damp meadows and farmland; also seen around reservoir and lake edges on migration.

A slim, thin-legged wagtail of open areas, the Yellow Wagtail is greenish above, with browner wings, pale wingbars, and a long, black, white-sided tail. Males are bright yellow below, females paler. UK birds have yellow and green heads; others have variable, blue-grey to charcoal-grey heads, some with white over the eyes. Its call is a full, loud *tsew* or *tsw-ee*.

Pied Wagtail

Family Motacillidae **Species** *Motacilla alba*

Length 18cm (7in) **Wingspan** 25–30cm (10–12in)

Distribution Resident in W and S Europe, a summer visitor elsewhere, in all kinds of open areas from moors and rocks to towns and wooded parks.

This slim wagtail has a dark bib, white wingbars, and a white-sided tail; summer males are black above in the UK ("Pied Wagtails"), or pale grey with browner wings in most of Europe ("White Wagtails"). Females of both are duller, Pied being smoky grey. The Pied Wagtail has darker flanks and a blacker rump than the White. Its black cap, white face, and black bib are distinctive; its throat is also white in winter leaving just a narrow breastband. Juveniles are paler, buff on the face at first with little black. It is often found on roofs, footpaths, roads, and car parks, walking with a bobbing tail. Its call is a bright, cheery *chre-weeep* and a harder, double *tiss-ick*.

White streaks on wings

Grey Wagtail

Family Motacillidae **Species** *Motacilla cinerea*

Length 18–19cm (7–7½in)

Wingspan 25–27cm (10–11in)

Distribution Breeds locally except in far N Europe, along fast-flowing streams. In winter, it is seen by lowland lakes and ponds.

The longest-tailed wagtail, the Grey is pale grey above, with a green-yellow rump, a yellow area under the tail, and dark wings with a long, white bar, obvious in flight. In summer, the male has a black bib and bright yellow underparts. Winter birds are more buff below with a pale throat, but still yellow under the tail. Its pale legs are also distinctive. The call – *chik!* – is sharper, higher, and more explosive than the Pied.

Wrens, dippers, waxwings, and accentors

A mixed group of small songbirds: wrens are diverse in America but only one species is found in Europe; the Dipper is a songbird that feeds in and under water; waxwings live in the far north but occasionally migrate south in large numbers; accentors are small, Eurasian birds.

Wren

Family Troglodytidae **Species** *Troglodytes troglodytes*

Length 9–10cm (3½–4in) **Wingspan** 13–17cm (5–6½in)

Distribution Found almost throughout Europe, a summer visitor in the north, from woods and gardens to moors, clifftops, and isolated marine islands.

The Wren is tiny but irascible, its short tail often cocked. It flits up to a perch, calls a few scolding notes, then dives out of sight, showing its warm, rusty plumage, a pale line over the eye, and short, barred wings. Sexes are alike. Its calls are dry, chattering, or grating notes, often repeated, such as *tch-tch-tch-tchrr-rrr* or *tik-tik-tik*. The song is loud, vibrant, full-throated, and very rapid, with a trill at or near the end.

Dipper

Family Cinclidae **Species** *Cinclus cinclus*

Length 18cm (7in)

Wingspan 25–30cm (10–12in)

Distribution A widespread but local resident in much of upland Europe, on fast-flowing streams; a few from the far north move south in winter.

A small, round bird with a striking, white bib, a short tail, and strong feet, the Dipper is always beside water. It wades, swims, and dives easily, even in a fast-flowing stream. Adults are dark brown above (blacker in some races), black below, and in some races with a brown breastband below the white chest. Juveniles are greyer. Call is a hard *zit*.

Waxwing

Family Bombycillidae

Species *Bombycilla garrulus*

Length 18cm (7in)

Wingspan 32–35cm (12–14in)

Distribution Breeds in far northern forests; large numbers move S and W in winter in some years.

An unusual, stocky, short-tailed, upright bird with a wispy crest and very short bill. Its general colour is pinkish-brown, grey on the rump, paler below, with white wing marks, and a black tail with a yellow tip. The face is fox-red, around a black eyestripe and bib. In flight, it is Starling-like but longer- and paler-bodied. It is tame in winter. Its call is a shrill, silvery trill, *schr-r-r-r-r-r*.

Dunnock

Family Prunellidae **Species** *Prunella modularis*

Length 14cm (5½in)

Wingspan 19–21cm (7½–8in)

Distribution A summer visitor in N and W Europe, resident in the W, found in woods and gardens, on heaths and moors, and high, scrubby slopes.

Small, secretive, and shuffling, the streaky, brown Dunnock is often overlooked. It has a very thin bill and thin, orange-brown legs; it is streaked brown above, grey on the face and breast, and streaked on the browner flanks. Sexes and ages are alike at all seasons. It flicks its tail as it feeds on the ground. Its call is a thin, sharp *see*; the song is a fast, slightly flat, musical warble.

Alpine Accentor

Family Prunellidae **Species** *Prunella collaris*

Length 15–17cm (6–6½in)

Wingspan 22cm (9in)

Distribution Breeds in the mountains of C and S Europe, wintering lower down and farther south, usually on exposed rocky or grassy hilltops.

Larger than a Dunnock, but similar in form and actions, the Alpine Accentor is more strongly marked with dark streaks above, a broad, black wingbar, a pale throat, and brighter, more obviously striped flanks with broad, rufous streaks. At a distance, it nevertheless looks rather pale and plain, the dark wingbar being the best clue. Its calls are sharp and thin notes.

Chats and thrushes

This group of small to medium-sized songbirds, with strong legs, short bills, and slim to thick-set bodies, includes some of Europe's best songsters. Most are solitary or found in family groups, but some species are social, especially outside the breeding season, often in mixed flocks.

Robin

Family Turdidae **Species** *Erithacus rubecula*

Length 14cm (5½in)   **Wingspan** 20–22cm (8–9in)

Distribution Breeds widely in woods and gardens in Europe except for the extreme N; most birds from the N and E move south or west in winter.

Short, flitting flight

Adult robins are identified by their red-orange face and gorget bordered with grey-blue on the neck, warm brown upperparts, and buff underside. They have an alert, rather upright shape, a small bill, thin legs, and bold, dark eyes. The tail is often raised above drooped wingtips. Juveniles share the shape and character but are mottled buff and brown at first, gaining spots of red with age. Calls include a high, metallic *tik*; the song is a fluent, strong, musical warble, with a wistful character in autumn, but brighter and more forceful in spring.

Nightingale

Family Turdidae **Species** *Luscinia megarhynchos*

Length 16–17cm (6–6½in)

Wingspan 23–26cm (9–10in)

Distribution A summer visitor to woods of S and C Europe; a widespread migrant throughout the Mediterranean area.

Larger than a Robin but smaller than a Song Thrush, this bird is plain brown, marked with a pale eyering; it has a pale, greyish underside and is warm rufous on the wings, rump, and tail. Its body tapers to a rather long, thick tail. The Nightingale's calls include a croaking *krrrr* and musical *hweet*; its song is a rich mixture of hesitant notes and fast, throaty warbles, with sudden changes of pace and pitch.

Bluethroat

Family Turdidae **Species** *Luscinia svecica*

Length 14cm (5½in)

Wingspan 20–22cm (8–9in)

Distribution Breeds in N and NE Europe and locally in C Europe; it is a migrant over most of the continental area.

This Robin-like bird has a similarly flirted or slightly cocked tail, but is grey-brown above, whiter below, with a white stripe over the eye and prominent rectangle of rufous at each side of the tail. Males have a vivid blue bib with a red or white central spot, females a black moustache and variable black, blue, and rufous markings on the breast.

Redstart

Family Turdidae

Species *Phoenicurus phoenicurus*

Length 14cm (5½in)

Wingspan 20–24cm (8–9in)

Distribution Seen in summer only throughout Europe, except Iceland, in wooded habitat.

Slimmer and longer-tailed than a Robin, the Redstart constantly flickers its tail and has eyecatching, orange-rufous rump and tail sides. Males have a white forehead, black bib, rich orange underside, and a grey back; browner females have a pale eyering in a plain, buffish face. In autumn, white speckling obscures the male's dark face.

Black Redstart

Family Turdidae **Species** *Phoenicurus ochruros*

Length 15cm (6in)

Wingspan 23–26cm (9–10in)

Distribution Breeds very locally in UK, but quite common in most of Europe except extreme N and NE; widespread in winter.

Whereas the Redstart is a woodland bird, the Black Redstart prefers cliffs, quarries, rocky coasts, and buildings, and has less rufous on its rump and tail. Males are sooty grey to black, blackest on the face, with white wing panels; females and young males are sooty grey-brown with a weak greyish wing panel. Its song is a short warble with a rough, dry rattle near the end.

Wheatear

Family Turdidae **Species** *Oenanthe oenanthe*

Length 14–15cm (5½–6in)

Wingspan 25–30cm (10–12in)

Distribution Breeds in almost all of Europe on heaths and moors. A widespread migrant in early spring and autumn; absent in winter.

The Wheatear is a small, lively bird with long wings and a short tail. Its rump and the sides and base of the tail are white, with a central black "T" shape on the tail. Males have a grey back and dark mask; females are browner. In autumn, adults and young of both sexes are brighter and mostly gingery-buff.

Black-eared Wheatear

Family Turdidae **Species** *Oenanthe hispanica*

Length 13–15cm (5–6in)

Wingspan 25–30cm (10–12in)

Distribution A summer visitor to stony, bushy areas in S and SE Europe; a rare vagrant farther north. Migrates to Africa in winter.

Slimmer than the Wheatear, this bird is more likely to perch on slim twigs and bushes; the tail has less black, but a narrower band of black at the tip curls around the outer edges. The male Wheatear has a black mask or throat and a whitish to orange-buff back. The female is duller and browner, with a plain face and a darker breast.

Black Wheatear

Family Turdidae **Species** *Oenanthe leucura*

Length 16–18cm (6–7in)

Wingspan 30–35cm (12–14in)

Distribution Resident in rocky areas in Iberia, and seen locally north to the southern Pyrenees; almost unknown elsewhere in Europe.

This is a large, blackish, stout-bodied, long-billed wheatear with a large splash of white around the rump, undertail, and tail; the tail has a broad black "T" shape. The male is dull black, the female slightly duller and browner black; both show paler wings especially in flight. It has a scratchy, warbling song with harsh notes.

Stonechat

Family Turdidae **Species** *Saxicola torquata*

Length 12cm (4½in)

Wingspan 18–21cm (7–8in)

Distribution Resident and also a winter visitor in bushy heaths over much of W and S Europe; a summer visitor in NE and E Europe.

This is a small, deep-bodied, upright chat with a short, all-dark tail and quick, whirring flight. The male has a black head and throat, white neck and wing patches, and a rusty breast. Females are browner and subtly paler on the side of the neck and at the lower edge of the bib, with a brown throat and a more uniformly rufous-brown underside.

Whinchat

Family Turdidae **Species** *Saxicola rubetra*

Length 12cm (4½in) **Wingspan** 21–24cm (8–9in)

Distribution A summer visitor to heaths and moors in most of Europe but increasingly scarce and localized; a migrant on many coasts in autumn.

A small chat, the Whinchat is slimmer than the Stonechat with a more tapered body shape and a white panel at each side of the tail. The male has a dark cap and blackish mask, a broad, white stripe over the eye and under the cheek, and a rich apricot to yellow-buff throat and breast; the back is streaked black and cream. Females are browner, with a buffish stripe over the eye and a whitish throat. Juveniles in autumn are duller still, with more buff, and the stripe over the eye is less clear and almost matched by the palest Stonechats; the white on the tail base remains a good feature. It calls *wheet chat chat* and sings with a warbling, Robin-like song mixed with chattering notes.

Female in flight

Spring male with bold head pattern.

Autumn

Song Thrush

Family Turdidae **Species** *Turdus philomelos*

Length 23cm (9in) **Wingspan** 33–36cm (13–14in)

Distribution Breeds widely in woods and gardens in most of Europe except Iceland; large numbers move south and west in winter.

Orange-buff underwing

This is a small thrush, spotted with dark brown-black "V"-shaped marks beneath. It is warm brown above, its face weakly marked with a paler area over the eye and a dark moustache. Beneath, the breast is yellow-buff and the flanks are buff-brown, leaving the belly clean white, with copious spots that are smallest and sparsest in the centre of the belly. The Mistle Thrush is larger, greyer, and more uniform below, with yellow-buff flanks and larger spots over the whole underside. The Song Thrush is the typical garden worm- and snail-eater. It has a pale orange-buff underwing and plain tail. Its call is a short, sharp *sip*; the song is rich, often rather strident, loud, and repetitive, with each group of two to five notes usually repeated two or three times, creating an easily recognized pattern.

Berries supplement a diet of worms and snails.

Mistle Thrush

Family Turdidae **Species** *Turdus viscivorus*

Length 27cm (11in)

Wingspan 42–48cm (16–19in)

Distribution Breeds in most of Europe, except the extreme north, in woods, heaths, farmland with trees, parks, and large gardens.

The largest, most heavily-built thrush, with a small-headed look; it has a pale, greyish- or olive-brown back, distinct pale edges to its wing feathers, and whitish sides to the tail. Beneath, it is uniform yellow-buff with large, black, rounded spots. Its underwing is white. Its call is a dry, harsh, chattering note; the song is loud, musical, and usually not very varied.

Blackbird

Family Turdidae **Species** *Turdus merula*

Length 24–25cm (9–10in)

Wingspan 34–38cm (13–15in)

Distribution Breeds across most of Europe, except Iceland, in woods, parks, gardens, and bushy places. Many move west in winter.

This large thrush has obvious male–female differences. Males are all-black except for a bright yellow bill and eyering. Females are dark brown, paler below, often whitish and streaked on the throat; juveniles are more gingery-brown. It calls with loud alarm rattles, a thin *srree*, and a loud *pink*; its song is mellow and musical.

Redwing

Family Turdidae **Species** *Turdus iliacus*

Length 21cm (8in)

Wingspan 33–35cm (13–14in)

Distribution Breeds mostly in N and NE Europe in bushy woods; widespread in farmland and heathy ground in winter.

Small and gregarious, the Redwing is dark brown above, silvery-grey or white below, with a bold stripe over the eye, another under the dark cheek, and a dark moustache. The underside is striped more than spotted and the flanks show a patch of dull red, which extends under the wing. Its call is a thin but loud *seeeep*, its song a simple, repetitive phrase.

Fieldfare

Family Turdidae **Species** *Turdus pilaris*

Length 25cm (10in)

Wingspan 39–42cm (15–16in)

Distribution Breeds in woodland and farmland across much of C, N, and E Europe; much more widespread throughout Europe in winter.

A big, bold, strikingly patterned thrush, the Fieldfare looks dark with white underwings at long range. It has grey on the head and rump, black on the face and tail, and a brown back. Beneath, it is white with a rich orange-buff breast and many black spots, often coalescing into a black area on the flanks in summer. It is often seen in flocks, frequently with Redwings and Blackbirds, calling a deep, chuckling, *tchak-ak-ak* or nasal, mewing *weeep*.

Ring Ouzel

Family Turdidae **Species** *Turdus torquatus*

Length 23–24cm (9in)

Wingspan 38–42cm (15–16in)

Distribution A summer visitor from March to October to mountains and high moors of N, W, and S Europe; seen on coasts on migration.

A large, long-tailed thrush, slimmer than a Blackbird, with a crescent of white on the chest. Males are sooty, blacker below, with a bright white gorget; females are browner with a less clear gorget. Males show a large, pale area on the upperwing. In flight, this is a long-winged thrush, like a Mistle Thrush in shape. Its calls are hard, rattling notes; its song is short, wild, and repetitive.

Rock Thrush

Family Turdidae **Species** *Monticola saxatilis*

Length 17–20cm (6½–8in)

Wingspan 30–35cm (12–14in)

Distribution Breeds on high altitude pastures, hillsides, cliffs, and stony areas in S Europe; winters in Africa.

Small and chat-like, the Rock Thrush has a tapered body and short tail. Males are strongly patterned with blue-grey on the head, dark brown on the back, and rusty-orange on the tail, the underwing, and the underside; there is a variable white patch on the back. Females are dark brown and closely barred all over, with paler mottles on the back. The bird is identified by its rusty-red tail and size. Its calls include *diu* and a hard *chak*.

Blue Rock Thrush

Family Turdidae **Species** *Monticola solitarius*

Length 21–23cm (8–9in)

Wingspan 35–40cm (14–16in)

Distribution Breeds on cliffs and in gorges in S Europe; resident in most areas but only in summer in the Alps.

Larger and darker than a Rock Thrush, this bird looks more like a Blackbird in rocky situations; good views reveal quite bright blue on the male, but at a distance it looks dull and dark. The female is dark brown, barred below, with a dark tail lacking any rufous; the long bill is a useful clue. Calls include an occasional *chak*; its song is rich and Blackbird-like.

Warblers

A varied group, each genus with its own character: *Sylvia* warblers are stocky, with fine songs and hard calls; *Phylloscopus* slimmer, greener, and slipping easily through foliage; *Locustella* are secretive, hard to see, with whirring songs; *Hippolais* are greenish or pale brown, strong-billed, and heavy; and *Acrocephalus* are reedbed birds with fast, repetitive songs.

Blackcap

Family Sylviidae **Species** *Sylvia atricapilla*

Length 13cm (5in) **Wingspan** 20–23cm (8–9in)

Distribution Mostly a summer visitor to thickets and woods, but also seen in winter in S and SW Europe and increasingly in the UK, where it is often found in gardens.

This medium-sized warbler has a hard *tak* call. Males are grey-brown, greyer on the neck, and paler below, with a neat, small, black cap extending down to eye level. Females have browner plumage and less obvious red-brown caps. The song is a sudden, rich, fast-flowing outburst, increasing in depth and volume in the middle, but very like the more even song of a Garden Warbler.

Greyish wings and tail

Garden Warbler

Family Sylviidae **Species** *Sylvia borin*

Length 14cm (5½in)

Wingspan 20–24cm (8–9in)

Distribution A summer visitor to most of Europe, breeding in thickets and woodland; rare in Ireland and absent from Iceland.

A quite heavy warbler, with a short, stubby, dark bill and grey legs. It is almost uniformly pale olive-brown, buffer below, with a subtle, greyer patch on the side of the neck and a hint of a pale mark over the eye but no other real pattern. Its call of *tchak* or *chuff* is softer than a Blackcap's; its rich, musical song is longer, and with less acceleration midway than a Blackcap's.

Whitethroat

Family Sylviidae **Species** *Sylvia communis*

Length 14cm (5½in) **Wingspan** 19–23cm (7½–9in)

Distribution Breeds widely except for Iceland and far N; a summer visitor to heaths, farmland, bushy places, and woodland edges.

Rufous patch

Quite small, but slim and long-tailed, the Whitethroat is lively and active in low vegetation. Males have pale grey heads, females are browner, and both have large, puffy, silvery-white throats. They have warm brown upperparts and a characteristic patch of rufous or gingery-brown on the wing. Underneath, they are whitish or buff and pinker on the breast; the long, grey tail has white sides. The eye has a whitish ring and the bill is pale buff or yellowish at the base; the legs are pale pink-brown (Lesser Whitethroats have dark legs). Males sing from bushes or wires, or in a quick, rising song flight, with a fast, chattery, pleasing but not very musical phrase. Calls include a light, nasal *whichity*, a harder *chek*, *cheer* and a rhythmic *ved ved ved ved*.

Lesser Whitethroat

Family Sylviidae **Species** *Sylvia curruca*

Length 13cm (5in)

Wingspan 17–19cm (6½–7½in)

Distribution Breeds in the UK, N, NW, and E Europe in thickets and hedges; migrates south-east in autumn, so very rare in SW Europe.

Shorter-tailed, darker-legged, and duller-winged than the Whitethroat, the Lesser is both quieter and less conspicuous. Males have a variable, dark cheek and a grey cap; females are plain grey-headed. Both have a clear, white throat, an off-white breast, brown wings, and a white-edged tail. Calls include a sharp *tek*; its song is a hollow, quick rattle.

Sardinian Warbler

Family Sylviidae **Species** *Sylvia melanocephala*

Length 13–14cm (5–5½in)

Wingspan 15–18cm (6–7in)

Distribution Breeds across S Europe, mostly resident and very rare farther north; found in bushy places, gardens, and thickets.

This is a long-tailed, slim warbler of low vegetation, where it can be secretive. It is typically seen in pairs or family groups. Males are grey above, paler below, with a bold, white throat, large, black hood, and red eyering; females are duller and browner with a greyer head, pink-red legs, and red eyering. Its calls include a hard, fast, scolding rattle or chatter, *chret-tret-tret-tret*.

Subalpine Warbler

Family Sylviidae **Species** *Sylvia cantillans*

Length 12–13cm (4½–5in)

Wingspan 13–18cm (5–7in)

Distribution A summer visitor to gardens, orchards, farmland, and thickets across S Europe; a rare vagrant farther north.

Very small, but stocky and long-tailed, this warbler is often seen diving into a bush or in short, high song flight. Males are blue-grey above and rusty orange-pink below, with a bold, white moustache; brick-red legs and eyering are helpful clues for identification. Females are browner and paler, with a whitish moustache, yellowish legs, and a pale buff breast.

Dartford Warbler

Family Sylviidae **Species** *Sylvia undata*

Length 12–13cm (4½–5in)

Wingspan 13–18cm (5–7in)

Distribution A localized resident in the southern UK, parts of France, Iberia, and Italy; seen in low thickets, heaths, and bushy places.

Quite a squat little warbler except for its long, narrow, sometimes cocked tail. Males are dark, with a grey head and bright red eyering, brown above, deep red-brown below; females are paler, buffer beneath, and browner on the head. Juveniles are paler and greyer. Calls are distinctively buzzy and churring, a low *dzzz* or *dchurr*; song is a fast, buzzy, chattery warble.

Cetti's Warbler

Family Sylviidae **Species** *Cettia cetti*

Length 14cm (5½in)

Wingspan 15–19cm (6–7½in)

Distribution Resident locally in the UK, France, SW, and S Europe, in waterside thickets, reedbeds, and quite dry ditches.

This thick-set, broad-tailed, stout-billed, warbler is hard to see but easy to hear. It is red-brown above, grey below, with a pale stripe over the eye and dark rusty tail. Its call is a hard, sharp, loud *quit*, the song a sudden, abrupt outburst of loud, fast, musical notes, *chwee! chuwee-wee-wee-wee-wee*, repeated a little while later from a different location.

Sedge Warbler

Family Sylviidae **Species** *Acrocephalus schoenobaenus*

Length 13cm (5in) **Wingspan** 17–21cm (6½–8in)

Distribution A summer visitor to most of Europe. Absent from Iceland and only a migrant in the south; breeds in waterside scrub, thickets, and reeds.

A small, upright warbler of tall, slender waterside vegetation and bushes, the Sedge Warbler has a bold, silver-white stripe over the eye and a dark, streaked cap. It is a pale, warm brown colour above with soft, dark streaks, unmarked on the paler, gingery rump; beneath it is plain, pale buff. Juveniles have a little streaking on the breast and a paler crown. Its calls include a low *tchrrrt* and hard *tek*; its song is quick, lively, urgent, and varied, with a mix of sweet notes and harsh chattering sounds.

Pale rump

Often sings from the top of a bush.

Great Reed Warbler

Family Sylviidae

Species *Acrocephalus arundinaceus*

Length 16–20cm (6–8in)

Wingspan 25–26cm (10in)

Distribution A summer visitor to S and C Europe north to the Baltic; very rare in the UK.

The size of a small thrush, the Great Reed Warbler is big and stocky, making the reeds shake as it hops about from stem to stem. It has a bold stripe over the eye and a strong, pale-based bill. It is a warm, pale, sandy-brown colour with a white throat. Its song is distinctive, frog-like, hesitant or strong, with a series of repeated, musical, strident, and grating notes, such as *chick chick, grrr grrr, grik grik grik, cherry cherry*.

Grasshopper Warbler

Family Sylviidae **Species** *Locustella naevia*

Length 13cm (5in)

Wingspan 15–19cm (6–7½in)

Distribution A local, scarce summer visitor to grassy places and moors in the UK, Ireland, and much of middle Europe to southern Scandinavia.

A slender, secretive warbler, often allowing a very close approach but simply impossible to see in deep grass or a thorny bush. It is softly streaked, with a more mottled crown and a plainer, rounded, wide, brown tail; often yellower below. The song, often at dusk, is a remarkable, sustained, even, mechanical, reeling trill (a more metallic rattle at very close range), occasionally seeming to fade.

Reed Warbler

Family Sylviidae

Species *Acrocephalus scirpaceus*

Length 13–15cm (5–6in)

Wingspan 18–21cm (7–8in)

Distribution Breeds throughout N Europe to Scandinavia; a summer visitor to reedbeds.

A slim, long-billed, longish-tailed, pale brown warbler of reeds and waterside bushes, the Reed Warbler is one of several plain species, and is usually much the commonest. It is a warm brown, a little more rufous on the rump, especially on juveniles. Its call is a low, soft *trrsch*, its song a relaxed, repetitive, rhythmic series of churring and rolling notes.

Chiffchaff

Family Sylviidae **Species** *Phylloscopus collybita*

Length 10–11cm (4–4½in) **Wingspan** 15–20cm (6–8in)

Distribution Breeds widely in European woodlands, except in Iceland and the extreme N; a few winter in W Europe and many in Mediterranean areas.

Short, round wings

A small, sleek, dull greenish bird, the Chiffchaff is very like the Willow Warbler, but is readily distinguished by its song. Adults are rather brownish-green above, dull yellow-buff below, but autumn juveniles are brighter with a longer, yellower stripe over the eye and yellower underparts. All show a thin, white crescent under the eye, blackish legs, and, compared with the Willow Warbler, rounder heads and shorter wingtips. The Chiffchaff also has a characteristic down–up dip of the tail as it feeds, which the Willow Warbler lacks. It is a bird of tall trees and also bushy undergrowth, feeding on insects from the foliage. Its song is a simple, repetitive, cheerful series of bright notes in uneven sequence, such as *chiff chiff chaff chep chaff chiff chaff chep*, often with a low growling *churr* at the end. Its call – a sweet or slightly sad, rising *hweet* – is closer to a single syllable than the Willow Warbler's.

Wood Warbler

Family Sylviidae **Species** *Phylloscopus sibilatrix*

Length 13cm (5in)

Wingspan 19–24cm (7½–9in)

Distribution Breeds locally over most of Europe in mature deciduous and larch woods with little or no undergrowth; winters in Africa.

Larger than a Willow Warbler and brighter green above, the Wood Warbler has a pale yellow throat and silky-white underside. Its long, often drooped, brown wings are lined with yellow-green edges. A broad yellow stripe runs over each eye, above a wide, dark green eyestripe. Males sing a distinctive, accelerating, ticking note that runs into a short, metallic, silvery trill, *tit-it-it-'t't't't't'ttrrrrrrr*, and a sad, rich *sweee-sweee-sweee*.

Willow Warbler

Family Sylviidae **Species** *Phylloscopus trochilus*

Length 11cm (4½in)

Wingspan 17–20cm (6½–8in)

Distribution Breeds widely in N and C Europe. A widespread migrant in the S in wooded and bushy places; winters in Africa.

Slightly longer, longer-winged, and flatter-headed than the Chiffchaff, the Willow Warbler tends to be cleaner, green-brown or grey-brown above and yellowish-white below, with a pale stripe over the eye; the legs are almost always pale brown or grey-brown. The song is a lovely, sweet cascade of notes; the call a two-syllable *hoo-eet*.

Bonelli's Warbler

Family Sylviidae **Species** *Phylloscopus bonelli*

Length 11–12cm (4½in)

Wingspan 19–22cm (7½–9in)

Distribution A summer visitor to southern Europe, France, and the Alps, where it favours oak and pine woods; winters in Africa.

Compared with other warblers described here, Bonelli's is cleaner, and has a plainer face; the light stripe above the eye and the dark stripe through the eye are weaker. It is silky-white below with little or no yellow, and the wings are fringed brighter green and the rump is yellower. Its song is a trill with no accelerating start.

Icterine Warbler

Family Sylviidae **Species** *Hippolais icterina*

Length 13cm (5in)

Wingspan 20–24cm (8–9in)

Distribution Breeds in NE and E Europe in leafy woodland; a migrant in the SE and a rare but regular migrant on some UK coasts.

A size above the *Phylloscopus* warblers, the adult Icterine is green above, yellow below, with a pale wing panel; juveniles are duller and browner, the wing panel dull buff or whitish. All have a bland face pattern with no dark line between the eye and bill, a dagger-like, orange- or pink-based bill, and greyish legs. Its calls include a hard *tik*.

Juvenile

Melodious Warbler

Family Sylviidae **Species** *Hippolais polyglotta*

Length 12–13cm (4½–5in)

Wingspan 18–20cm (7–8in)

Distribution Breeds in France, Iberia, and Italy in bushy areas and woods; a rare but regular migrant on some UK coasts; winters in Africa.

Like the Icterine Warbler, this is a high-crowned warbler with a pale orange-pink dagger-bill, a long, square tail, and strong legs and feet. Adults are pale green above, with a weak, pale wing panel, and pale yellow below; juveniles are duller. They have shorter wingtips than the Icterine Warbler but can be hard to separate, especially in autumn.

Goldcrest

Family Sylviidae **Species** *Regulus regulus*

Length 9cm (3½in)

Wingspan 13–15cm (5–6in)

Distribution Breeds in most of Europe in mixed and coniferous woods; widespread in trees and bushy places in winter.

A minute, rounded, warbler-like bird with a fine bill and spindly legs, the Goldcrest is pale olive-green with a broad, L-shaped, pale wingbar and black wing patch. Adults have a thin, yellow crown stripe (fanned to reveal the orange centre when the male displays). The call is a high, thin *seee-seee-seee*, the song a rhythmic *seedli-ee seedli-ee seedli-ee* with a terminal flourish.

Firecrest

Family Sylviidae **Species** *Regulus ignicapillus*

Length 9cm (3½in)

Wingspan 13–15cm (5–6in)

Distribution Breeds in forests in much of S and C Europe; more widespread as an autumn and spring migrant.

Like the Goldcrest, but often fractionally slimmer, cleaner, silky white beneath, and usually brighter green above, the Firecrest is best identified by a bold, white wedge over the eye, a dark eyestripe, and a golden forehead. A bright bronzy-orange shoulder patch may show well. The call is a firm *zeet* or *zit*; the song is a simple, accelerating *zi-zi-zi-zizizizeeee*.

Flycatchers

European flycatchers are small, very short-legged birds that tend to perch rather upright; they are long-winged and fly with great agility to catch insects on the wing. The "pied" group also catch food on the ground. They are long-distance migrants, often encountered far from their breeding areas in spring and autumn.

Pied Flycatcher

Family Muscicapidae **Species** *Ficedula hypoleuca*

Length 13cm (5in)

Wingspan 21–24cm (8–9in)

Distribution A summer visitor to open woodland with little undergrowth in much of N and NW Europe; a widespread autumn migrant.

Unique in the west but very like Collared and Semi-collared Flycatchers in the east, the Pied Flycatcher has white underparts and a bold, white wing panel. Spring males are black above; females and autumn birds are dull chocolate brown with a smaller creamy wing patch and often a dusky moustache.

Spotted Flycatcher

Family Muscicapidae **Species** *Muscicapa striata*

Length 14cm (5½in) **Wingspan** 23–25cm (9–10in)

Distribution A summer visitor to most of Europe except Iceland, arriving very late in spring in open woods, parks, and gardens.

While many warblers slip quietly through foliage, the long-winged Spotted Flycatcher sits on more open perches, from fence posts to treetop height; it flies out and returns to the same perch. It is a very pale grey-brown bird, silvery whitish below, with faint streaks on the crown and chest; juveniles have pale buff spots above. Calls are simple but distinctive short, metallic *tzic* or *tzee* notes; the song is short and unmusical.

Tits, nuthatches, and treecreepers

Tits are small, often colourful, sociable birds with quick, jerky movements. They are usually noisy, with sometimes confusing calls but distinctive songs. The Nuthatch is an agile climber on trees, also with loud, varied calls, while the Treecreeper literally creeps close to the bark, typically spiralling up the tree trunk as it searches for food.

Great Tit

Family Paridae **Species** *Parus major*

Length 14cm (5½in) **Wingspan** 22–25cm (9–10in)

Distribution A widespread resident in forests and woodland of all kinds, gardens, and scrub; wanders in winter.

A bold, striking tit with a black cap and big, white cheeks, the Great Tit is green above, blue-grey on the wings, and yellow beneath, with a black central stripe (widest on the male). Young birds have yellower cheeks. The grey tail has white sides. Calls are very variable, and include a ringing *pink* or *chink*, a whistled *tui tui tui*, and a nasal, buzzy *churrr*. The Great Tit also often taps loudly with its bill. The song is a strident, musical *tea-cher tea-cher* or *seetoo seetoo seetoo*.

Blue Tit

Family Paridae **Species** *Parus caeruleus*

Length 11cm (4½in)

Wingspan 17–20cm (6½–8in)

Distribution Breeds widely in woods and gardens of all kinds across most of Europe, except in the extreme north.

A small, lively bird with a blue cap ringed with white, white cheeks, and a black bib, the Blue Tit is green above, yellow below, and blue on the wings and tail (brightest in spring males). In summer, it often looks faded and pale, its bright colours dimmed by wear and tear. Calls include a bouncy *tsee-tsee-tsee-sisisisi*, a thin *see-see-see*, and a scolding *churrr*.

Coal Tit

Family Paridae **Species** *Parus ater*

Length 11cm (4½in)

Wingspan 17–21cm (6½–8in)

Distribution Breeds widely in mixed and coniferous woods and often visits gardens and parks; more widespread in winter.

One of Europe's tiniest birds, the Coal Tit has no green, blue, or yellow at all. The large head is black with big, white cheeks and a clear rectangle of white on the back of the neck; the grey-brown wings have two white bars. Calls are very high and thin, or a sharp, piping *tseu* or *tsooo*; its song is a repetitive, bright *sweetu sweeetu*.

Crested Tit

Family Paridae **Species** *Parus cristatus*

Length 11cm (4½in)

Wingspan 17–20cm (6½–8in)

Distribution Breeds in mixed or coniferous woodlands in much of continental Europe and locally in northern Scotland.

A tiny, brown-backed tit with no strong markings on its wings or body and no bright colours, the Crested Tit has a distinctive, pointed, speckled crest and white cheeks edged in black. Its underside is buff, and its black neck ring extends into a black bib. Its call is typically buzzy and stuttering, a rather soft trill, *b'd-rrrr-rrup*, or a thin, high note, *zit* or *zee*.

Long-tailed Tit

Family Aegithalidae **Species** *Aegithalos caudatus*

Length 14cm (5½in)

Wingspan 16–19cm (6–7½in)

Distribution A widespread resident, wandering in winter in woodland and bushy areas almost throughout Europe.

Not a true *Parus* tit, but sharing many of their quick, agile actions, the Long-tailed Tit is almost always found in small groups that fly in single file from bush to bush. Adults are slightly scruffy, black, pink, and white (greyer in S Europe) with a black band across the head (lacking in N Europe) and a very long, thin tail. Juveniles are black and white.

Marsh Tit

Family Paridae **Species** *Parus palustris*

Length 11cm (4½in)

Wingspan 18–19cm (7–7½in)

Distribution Breeds in deciduous and mixed woodland with bushy undergrowth across the middle of Europe; absent from the north.

A grey-brown tit with no bright colour, the Marsh Tit has plain brown wings, a neat, glossy black cap, and a smallish black bib (unlike the greyer, fine-billed Blackcap). Its call – a distinctive, loud, bright, whistled *pit-chew!* – helps distinguish it from the similar Willow Tit. It also calls *chik-a-dee-dee-dee*. The song is a repetitive *schupi-schupi-schupi-schupi*.

Willow Tit

Family Paridae **Species** *Parus montanus*

Length 11cm (4½in)

Wingspan 18–19cm (7–7½in)

Distribution Breeds widely N and C Europe in damp willow thickets, hedgerows, and woodland with dense undergrowth.

Very like a Marsh Tit, the Willow is thicker-necked and bulkier, with a longer, rougher, duller black cap and a pale lengthwise wing panel (but not a crosswise white wingbar like the Coal Tit). It never calls *pitchew*, but has a distinctive, harsh, nasal, buzzing *chair chair chair* and a thin, sharp *zi zi zi*. Its song is usually a piping *tyoo tyoo tyoo*, rarely a musical warble.

Bearded Tit

Family Timaliidae **Species** *Panurus biarmicus*

Length 13cm (5in)

Wingspan 16–18cm (6–7in)

Distribution Breeds very locally in reedbeds across Europe; more widely dispersed in reeds and reedmace in winter.

Not closely related to the true tits, this is a bird that is restricted entirely to reeds in the breeding season, and reeds, reedmace, or tall grass in wet marshes in winter. It is rusty-brown with streaked wings and a very long, rufous tail. Males have blue-grey heads with bold black "moustaches". Best located by its loud, ringing *ping* or *psching* calls.

Penduline Tit

Family Remizidae **Species** *Remiz pendulinus*

Length 10–11cm (4–4½in)

Wingspan 20cm (8in)

Distribution Breeds in and around freshwater marshes, mostly in E and S Europe; more widespread in reeds in winter.

A tiny bird, this tit is an acrobatic inhabitant of marshy places and tall riverside willows and poplars (making its "pendulous" nest of down from their flowers). Adults are rich brown above, pale buff below, grey on the head, with a bold, black mask (strongest on the male). Juveniles have plain heads. The call is distinctive, a high, thin, fading-out *psieeeeee*.

Nuthatch

Family Sittidae **Species** *Sitta europaea*

Length 13cm (5in) **Wingspan** 16–18cm (6–7in)

Distribution Breeds in mature woods with big trees throughout most of Europe except the far north, Scotland, and Ireland.

Restricted almost entirely to trees, but feeding now and then on the ground or old stone walls, the Nuthatch clings on with its strong feet, not using its tail as woodpeckers do, whether upside down, the right way up, climbing up, or coming down head first. It is stocky and short-tailed, with a dagger bill. The upperparts are blue-grey with a long, black eyestripe, the underside buff with a rusty flank and pale spots under the tail. It has loud, ringing calls of several types: a whistled *pew pew pew pew pew*; a trilled *trr-rr-rr-rr-rr*; a short *chwit;* and variations on these themes, with a distinctive "boy whistling" character.

Hops jerkily over the leaf litter.

Broad wings

145

Short-toed Treecreeper

Family Certhidae **Species** *Certhia brachydactyla*

Length 13cm (5in)

Wingspan 18–21cm (7–8in)

Distribution Breeds in mixed and coniferous woods in SW, C, and SE Europe, rarely moving outside its breeding range.

Extremely similar to the Treecreeper, this small, brown-and-whitish bird of tree trunks and branches (rarely on rocks) is best told by its song. It has a fine curved bill, and its underside usually looks dull except for a clear, white throat. Calls include a hard *tsoit*; the song – a series of discrete notes, such as *stit stit steet, stit-it steroi-tit* — lacks the smooth flow and flourish of a Treecreeper's.

Treecreeper

Family Certhidae **Species** *Certhia familiaris*

Length 13cm (5in) **Wingspan** 18–21cm (7–8in)

Distribution Breeds in woods of all kinds in Ireland, Britain, N and E Europe, and locally in S Europe; wanders south from northern parts of its breeding range in winter.

This little bird creeps about on tree bark, climbing upwards, spiralling around branches, and often hanging underneath them, but not coming down head-first like a Nuthatch. It uses its tail as a support. It is finely marked rusty-brown above, with a white stripe over the eye; the underside is silky white, sometimes with a little pale, clean, buff-brown on the flanks, but without the contrasted dull breast and white throat of the Short-toed Treecreeper. Tiny detailed differences in the wing pattern are best appreciated on photographs, rather than the living bird. The best differences are the call, a longer, thin *seeee* (but there is some overlap), and better still the song, typically a longer, flowing, musical sequence with a flourish at the end recalling a Willow Warbler: *tsi-tsi-tswee-sweesweeswee swity-sweeoo.*

Long, pale wing bars

Shrikes

Shrikes are predatory songbirds, eating small mammals and small birds as well as big insects, which they catch in flight or on the ground. They perch prominently when hunting but can equally be elusive. Their bills are slightly hooked, their feet strong; sexes are almost alike in some species but different in others.

Red-backed Shrike

Family Laniidae **Species** *Lanius collurio*

Length 16–18cm (6–7in) **Wingspan** 24–27cm (9–11in)

Distribution A summer visitor from Africa, breeding over much of Europe except the north and far south-west, in bushy areas and woodland edges.

A small, colourful shrike, the Red-backed has an upright, alert stance, often swaying its long tail from side to side. The male has a grey head and rump, a black mask, a pink breast, and a boldly black-and-white tail; females are plainer and browner, but finely barred on the underside, with just a hint of a dark mask and a plain, rusty-brown tail. Autumn juveniles are slightly more rufous with scaly barring above as well as below. It is slightly smaller than a Song Thrush, much more upright when perched, and unlikely to hop about on the ground. Calls include a harsh *chek* or *chak* and the song is a hurried warble with rough notes and mimicry included.

Woodchat Shrike

Family Laniidae **Species** *Lanius senator*

Length 17–19cm (6½–7½in)

Wingspan 25–30cm (10–12in)

Distribution A summer visitor to SW and S Europe, in warm, open, bushy places, orchards, and light woodland; winters in Africa.

A boldly-patterned shrike, the Woodchat is black and white with a large rufous cap. Males have a more solid black mask than the females. The white "V" on the upperside is distinctive. Juveniles are grey-brown with rufous-buff feather edges, less rusty than young Red-backeds, with obvious whitish feathers along the shoulder area. In flight, adults have a large white wing patch, absent in birds nesting in the Balearics.

Crows and orioles

Crows form a mixed group, typically large and all or mostly black, with short, stout bills and strong legs; in flight they are large, steady birds with an even, direct action. Others, however, are more colourful or pied. Orioles are smaller, rather thrush-like; males are much brighter than females but are elusive in dense foliage; they have loud songs.

Jay

Family Corvidae **Species** *Garrulus glandarius*

Length 34–35cm (13–14in) **Wingspan** 52–58cm (20–23in)

Distribution Breeds widely except in Iceland and northern Scandinavia; some northern birds wander in winter. Found in all kinds of wooded areas, especially oak woods.

This is a strikingly patterned but often elusive, shy crow. It is often seen flying away, showing its big, white rump, white wing patch, and black tail; the blue wing patches are usually much less conspicuous. A black moustache is striking in close views. Typically, it is heard more than seen, with a loud, "ripping" note like tearing cloth, *skairk!* and occasional softer mewing notes.

Magpie

Family Corvidae **Species** *Pica pica*

Length 44–46cm (17–18in)

Wingspan 52–60cm (20–23in)

Distribution Breeds almost throughout Europe except for Iceland, in open, bushy or well-wooded areas, including suburban gardens.

A large, long-tailed, often gregarious crow, with similar plumage in both sexes at all ages and seasons (juveniles have shorter tails at first). The big, white shoulder patch, flanks, and belly are as striking as the long tail; in flight the wingtips are also largely white. Calls include a loud, fast rattling chatter, *tcha-tcha-tcha-tcha-tcha.*

Nutcracker

Family Corvidae **Species** *Nucifraga caryocatactes*

Length 32–35cm (12–14in)

Wingspan 49–53cm (19–21in)

Distribution Breeds in high altitude pine forests in N and C Europe, periodically wandering west and south in autumn and winter.

A medium to small, boldly-spotted crow, dependent on pine seeds for food, the Nutcracker occasionally "erupts" out of its normal range if food supplies fail. The dark cap, dagger bill, pale-spotted body, and white ventral area are striking (Starlings are much smaller and lack the white vent and tail tip). It often perches on top of a tall tree.

Chough

Family Corvidae **Species** *Pyrrhocorax pyrrhocorax*

Length 37–41cm (14–16in)

Wingspan 68–75cm (27–29in)

Distribution Breeds on coastal cliffs and in mountainous areas inland, in Ireland, western UK, Iberia, the Alps, Italy, and SE Europe.

A glossy, black crow with a curved, red bill and red legs, the Chough is blacker than a Jackdaw and even more aerobatic in flight, with confident dives, swoops, and high soaring. It has a short, square tail and very square, fingered wingtips. Its calls include a loud, joyful, ringing *chee-yaah*, *pee-yaa* and shorter *chuk* notes.

Alpine Chough

Family Corvidae **Species** *Pyrrhocorax graculus*

Length 36–39cm (14–15in)

Wingspan 65–74cm (25–29in)

Distribution Breeds at high altitude in the mountains of SW, C, and SE Europe, moving lower down in winter or during poor weather.

A glossy crow, often seen in large, mixed flocks with Choughs, from which it may be separated by its shorter, pale yellow bill and tighter plumage. In flight, it has a subtly two-tone underwing, a longer, rounder tail, and rounder wings than the Chough. Its calls include a sharp *zeee-up* and a rippling, hissy *chirrish.*

Rook

Family Corvidae **Species** *Corvus frugilegus*

Length 44–46cm (17–18in)

Wingspan 81–99cm (32–39in)

Distribution Breeds in farmland and woods across much of Europe except the far N and S; eastern birds move south in winter.

This big black crow has a slim bill and a peaked crown with a steep forehead. Adults have a bare pale "parchment" coloured face, while juveniles have blacker faces. In flight, Rooks appear rather round-tailed; they are able to soar well over their treetop colonies. Their calls include relaxed cawing, *caar* or *grah-gra-gra*.

Hooded Crow

Family Corvidae **Species** *Corvus cornix*

Length 44–51cm (17–20in)

Wingspan 93–104cm (36–41in)

Distribution Breeds on cliffs and moorland with scattered trees in Ireland, Isle of Man, Scotland, much of Europe where Carrion Crow absent.

This handsome grey and black crow replaces the Carrion Crow in parts of Europe. In a narrow band in northern Scotland the two hybridize and produce intermediate plumage patterns, but the vast majority of both remain pure and behave as separate species. The Hooded Crow is especially fond of rocky moorland, but it is also a great scavenger on all kinds of shorelines.

—— Grey body

Carrion Crow

Family Corvidae **Species** *Corvus corone*

Length 44–51cm (17–20in)

Wingspan 93–104cm (36–41in)

Distribution Breeds in farmland and open areas of UK and east to Denmark and C Europe.

A big, black crow, easily taken for a Rook or Raven. Carrion Crows do not swirl in flocks above trees like Rooks, but do gather on fields and beaches, so a flock is not an infallible guide to the Rook. Rooks soar and perform aerobatics better than crows, which fly more sedately. Crows have squarer wingtips and tails than either the Rook or Raven.

Raven

Family Corvidae **Species** *Corvus corax*

Length 54–67cm (21–26in)

Wingspan 120–150cm (47–59in)

Distribution Breeds in mountains, on moors and cliffs, and in extensive woodland almost throughout Europe, but very local in most areas.

The Raven is the biggest crow, but its size is hard to judge. The heavy head, often with a bristly "beard", and the long, thick, arched bill are useful clues. In flight, it is easier, with a long, diamond- or wedge-shaped tail, and angled, fingered wings. Calls are a very abrupt, loud, *cra cra*, *cronk cronk* or *tuk tuk*.

Jackdaw

Family Corvidae **Species** *Corvus monedula*

Length 33–34cm (13in)

Wingspan 67–74cm (26–29in)

Distribution Breeds in woods, on cliffs, and in buildings in most of Europe except for the far north; north-eastern birds move west in winter.

A pigeon-sized, rather grey crow with a black cap and grey shawl around the neck, the Jackdaw is also more pigeon-like in flight (with a short head, rounded wings, and a quicker action) than other crows. It often mixes with Rooks. Calls include short, squeaky *tchak* and *kyak* notes and longer, higher *che-yar* sounds.

Golden Oriole

Family Oriolidae **Species** *Oriolus oriolus*

Length 22–25cm (9–10in)

Wingspan 35cm (14in)

Distribution Breeds in deciduous woods, especially of oak and poplar, across most of Europe; winters in Africa.

Shaped like a slim, long-winged thrush, the Golden Oriole lives in dense foliage high in trees, now and then flying across open spaces between clumps. Males are brilliant yellow and black; females are greener or paler yellow with duller wings, and lack the male's black mask. Juveniles are streaked below. Calls include cat-like squawling notes; the song is a very rich, fluty, short yodel, such as *whee-dlo*, *wee-dl-eeu*, or *wee-wee-edl-oo*.

Starlings

Noisy, quarrelsome, and even bullying, starlings are busy birds, rarely still for long. They move in small parties or large flocks, sweeping in co-ordinated movements; on the ground they have a quick, bustling walk and probe into short grass for food. They are short-tailed and sharp-billed. Their songs are quick and varied but not really musical.

Starling

Family Sturnidae **Species** *Sturnus vulgaris*

Length 21cm (8in) **Wingspan** 37–42cm (14–16in)

Distribution A widespread breeder in woods, farmland, and suburbs except in Iberia and Iceland; northern and eastern birds move south in winter.

Smaller than a Blackbird, with a shorter, square tail and much more pointed, triangular wings, the Starling is glossy black, with a green and purple sheen. In winter, it has copious white spotting, almost solidly whitish on the throat. Young birds are dull brown with a dark mask, gaining black and white on the body by late summer. Varied calls include a loud *cheer* and *shweee*.

Spotless Starling

Family Sturnidae **Species** *Sturnus unicolor*

Length 21cm (8in)

Wingspan 37–42cm (14–16in)

Distribution Breeds in Iberia and North Africa. Resident in towns, villages, and farmland areas; may mix with common Starlings in winter.

Like a Starling with longer, spiky underside feathers, the Spotless Starling is dull, oily black, with a deep green and purplish sheen but no obvious spots in summer and only small, pale ones in winter (when Starlings often join it in Iberia). Its bright pink legs are obvious, its calls loud and ringing.

Sparrows

Sparrows are small, finch-like birds with stout, short bills and short legs. They are sociable, often in dense flocks or family parties, usually living on or near the ground or in thick bushes and hedgerows. Some species live in gardens and towns. Sexes may be alike or very different in appearance; juveniles look much like adult females.

House Sparrow

Family Passeridae **Species** *Passer domesticus*

Length 14cm (5½in) **Wingspan** 20–22cm (8–9in)

Distribution Breeds widely in open areas, near farms, and in gardens and suburbs almost everywhere, but local in northern and upland areas.

A typical "little brown bird" in many towns and villages, the House Sparrow is gregarious and noisy, with frequent outbursts of calling and squabbles. Males are streaked above, unmarked grey below, with a black bib and a grey-centred crown; females are streaked above, pale grey-buff below and have a broad, pale stripe behind the eye. Calls include cheeping and chirrupy notes.

Tree Sparrow

Family Passeridae **Species** *Passer montanus*

Length 14cm (5½in)

Wingspan 20cm (8in)

Distribution Breeds widely but locally in many areas, in woods, wooded farmland, and villages; wanders a little more widely in winter.

This neat sparrow has a plumage recalling a male House Sparrow but with a completely red-brown cap, a white collar, and white cheeks with a bold, black spot. Males and females are alike. In flight, their distinctive calls are a short *tek tek*; the chirrupy chorus from a flock, and the undistinguished song are much like the House Sparrow's.

Finches

While the Chaffinch and Brambling are similar species, other finches are more varied. All have thick bills, some are short, others more pointed, for manipulating their favoured food. Males and females may be different. They are small, rather short-tailed birds, often in flocks outside the breeding season. Calls and songs are useful in identification.

Chaffinch

Family Fringillidae **Species** *Fringilla coelebs*

Length 14cm (5½in) **Wingspan** 25–28cm (10–11in)

Distribution Breeds widely except in Iceland, in all kinds of woods and gardens; northern and eastern birds move south and west in winter.

All Chaffinches have two bold white bars on each wing and white sides to the tail. Males have a grey hood (obscured by ochre-brown in winter), a pale red-brown back, and brownish-pink underparts. Females are duller, more olive, with unstreaked, olive-grey underparts. Calls include a loud *pink pink!* and a soft *chup* in flight; the loud, cheery, rattling song has a flourish at the end.

Brambling

Family Fringillidae **Species** *Fringilla montifringilla*

Length 14cm (5½in)

Wingspan 25–28cm (10–11in)

Distribution Breeds in N and NE Europe in open woods; in winter, it is much more widespread in woods and farmland.

A mirror-image of the Chaffinch in structure and pattern, the Brambling has orange-buff wingbars instead of white, and a long, narrow, white rump. The breast is orange-buff above, with a clear, white belly. Females and winter males have buff-brown heads, with a pale nape panel; spring males have jet black hoods and black on the back. Calls include a nasal *tsweek* and a hard *tchek* in flight.

Winter

Linnet

Family Fringillidae **Species** *Carduelis cannabina*

Length 13–14cm (5–5½in)

Wingspan 21–25cm (8–10in)

Distribution Breeds in open, heathy, or bushy places across most of Europe; moves south and west in winter.

This small, fork-tailed, small-headed finch has white streaks in the wing and tail; males have unmarked, tawny-brown backs; females are slightly streaked above, with dark streaks on the chest and a pale spot below the eye. Spring males are pink-red on the forehead and breast. Its calls include a light, *tidit tiditititi* and a nasal *tseeoo*; its song is a musical warbling.

Twite

Family Fringillidae **Species** *Carduelis flavirostris*

Length 13–14cm (5–5½in)

Wingspan 21–25cm (8–10in)

Distribution Breeds very locally in meadows in the UK and Scandinavia; more widespread in winter, especially on coasts.

Sharing the size, shape, and white wing streaks of the Linnet, the Twite also has the buff wingbar and generally tawny-brown, streaky colour of a Redpoll. Its white tail sides can be eyecatching; in winter, the yellow bill and wide, tawny throat patch are also good clues. The male has a dull pink rump. Calls include a twangy *chwai-it* and a harder twitter than the Linnet's notes.

Redpoll

Family Fringillidae **Species** *Carduelis flammea*

Length 11–15cm (4½–6in)

Wingspan 20–25cm (8–10in)

Distribution Breeds widely in N and NW Europe, and locally in C Europe in pine and birch woods; wanders widely in winter.

Probably best split into two closely related species (the northern "Mealy" being bigger and paler, with whiter wingbars than the western "Lesser"), the Redpoll is streaky brown with a buff wingbar, small, red forehead, and black chin. Summer males are variably red or pink on the breast. Flight calls are useful clues: a hard, fast chatter, *chuch-uch-uch-uch*, and short, rapid, metallic trill. Perched birds also call with a twangy, nasal *tsoo-ee*.

Goldfinch

Family Fringillidae **Species** *Carduelis carduelis*

Length 13cm (5in)

Wingspan 21–25cm (8–10in)

Distribution Breeds in open, scrubby, and heathy areas across Europe, except in the far north; eastern birds move south-west in winter.

A small finch with black wings crossed by a broad, yellow band, the Goldfinch has a light, airy, bouncy flight and slurred, lilting calls, *skip-i-lip* or *swililililp*. Adults have black-and-white heads with deep red faces; juveniles have plain, greyish heads and large, buff tips to the wing and tail feathers. They are often in small groups, on low plants or in alders, but nest in taller, leafy trees.

Greenfinch

Family Fringillidae **Species** *Carduelis chloris*

Length 15cm (6in)

Wingspan 25–27cm (10–11in)

Distribution Breeds in woods, orchards, and bushy farmland over most of Europe; wanders in more open areas in winter.

A stocky, thick-billed finch with bold, yellow marks on the wing and tail, the Greenfinch is unstreaked (adults) or only softly marked with dull brown (juveniles). Spring males are pale to bright green, females similar but with a little less yellow in the wing; they have large, pale bills and small, dark masks. Calls include a chattering *tit-it-it-it-it* and a loud *zwee*; the song is a varied, loud, ringing or rattling trill.

Siskin

Family Fringillidae **Species** *Carduelis spinus*

Length 12cm (4½in)

Wingspan 20–23cm (8–9in)

Distribution Breeds in mixed and coniferous woods in NW, N, and NE Europe, and locally in C Europe; wanders widely in winter.

A bird of coniferous woods in summer, in winter it favours birch, alder, and larch woods, and will visit garden feeders. The Siskin is a tiny finch with a fine bill. The male has a black cap and bib and black wings crossed by a green-yellow band; the female is greyer, whitish below with black streaks. Calls include a loud, bright, metallic *tsy-zee*.

Serin

Family Fringillidae **Species** *Serinus serinus*

Length 11–12cm (4½in)

Wingspan 18–20cm (7–8in)

Distribution Breeds in bushy farmland, woods, and gardens in C and S Europe; moves south-west in winter

The Serin is a tiny, long-tailed, stub-billed finch with a yellow rump and plain brown wings and tail. The male has a broad, yellow forehead and yellow breast; the female is duller; and juveniles are browner, with more streaks below, and a pale buff wingbar. The song is a sharp, "splintering glass" jingled twitter.

Bullfinch

Family Fringillidae **Species** *Pyrrhula pyrrhula*

Length 15cm (6in) **Wingspan** 22–26cm (9–10in)

Distribution Breeds in bushy woodland over most of Europe except Iceland and the far south; wanders in winter.

A thick-set, bull-necked, round-billed finch, the Bullfinch eats soft buds and shoots and is usually seen in pairs or small groups in hedgerows or bushes. The adult has a jet black cap and bill, black wings crossed by a broad, pale grey band, a wide, white area across the rump and beneath the tail, and a square, black tail. Males are blue-grey above and bright red-pink beneath; females are grey-brown above and dull pink-grey or buffish below. Juveniles are like females but lack the black cap at first. The song is infrequent, creaky, and quiet, but the usual call is very distinctive: a soft, even, whistled *peeeuw, tooo,* or *deu*.

A bright male calls from a hedgerow.

Hawfinch

Family Fringillidae **Species** *Coccothraustes coccothraustes*

Length 18cm (7in) **Wingspan** 29–33cm (11–13in)

Distribution Breeds in woodland and orchards across much of S and C Europe, but scarce and local almost everywhere; wanders south in winter.

One of the larger finches, the Hawfinch has a bull neck, heavy head, and thick bill, combined with very short legs, to give it a top-heavy appearance when perched (often upright) or on the ground. It is generally dark brown with a bright tawny rump, bright forehead and cheeks, and grey neck. The wings are crossed by a pale band, with white streaks on the outer wing prominent in flight. It often feeds on the ground in small, inconspicuous groups and flies off rapidly with sharp, ticking, Robin-like *tik* or *titik* calls.

Broad buff-white bar

Large bill to crush seeds.

Crossbill

Family Fringillidae **Species** *Loxia curvirostra*

Length 16cm (6in)

Wingspan 27–30cm (11–12in)

Distribution Breeds locally, and often erratically, across Europe, wandering widely in late summer and autumn in pine, spruce, and larch woods.

A large, stocky finch, the Crossbill has a thick, cross-tipped bill. Its dark brown wings and tail and its bright rump are obvious in flight. Males are red, with pale pink-red rumps; females are greenish, with yellow rumps. Their calls are loud, hard, staccato *jup-jup-jup* or *chip-chip-chip* notes. Scottish Crossbills and Parrot Crossbills (Scandinavia) are confusingly similar.

Buntings

Much like finches apart from detailed differences in the structure of the bill, buntings are mostly rather long and slim, with quite long tails (in many species, edged with white). Males and females often differ and winter plumages are generally duller. They have simple, repetitive songs. Most feed on or near the ground, often in small flocks.

Reed Bunting

Family Emberizidae **Species** *Emberiza schoeniclus*

Length 15cm (6in) **Wingspan** 21–26cm (8–10in)

Distribution Breeds in and around reeds and marshy areas in most of N and C Europe; northern birds wander south in winter.

A slim bunting of marshy places, the Reed Bunting is streaked above, less so below, with a broadly white-edged, black tail. A spring male has a black head above a broad, white collar; in winter, this pattern is partially obscured. Females are browner, with a hint of a dark hood and moustache, a pale streak over the eye, and another below the reddish cheek. Calls include a loud *tseeu* and a high, thin *sweee*; the song is a short, simple, repeated phrase, such as *srip srip srip sea-sea-sea-sitip-see*.

Lapland Bunting

Family Emberizidae **Species** *Calcarius lapponicus*

Length 14–15cm (5½–6in)

Wingspan 25–28cm (10–11in)

Distribution Breeds in Arctic areas of N Europe; moves south to coastal regions of the North Sea and Baltic in winter.

A long-bodied, short-tailed bunting; the summer male has a black head and breast with a bold, white stripe from the eye, around the cheeks, to the side of the breast. In winter, this is obscured, more like a female's, with dark cheek corners, a pale central crown stripe, a dark moustache, and dark streaks on each side of the breast. The wing has a central rufous panel.

Winter

Ortolan Bunting

Family Emberizidae **Species** *Emberiza hortulana*

Length 15–16cm (6in)

Wingspan 22–26cm (9–10in)

Distribution Breeds locally but very widely across Europe on high pastures and warm, bushy slopes; winters in Africa.

This bunting is characterized by its sharp, pink bill and rather plain face with a yellow moustache and pale eyering. Males are pale green on the head and breast, rusty orange below; females are paler and more streaked. Young birds are buff-brown and streaked, leaving the eyering and bill as the most reliable clues to identification. The song is a short, simple phrase.

Yellowhammer

Family Emberizidae **Species** *Emberiza citrinella*

Length 16cm (6in)

Wingspan 23–29cm (9–11in)

Distribution Breeds in bushy, heathy places and farmland over most of Europe; some move south and west in winter.

A sharp-faced bunting, the Yellowhammer has a dark-tipped bill, a bright rufous rump, and a white-sided tail. The male is bright yellow with a variable dark crown and cheek marks; the female is paler, duller yellow with more streaks. The call is a metallic *tsi-wik* or *tsik*; the song is a metallic trill with a longer note near the end, *tsi-tsi-tsi-tsi-tsi-tseee-sip*.

Cirl Bunting

Family Emberizidae **Species** *Emberiza cirlus*

Length 15–16cm (6in)

Wingspan 22–26cm (9–10in)

Distribution Breeds widely but very locally in warm, bushy places over SW, C, and SE Europe; rare in the extreme southwest UK.

Compared with the Yellowhammer, the male Cirl Bunting has a darker, red-brown back, a redder breastband, and a greenish crown, dark eyestripe, and black bib. Females are best told by their dull olive rumps. The call is a short, thin, quiet and elusive *sip*; the song is a simple trill, fast or slightly slower and more ticking, like *t-r-r-r-r-r-r-r-r-r* or *titititititit*.

Rock Bunting

Family Emberizidae **Species** *Emberiza cia*

Length 15cm (6in)

Wingspan 22–26cm (9–10in)

Distribution Breeds on rocky slopes and higher cliffs in S Europe; makes minor movements to lower ground in winter.

The Rock Bunting is characterized by its black-streaked, rusty-brown back, rufous rump and underside, and grey head with bold, black streaks; the black head marks are least obvious on females and winter males. The usual call is infuriatingly hard to pinpoint, a simple, sharp, short *si*.

Corn Bunting

Family Emberizidae **Species** *Miliaria calandra*

Length 18cm (7in)

Wingspan 26–32cm (10–12in)

Distribution Breeds on farmland across S Europe and more locally farther N and NW; some movement west and south in winter.

This big, pale, streaky bunting is a little like a Skylark. Often seen perching on bushes and wires, it has a plain, brown tail and thick, pale bill, sometimes with a defined dark edge to the cheeks. It has a pale crown stripe and dark streaks coalescing on the centre of the breast. The sexes are alike. Calls include an abrupt *plip*; the song is a twitter ending in a metallic "rattling keys" splutter.

Snow Bunting

Family Emberizidae **Species** *Plectrophenax nivalis*

Length 16–17cm (6–6½in)

Wingspan 32–38cm (12–15in)

Distribution Breeds on tundra or mountains in the far north, but rare in Scotland; wanders to coasts and hills inland in winter.

This is a long, thick-set, short-legged, low-slung bunting, with variable amounts of white in the wing. In winter, the pale head and breast have extensive, bright rusty-orange marks and the bill is yellow. In summer, males are white with black backs and wingtips. The calls include a sweet *tseeu* and a light, tinkling trill, *tiri-lil-ili-il-ip*.

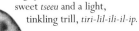

Winter

Where to watch

Birdwatching adapts to your lifestyle. You can observe birds in your own back garden, or travel the world in search of new experiences. The following pages will lead you to the best sites in Europe, telling you how to get there and what to expect to see once you have arrived.

England

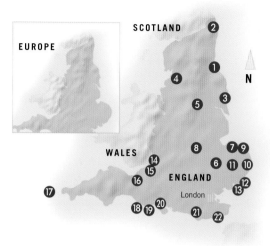

A LARGE AND VARIED COUNTRY, England has low-lying, soft coasts with small stretches of cliffs that have occasional seabird colonies and nesting Peregrines. Headlands and islands around the coast are good sites for watching seabirds offshore and other migrants, especially in the autumn, and the country has an exceptional range of estuary birds throughout the year. Southern heathlands, oak woods, high moorland, and rich agricultural land add to the variety of bird life. England is blessed with an unusually high occurrence of rare species from North America, Europe, and Asia.

❶ Teesside

Tree-lined banks of the River Tees.

Location The lower reaches of the River Tees in northeast England, in and around Hartlepool.
Access Explore the mouth of the River Tees and south of Hartlepool (Seaton Carew). There are good wader pools off the A178 near Saltholme.
Contact English Nature, Stocksfield Hall, Stocksfield, Northumberland NE43 7TN
Web: www.naturalengland.org.uk

Teesmouth is an industrial area studded with interesting wildlife spots. Seabirds can be really exciting, with Manx and Sooty Shearwaters, Gannets, Fulmars, Little Gulls, and Great, Arctic, Pomarine, and Long-tailed Skuas seen in surprising numbers. Late autumn can be good for skuas and Little Auks, especially after a northerly gale, which brings in many birds. Snow Buntings and Shore Larks are usually around in winter.

❷ Lindisfarne (Holy Island)

Location An island off northern Northumberland, 20km (12½ miles) southeast of Berwick-upon-Tweed.
Access Lindisfarne, including Holy Island, is signposted off the A1. It is joined to the mainland by a causeway that is covered at high tide.
Contact English Nature, Stocksfield Hall, Stocksfield, Northumberland NE43 7TN
Web: www.naturalengland.org.uk

This area has a terrific mixture of marshland, dunes, mud and sand flats, rocky coasts, and islands. In summer, there are terns, Fulmars, and nesting waders and wildfowl, including Eiders. In winter, vast numbers of waders and wildfowl are found, including the pale-bellied race of Brent Geese and Long-tailed Ducks. Autumn migration is excellent, both onshore and offshore. It is also worth making a expedition to the mudflats further south on the Northumberland coast, including those around Fenham, Elwick, and Fenham-le-Moor.

Long-tailed Duck

The impressive cliffs at Bempton are wonderful for breeding seabirds.

❸ Bempton Cliffs/ Flamborough Head

Location A large headland north of Bridlington in East Yorkshire.
Access From Bridlington, take the B1255 then B1259 to reach the car park near Flamborough Lighthouse. The RSPB centre at Bempton cliffs is signposted off the B1229 that runs along the north side of the headland.
Contact The RSPB, Bempton Cliffs
Tel: 01262 851179
Web: www.rspb.org.uk

A long, cliff-bound coast runs from Filey Bay southeast to the headland of Flamborough. The whole stretch is magnificent in summer, with tens of thousands of breeding seabirds concentrated around the RSPB reserve at Bempton.

Here is England's only Gannet colony, as well as thrilling numbers of Guillemots, Kittiwakes, Fulmars, and Herring Gulls. Puffins are less abundant but usually easy to see with a little effort. Safe vantage points give good viewing. In spring and autumn, the area is famous for its migrants, including many rarities, especially in the Flamborough area. Migrant Great, Arctic, Pomarine, and Long-tailed Skuas are regulars, along with Manx and Sooty Shearwaters and, in November, Little Auks, but much depends on the weather conditions on the day and during the preceding week.

❹ Morecambe Bay

Location An estuary in northwest England, north of Lancaster.
Access Good points to view the high tide wader roosts include Hest Bank, about 3km (2 miles) north of Morecambe on the A5015; Flookburgh Marshes; the sea wall at Heysham on the A589; and the Kent Estuary.
Contact The RSPB Hest Bank
Tel: 01524 701601
Web: www.rspb.org.uk

This wonderful, wide estuary is set between hills and marshes. Much of it is sandy with shallow, winding creeks at low tide. From early autumn to late spring, waders number tens of thousands, many coming to roost at high tide at Hest Bank on the eastern side of the bay. The area is worth exploring for views of Knots, Oystercatchers, Bar-tailed Godwits, Grey and Ringed Plovers, Turnstones, and Curlews. In winter, wildfowl are numerous especially on salt-marshes, with many Wigeon, Shelducks, and Eiders offshore. In spring and autumn, migrants add still more variety.

❺ Fairburn Ings

Watching in wetlands at Fairburn Ings.

Location Adjacent to the A1 road, 8km (5 miles) northeast of Castleford, West Yorkshire.
Access Fairburn is signposted off the A1 and A656. The reserve has hides, wheelchair-accessible trails, a visitor centre, and good roadside views.
Contact The RSPB
Tel: 01977 628191
Web: www.rspb.org.uk

This extensive reserve owes its existence to mining subsidence, which has created a number of shallow lakes. Around them are patches of scrub, wet meadows, reedy marsh, and mining spoil, much of it overgrown with willow scrub. These varied habitats are especially rich in summer, when Reed and Sedge Warblers and other songbirds breed, and Little Ringed Plovers, Lapwings, and Redshanks nest on the spoil and pastures. In autumn, terns and migrant waders are frequent and may include an occasional rarity. In winter, the pools are full of wildfowl, including Tufted Ducks, Goldeneyes, and Goosanders, and a regular herd of Whooper Swans.

❻ Ouse Washes

Location Between King's Lynn and Cambridge in the East Anglian fens.
Access The Wildfowl & Wetlands Trust centre at Welney is signposted just off the A1101 northwest of Littleport. The RSPB reserve is at Purl's Bridge, south of Manea on the B1093.
Contact WWT, Hundred Foot bank, Welney, Wisbech PE14 9TN
Tel: 01353 860711
Web: www.wwt.org.uk
or The RSPB
Tel: 01354 680212
Web: www.rspb.org.uk

Two straight, parallel channels carry drained water off the East Anglian fens to the Wash. If they are overburdened after heavy rain, excess water is diverted on to the fields between the two channels, forming a shallow lake. These washes are usually excellent in spring and summer, but unseasonal spring rains have recently reduced the numbers of breeding birds. Nevertheless,

The Ouse Washes are an important habitat for breeding wildfowl.

Snipe, Lapwings, Yellow Wagtails, and wildfowl still breed in impressive numbers. In winter, you can observe Wigeon, Pochards, Tufted Ducks, Pintails, Teal, and Shovelers. The chief attraction, however, is the concentration of Bewick's, Whooper, and Mute Swans.

❼ Titchwell Marsh

Marshland at the Titchwell reserve.

Location On the north Norfolk coast, 8km (5 miles) east of Hunstanton.
Access Signposted off the A149 north Norfolk coast road, just west of the village of Titchwell.
Contact The RSPB
Tel: 01485 210779
Web: www.rspb.org.uk

This large RSPB reserve has as much bird variety as anywhere on the magical north Norfolk coast. It includes areas of farmland, willow scrub, and woodland, and a broad freshwater reedbed with lagoons, as well as salt-marsh, dunes, and a wide, sandy beach. It is well provided with hides and good trails.

Wood Sandpiper

❽ Rutland Water

Location About 35km (22 miles) east of Leicester.
Access The birdwatching centre and reserve is at Egleton between the two main roads converging on Oakham.
Contact Leicestershire and Rutland Wildlife Trust, Fishponds Cottage, Hambleton Road, Oakham, Rutland LE15 8AB
Tel: 01572 770651
Web: www.rutlandwater.org.uk

This huge lowland reservoir is full of birds in winter, when large flocks of Mallards, Teal, Wigeon, Gadwalls, and Tufted Ducks are present, and Goosanders are regularly seen. Waders, including Common, Green, and Wood Sandpipers, Greenshanks, Ruffs, Dunlins, and Ringed Plovers, appear on migration in spring, late summer, and autumn. Common and Black Terns may be seen over the water in autumn. Tree Sparrows may still be observed here, and attempts are being made in the Egleton area to establish breeding Ospreys.

❾ Cley-next-the-sea

Location A famous reserve on the north Norfolk coast about 10km (6 miles) west of Sheringham.
Access There are several car parks signposted off the A149 north Norfolk coast road, just east of Cley-next-the-sea. A visitor centre immediately east of Cley gives access to hides and nature trails. Also explore the beach tracks at Salthouse, Kelling, and Weybourne. The car park near Walsey Hills leads on to the East Bank, a famous birdwatching walk.
Contact Norfolk Wildlife Trust, Oakeley centre, Cley Marshes, Cley, Holt, Norfolk NR25 7RZ
Tel: 01603 625540
Web: www.norfolkwildlifetrust.org.uk

This notable stretch of the Norfolk coast, including Cley marshes, is magnificent for birds in all seasons. It boasts one of the most varied lists of birds for any area of similar size in the UK. Summer sees breeding Avocets and Bearded Tits. Spring and autumn migrants include terns, occasional shearwaters, and skuas offshore, many pipits, wagtails, Wheatears, flycatchers, and chats, and a long list of warblers, regularly including Yellow-browed and Barred Warblers in autumn. The area is justly famous for its variety of migrant waders, often including rarities from Asia and North America. In winter, there are big numbers of Wigeon, Teal, Shovelers, and other ducks, and Brent Geese, as well as Snow Buntings and sometimes Shore Larks near the beach. Migrant Marsh and Hen Harriers are regulars. This special reserve has numerous hides and nature trails.

Wheatear

❿ Norfolk Broads

Picturesque Broadland landscape.

Location A complex of lakes, meres, reedbeds, and wet pasturelands in east Norfolk, north of Great Yarmouth.
Access Explore the many road and waterway routes: find Hickling Broad near Stalham from Hickling Heath or Potter Heigham; find Cockshoot and Ranworth Broads from Ranworth.
Contact Norfolk Wildlife Trust, 72 Cathedral Close, Norwich NR1 4DF
Tel: 01603 625540
Email: info@norfolkwildlifetrust.org.uk

The Broads remain excellent for birds despite the large numbers of tourists. In summer, there is a chance of viewing Bitterns, Bearded Tits, Reed Warblers, Marsh Harriers, and Egyptian Geese among other interesting birds. A tiny group of Cranes may be in the area in winter, along with Short-eared and Barn Owls, Hen and sometimes Marsh Harriers, Wigeon, and Gadwalls. Large flocks of Lapwings and Golden Plovers are all likely. There are many areas worth exploring in this extensive wetland.

⓫ Breckland

Location A large area of heathland and forest centred around Brandon, to the northwest of Thetford.
Access There are many roads and trails through the area. Try Weeting Heath north of Brandon; King's Forest north of Lackford; Grime's Graves north of Brandon; and Santon Downham east of Brandon.
Contact Norfolk Wildlife Trust, The Warden's House, East Wretham Heath, Thetford Road, Wretham, Thetford IP24 1RU
Tel: 01603 625540
Web: www.norfolkwildlifetrust.org.uk

The Brecks are sandy heaths, spread out across the borders of Norfolk and Suffolk. Many have been converted to farmland or planted with conifers, but patches of the original grass and heather heathland remain, and are worth seeking out. In summer, Weeting Heath is good for Stone-curlews, breeding Wheatears, and Woodlarks. Belts of Scots pine and mature plantations have Crossbills, while felled areas are excellent for Woodlarks and, late on summer evenings, Nightjars. Broadleaved woods have many interesting birds including Redstarts and elusive Hawfinches. Several small pools and clear rivers running through the Brecks attract Gadwalls and Kingfishers.

⓬ Walberswick/Dunwich

Varied habitats at Walberswick.

Location A marshland reserve on the Suffolk coast just south of Southwold.
Access Walberswick village is south of Southwold, on the B1387; the marshes lie between this road and Dunwich to the south, with access from the beach and also various tracks through the forest inland to the edge of the reeds.
Contact Suffolk Wildlife Trust, Brooke House, The Green, Ashbocking, Ipswich IP6 9JY
Tel: 01473 890089
Web: www.suffolkwildlifetrust.org

This is a wild area of marsh reaching to a shingle ridge along the coast, with shallow lagoons and wet pasture along its edges, and heathy hills and conifer woods inland. Its reedbed specialists include Marsh Harriers, Bitterns, and Bearded Tits, as well as large numbers of Reed and Sedge Warblers. Winter sees Snow Buntings and sometimes Shore Larks along the beach, Red-throated Divers in remarkable numbers offshore, and a good chance of Hen Harriers and Short-eared and Barn Owls. Footpaths inland and on embankments through the marsh allow plenty of scope for exploration. Nearby Dunwich Heath usually has a few Stonechats and Dartford Warblers.

⓭ Minsmere

Location On the Suffolk coast, about 10km (6 miles) south of Southwold.
Access The reserve is signposted from the A12 and Westleton village on the B1125 near Saxmundham. There are numerous hides, nature trails, and a visitor centre and shop.
Contact The RSPB
Tel: 01728 648281
Web: www.rspb.org.uk

This famous RSPB site is extremely varied, with sand dunes and a beach, lagoons, reedbeds, heath, marsh, and various types of woodland attracting close to 100 breeding species in most years. Highlights include Avocets, Bitterns, Marsh Harriers, and Bearded Tits. In spring and autumn, there are usually Common, Little, and Sandwich Terns about. Late summer is good for Spotted Redshanks, Black-tailed Godwits, and Ruffs. Autumn migrants are numerous.

Follow the numerous nature trails to explore the Minsmere reserve.

Purple Herons, while autumn regulars range from Short-toed Larks, Lapland Buntings, Barred and Yellow-browed Warblers, and Red-breasted Flycatchers, to Buff-breasted and Pectoral Sandpipers from America. There is the chance to see birds from central Asia, the Arctic, and North America within a short walk, some of them "once in a lifetime" encounters.

⑱ Portland Bill

Location A headland joined to the mainland by a causeway, just south of Weymouth on the south coast.
Access The A354 from Weymouth leads to Portland. A bird observatory is near the southernmost tip, with car parks close to the lighthouse.
Contact Portland Bird Observatory, Old Lower Light, Portland Bill, Dorset DT5 2JT
Tel: 01305 820553
Web: www.portlandbirdobs.org.uk

The headland, with its many sheltered quarries, offers an attractive landfall for incoming migrants in spring and "coasting" migrants in autumn. Occasional vagrants blown across from North America reach the headland, too. Regular migrants include Red-backed Shrikes, Tawny and Richard's Pipits, Yellow-browed and Barred Warblers, Red-breasted Flycatchers, and Ortolan Buntings. Birds over the sea include Storm Petrels, Manx and Mediterranean Shearwaters, and Arctic, Pomarine, and Great Skuas. Puffins breed on the cliffs on the western side of the headland.

⑭ Nagshead/ Forest of Dean

Location About 15km (9½ miles) southwest of Gloucester.
Access Nagshead RSPB reserve is signposted from Parkend village on the B4234. The forest area around Coleford is worth exploring. Highnam Woods west of Gloucester, on the A40, is also a RSPB nature reserve.
Contact The RSPB
Tel: 01594 562852
Web: www.rspb.org.uk

This region has ancient broadleaved forest, open heath, and some plantations. Summer birds include Nightingales, many Pied Flycatchers, Redstarts, Wood, Green, and Garden Warblers, Blackcaps, Treecreepers, Nuthatches, and woodpeckers. Sparrowhawks, Buzzards, and Ravens breed here. There are a few elusive Hawfinches and even some Mandarin Ducks along the forest streams.

⑮ Slimbridge

Location On the Severn estuary, about 35km (22 miles) northeast of Bristol.
Access Turn off the A38 near Dursley and head west.
Contact The Wildfowl & Wetlands Trust, New Grounds, Slimbridge, Gloucestershire GL2 7BT
Tel: 01453 891900
Web: www.wwt.org.uk

Slimbridge is the headquarters of the Wildfowl & Wetlands Trust, and has a comprehensive collection of captive waterfowl.

Visitors to Slimbridge enjoy spectacular views of wildfowl.

However, the wild birds are the prime attraction in winter. White-fronted Geese, Bewick's Swans, Wigeon, Gadwalls, Shovelers, Pintails, Teal, and Mallards make this site a mecca for wildfowl enthusiasts. Peregrines, Merlins, Hen Harriers, and other birds of prey add variety, and in the grounds, wild Water Rails mingle with the captive ducks.

⑯ Somerset Levels

Flooded farmland at Somerset Levels.

Location The extensive area east of Taunton in southwest England.
Access Many spots are worth a visit: try West Sedgemoor between North Curry, Curry Rivel, and Stoke St Gregory north of the A378; Shapwick, north of the A39 east of Bridgwater; and King's Sedge Moor, east of the A361 between Bridgwater, Street, and Somerton.
Contact English Nature, Roughmoor, Bishop's Hull, Taunton, Somerset TA1 5AA
Tel: 01823 283211
or The RSPB (for West Sedgemoor)
Tel: 01458 252805
Web: www.rspb.org.uk

Most UK farmland has long since been drained, but parts of the Somerset Levels retain low-lying, wet fields and deep drainage ditches. In summer, Redshanks, Snipe, and Lapwings breed in flowery meadows, filling the air with their various calls and dramatic display flights. On a ridge above West Sedgemoor is a large Grey Heron colony, with RSPB hides. Buzzards breed in nearby woods. In autumn and winter, floods attract vast numbers of Lapwings, Snipe, Golden Plovers, Wigeon, and other wildfowl, as well as a few Bewick's Swans.

⑰ Isles of Scilly

Location A group of islands about 45km (28 miles) off the southwestern tip of Cornwall.
Access By boat or helicopter from Penzance; local boats between islands.
Contact English Nature, Trevint House, Strangways Villas, Truro, Cornwall TR1 2PA
Tel: 01872 265710
Email: cornwall@english-nature.org.uk

These charming islands are justly famous for their staggering lists of rare birds, chiefly seen in spring and autumn when accommodation on St Mary's, Tresco, and St Agnes is hard to come by because of an annual influx of birdwatchers. Nothing is predictable, but spring migrants may include Hoopoes and

Richard's Pipit

left by decades of excavation, is a remarkable place for birds. It has variable numbers of seabirds breeding in summer, but it is in migration periods and winter that it excels. Spring migration extends from March to May, with waders, gulls, terns, passing skuas, divers, and wildfowl offshore. Warblers, chats, finches, and other small birds often include rarities. Wintering wildfowl on the flooded pits usually include Smews.

22 Pulborough Brooks

Location Near the south coast, 30km (19 miles) northwest of Brighton.
Access Signposted from the A283 between Pulborough and Storrington.
Contact The RSPB
Tel: 01798 875851
Email: pulborough.brooks@rspb.org.uk
Web: www.rspb.org.uk

This Sussex river valley provides extensive views across a low-lying wetland where ancient flood meadows and pools have been restored and recreated on an RSPB reserve. There is a large visitor centre, trails, and hides that allow easy exploration of open woodland, grassy meadows, the river, and its marshy floodplain. In summer, Snipe and Redshanks breed here, and other wetland birds, including Kingfishers, are frequent. Autumn brings migrant terns and waders, while winter sees duck numbers at their peak. Short-eared Owls and occasional Hen Harriers may be seen.

19 Arne

Colourful heathland at Arne.

Location The extensive harbour area to the southwest of Bournemouth on the south coast.
Access Explore west of Poole and Bournemouth, around Studland (on the B3351), Wareham, and Arne (signposted east of Wareham from the A351); Brownsea Island can be visited by boat from Poole.
Contact The RSPB
Tel: 01929 553360
Web: www.rspb.org.uk

Despite the clamour of expanding towns, this area offers good heaths with extensive tracts of gorse and heather. In some parts, it is overgrown by invading conifers; in others, the heath runs down to the coast where it adjoins salt-marsh and mudflats. The varied birdlife includes Woodlarks, Dartford Warblers, Nightjars, and Hobbies. The woodland has Buzzards and a wide selection of songbirds.

The estuaries are excellent in autumn with extensive flocks of Black-tailed Godwits; in winter, they attract small numbers of sea ducks.

20 New Forest

Location The area to the southwest of Southampton on the south coast.
Access There are abundant opportunities to walk in the forests and heaths around Lyndhurst, Beaulieu Road, Stockley, Stoney Cross, Fritham, and Burley.
Contact Forestry Commission, Great Eastern House, Tenison Road, Cambridge CB1 2DU
Tel: 01223 314546

This vast area merits lengthy exploration. The New Forest is not all wooded: much of it is open heathland with gorse, heather, and close-cropped pastures kept short by deer and horses. These open spaces have breeding Woodlarks and Dartford Warblers, as well as more widespread species such as Stonechats and Linnets. Hobbies hunt over the heaths. The woodland has large conifer plantations and old forest, especially of oak, where Hawfinches, Buzzards, and Ravens can be found. Rare Honey Buzzards and other birds of prey may sometimes be

The New Forest has a variety of exciting landscapes and habitats.

observed with patience. Nearby estuaries on the southern edge of the New Forest have wildfowl, waders, gulls, terns, and many Little Egrets.

21 Dungeness

Flooded pits at Dungeness.

Location A large shingle peninsula in southeast Kent, jutting out into the English Channel.
Access Signposted from the Lydd to Dungeness road east of Rye.
Contact Dungeness Bird Observatory, 11 RNSSS Cottages, Dungeness, Romney Marsh, Kent TN29 9NA
Tel: 01797 321309
Web: www.dungenessbirdobs.org.uk

This extensive, low-lying headland, composed of huge, sweeping shingle ridges, with areas of scrub, marsh, and lagoons

Kingfisher

Scotland

MORE THAN 800 ISLANDS and a long, indented coastline make Scotland a paradise for seabirds and waders. Its northern and western isles are often bleak and inhospitable, but sunny, still days in these environments are incomparable. Mainland cliffs are full of seabirds while the many estuaries welcome waders and wildfowl from all over northern Europe, Siberia, and the Canadian Arctic. High hills have tundra species, such as Ptarmigan and Snow Buntings, while ancient pine forests have one unique species – the Scottish Crossbill – as well as Crested Tits, Capercaillies, and Ospreys.

❶ Fair Isle

Magnificent rocky cliffs of Fair Isle.

Location A small island situated between the Shetland and Orkney Island groups.
Access By boat or air from Lerwick.
Contact Fair Isle Bird Observatory Trust, Fair Isle, Shetland ZE2 9JU
Tel: 01595 760258
Web: www.fairislebirdobs.co.uk

Fair Isle is one of the great bird islands of Europe, famous for its breeding Arctic and Great Skuas, other seabirds, and a great array of migrants in spring, autumn, and early winter. Late spring sees many small birds making landfall, with regular "scarce" species including Bluethroats, Red-backed Shrikes, and Wrynecks. Autumn brings Fair Isle specials such as Short-toed Larks, Richard's Pipits, Little, Yellow-breasted, and Rustic Buntings, and even species from eastern Asia and North America. Much of the island is bleak and offers little cover, so birds take shelter in tiny patches of crops, in sheltered ditches, or in gullies at the top of dramatic sea cliffs. It is a stimulating, unpredictable place to look for birds – an unmissable treat for the committed birdwatcher.

❷ Handa Island

Location A small island off the northwest coast of Scotland, just to the northwest of Scourie, Sutherland.
Access By boat from Tarbet, daily except Sundays between April and September.
Contact Scottish Wildlife Trust, Unit 4A, 3 Carsegate Road North Inverness IV3 8DU
Tel: 01463 714746
Web: http://scottishwildlifetrust.org.uk

Handa is seemingly rather low and gentle when seen from the mainland, but has dramatic sheer cliffs and giant stacks facing the north and west. These ancient rocks provide ledges for breeding Guillemots, Razorbills, and Kittiwakes, with smaller numbers of Fulmars and Puffins. The lower cliffs have Black Guillemots, while the moorland on the island centre has several pairs of Great and Arctic Skuas. Even Red-throated Divers breed on a small lochan, while Ringed Plovers and Oystercatchers nest near the beautiful sandy beaches of the small sheltered coves.

❸ Forsinard

Location Situated in the heart of the Flow Country of Sutherland, 40km (25 miles) northwest of Helmsdale.
Access The visitor centre can be reached by rail to Forsinard or by road on the A897 from Helmsdale.
Contact The Warden, Forsinard Station, Forsinard, Sutherland KW13 6YT
Tel: 01641 571225
Web: www.rspb.org.uk

The RSPB has its biggest nature reserve here, centred on the tiny village and railway station at Forsinard. The surrounding area is a mixture of ancient, rolling peatland and new, alien conifer plantations, many of which the RSPB is in the process of removing. Peatland, a rare habitat internationally, is seen here at its best, with innumerable pools and deep, quaking bogs. A safe walkway from Forsinard gives a good taste of this remote habitat, where Red-throated Divers, Greenshanks, Golden Plovers, and occasional Arctic Skuas nest. There are Hen Harriers, Merlins, and Short-eared Owls and, around the farmed areas at the edges, Twites, Wheatears, and Rock Doves can be seen.

Striking and important peatland habitats at Forsinard.

❹ Duncansby Head

Location The far northeastern corner of mainland Scotland, approximately 30km (19 miles) north of Wick, Caithness.
Access Take the minor road east from John O'Groats and explore the clifftops on both sides of the lighthouse.
Contact The RSPB, Dunedin House, 25 Ravelston Terrace, Edinburgh EH4 3TP
Tel: 0131 3116500

The wonderful sights and sounds at Duncansby Head are hard to beat; it is not the biggest cliff, nor does it have the largest seabird colonies, but it is a perfect stretch of sandstone coastline, with cliffs, gullies, and offshore stacks. Seabirds, often visible at close range, include Fulmars, Guillemots, Puffins, Razorbills, and Kittiwakes, and a few Arctic and Great Skuas. Rock Doves are frequent and Peregrines likely, with Gannets and perhaps Manx Shearwaters offshore.

❺ Abernethy/ Loch Garten

Abernethy Forest.

Location On the edge of the Cairngorm mountains near Aviemore, about 55km (34 miles) southeast of Inverness.
Access East of Aviemore off the B970 between Boat of Garten and Nethybridge.
Contact The Warden, Grianan, Nethybridge, Inverness-shire PH25 3EF
Tel: 07841 317027
Web: www.rspb.org.uk

Loch Garten is famous for its Ospreys, which returned to breed here in the 1950s. A centre overlooking the nest is open from April to late summer. Abernethy Forest is also justly famous among naturalists as a wonderful place

for birds, with Crested Tits, Common, Parrot, and Scottish Crossbills, Capercaillies, Black Grouse, Buzzards, Ravens, Golden Eagles, and many more common species breeding. The large reserve extends to the Cairngorm plateau, where there are Dotterels in summer and Ptarmigan and Snow Buntings all year round. Disturbance by visitors is a potentially serious problem in spring, so be sure that access is permitted.

❻ Fowlsheugh

Cliff-bound coast at Fowlsheugh.

Location 5km (3 miles) south of Stonehaven, or 25km (16 miles) south of Aberdeen on the east coast.
Access There is a car park at Crawton, which is signposted from the A92; take care as you follow the footpath along the clifftop.
Contact The RSPB
Tel: 01346 532017
Web: www.rspb.org.uk

This stretch of cliff remains wild and unspoiled, with glorious shows of gorse, broom, and campion at the top of the Old Red Sandstone cliffs. Around 30,000 pairs of

Guillemots and similar numbers of Kittiwakes breed here, along with smaller numbers of Fulmars, Puffins, Razorbills, Shags, and Herring Gulls. The cliffs are deeply incised in places, giving good views. It is best to visit between late March and late July.

❼ Loch of Strathbeg

Location In the northeast corner of Aberdeenshire between Peterhead and Fraserburgh.
Access The visitor centre is signposted from the A90 at Crimond, north of Peterhead.
Contact The RSPB, Starnafin, Crimond, Fraserburgh AB43 8QN
Tel: 01346 532017
Web: www.rspb.org.uk

This large loch close to the coast has an RSPB nature reserve, visitor centre, and hides overlooking damp meadows and shallow lagoons created for waders and wildfowl. In summer, Lapwings, Redshanks, and Snipe breed. In autumn, there are many Golden Plovers and migrant waders, gulls, and terns. Big numbers of Pink-footed and Greylag Geese arrive and many remain all winter, along with Whooper Swans, Wigeon, Teal, and smaller numbers of Goldeneyes, Goosanders, and other ducks, so that the loch is worth a visit at any time of the year.

Flocking birds in the sky over the Loch of Strathbeg, a large, natural loch.

Redshank

❽ Ythan Estuary/ Sands of Forvie

Location An estuary on the east coast, 30km (19 miles) north of Aberdeen.
Access The A975 from Newburgh, north of Aberdeen, crosses the estuary. The Forvie Visitor Centre lies to the north on the B9003 to Collieston.
Contact Aberdeen Office: Inverdee House, Baxter Street, Torry, Aberdeen, AB11 9QA
Tel: 01224 266500
Web: www.snh.gov.uk

This whole area of dunes, beach, and shallow estuary is exciting in autumn and winter, but in summer it is also full of birds, with nesting Eiders, Sandwich Terns, Curlews, and Short-eared Owls. Migrant waders and wildfowl abound in autumn, and wintering flocks include many Golden Plovers, Redshanks, Curlews, Wigeon, Teal, Shelducks, Eiders, Whooper Swans, and often Pink-footed Geese. Snow Buntings are regular.

❾ Fife Ness

Location The most easterly point of Fife, 40km (25 miles) southeast of Dundee.
Access The headland is reached from Crail on the A917. There are many footpaths and minor roads along the Kilminning coast and the Ness itself.
Contact Scottish Wildlife Trust, Cramond House, Cramond Glebe Road, Edinburgh EH4 6NS
Tel: 0131 312 7765
Web: http://scottishwildlifetrust.org.uk

The long-distance coastal footpath skirts excellent areas for migrants, and is worth a visit in spring and autumn when tired songbirds make landfall and can be watched in low scrub and bushes, and specially planted trees at Fife Ness Muir. In autumn, Barred Warblers, Wrynecks, Bluethroats, and Red-backed Shrikes are possible. Arctic, Pomarine, and Great Skuas, Manx Shearwaters, and Little Gulls may be seen offshore, along with a steady flow of Gannets, Fulmars, and Kittiwakes. Waders, including Whimbrels, also pause on the rocky shores at times.

❿ Aberlady Bay

Location On the southern shore of the Firth of Forth, just to the east of Edinburgh.
Access From various points along the A198 Berwick road.
Contact The Warden, 4 Craigielaw, Longniddry, East Lothian EH32 0PY
Tel: 01620 827847
Web: www.aberlady.org

The coast east of Edinburgh is full of surprises and provides good birdwatching at all times of year. Aberlady and Gosford Bays, and Gullane Bay a little farther east, are particularly worthy of exploration. A long walk will take you through areas of grassland, dunes, rocky headlands, and

Slavonian Grebe

sandy beaches, with sand and mud flats at low tide. Incoming tides from late summer to late spring bring in many waders and wildfowl, including Red-necked, Slavonian, and Great Crested Grebes. Red-breasted Mergansers, Common and Velvet Scoters, Eiders, and occasional Long-tailed Ducks are particularly interesting, while winter waders include Purple Sandpipers and Bar-tailed Godwits.

⓫ Bass Rock

Location A rocky island off the southern shore of the Firth of Forth, just northeast of North Berwick.
Access By boat from North Berwick.
Contact Scottish Seabird Centre, The Harbour, North Berwick
Tel: 01620 890202
Web: www.northberwick.org.uk
Email: seaton@northberwick.org.uk

The Rock is best appreciated on a visit by boat (subject to weather conditions). Landing is restricted to late in the breeding season to avoid disturbing the spectacular colony of Gannets (reaching up to 40,000 pairs) and lesser, but still impressive, numbers of Guillemots, Razorbills, Puffins, Fulmars, and Shags. Bass Rock is an extraordinary

The impressive and thriving colony of Gannets on Bass Rock.

place for any visitor, but is especially exciting and rewarding for the photographer or artist, who can wish for no more confiding or dramatic subjects.

⓬ Caerlaverock and the Solway Firth

View across the Solway Firth.

Location On the eastern shore of the mouth of the River Nith, which flows into the Solway Firth 15km (9½ miles) south of Dumfries.
Access Caerlaverock is approached via the B724 west from Annan. The Solway region is easily explored from roads, including the A710 and B725.
Contact WWT Caerlaverock, Eastpark Farm, Caerlaverock, Dumfries-shire, DG1 4RS
Tel: 01387 770200
Web: www.wwt.org.uk

The region is justly famed for its winter wildfowl, with large flocks of Greylag, Pink-footed, and Barnacle Geese, many Bean Geese, Whooper Swans, Scaup, and Goosanders, and always the chance of Barn Owls and Hen Harriers along with many Buzzards. Even Golden Eagles are possible over nearby hills.

⓭ Islay

Location One of the Inner Hebrides to the southwest of Jura.
Access By ferry from Tarbert; a good road system gives easy access to most places of interest, especially Loch Gruinart in the north.
Contact The Warden, Bushmill Cottage, Gruinart, Isle of Islay, Argyll PA44 7PP, or Islay Tourist Information Centre
Tel: +44 (0)1496 810254
Web: www.islayinfo.com

This large island has a variety of landscapes, from low-lying pasture land and salt-marshes, estuaries, and coastal cliffs to high, bleak, heathery ground and exposed mountains. In summer, it has many breeding species including handsome Rock Doves, Hen Harriers, Red Grouse, Oystercatchers, Black Guillemots, and Arctic Terns. In autumn, huge numbers of Barnacle and smaller numbers of Greenland White-fronted Geese arrive to stay the winter and into spring.

Wales

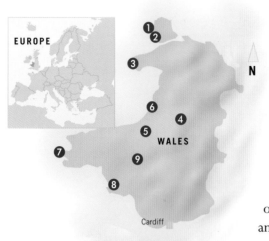

HIGHER PEAKS LIE to the north of Wales, but most of the land is rolling moors above wooded and farmed valleys. Woodland birds are common and birds of prey, including Buzzards as well as rarer Peregrines, Merlins, Red Kites, and Goshawks, have long attracted birdwatchers. Several estuaries, especially in the south, are good for waterfowl, while islands and cliffs of the west coast have seabird colonies, Ravens, and Choughs. Welsh lakes are generally cold and poor for birds, with the exception of a handful of shallow lowland lakes and reservoirs in the south and on Anglesey in the far northwest.

❷ Valley Lakes, Anglesey

Location Just south of Caergeilliog, near Valley, on Anglesey.
Access Easily reached from the A55; there are daily buses from Bangor and Holyhead.
Contact The Warden, Plas Nico, South Stack, Holyhead, Anglesey LL65 1YH Tel: 01407 764973
Web: www.rspb.org.uk

Valley Lakes are various small, reed-fringed pools in a strange setting of low pastures and rocky outcrops, located close to the coast. A nature trail 3km (2 miles) in length takes you through the best habitats. At any time, you are likely to see a variety of wildfowl. In summer, the area is good for breeding Sedge Warblers and assorted waders, such as Snipe, Lapwings, and Curlews.

Lapwing

❸ Lleyn Peninsula and Bardsey (Ynys Enlli)

Grassy clifftops of Lleyn Peninsula.

Location South of Anglesey. Bardsey Island is found at the end of the Lleyn Peninsula.
Access The A499 runs near the south coast of the long peninsula and the B4417 along the north. Minor roads lead to small bays and headlands.
Contact Bardsey Island Trust and Bardsey Bird Observatory, Cristen, Ynys Enlli, off Aberdaron, via Pwllheli, Gwynedd LL53 8DE
Web: www.bbfo.org.uk

This long, angular, unspoiled peninsula is less intensively farmed than adjacent areas. Its old pastures attract feeding Choughs that nest on the coastal cliffs, the prime attraction of the region. Peregrines are regularly seen along the cliffs. Offshore at the western tip is Bardsey, an island with Manx Shearwaters breeding in summer. Many migrants can be seen in spring and autumn.

❶ South Stack, Anglesey

Location West of Holyhead on Holy Island, off the west coast of Anglesey, in northwest Wales.
Access Take the minor road west from Holyhead for 3km (2 miles) to the car park and nearby visitor centre in Ellin's Tower. Trails lead over nearby maritime heath and pass along cliffs.
Contact The Warden, Plas Nico, South Stack, Holyhead, Anglesey LL65 1YH Tel: 01407 762100
Web: www.rspb.org.uk

This reserve is important for two habitats – its sea cliffs, and its colourful maritime heath (to the south of the cliffs), which is patricularly worth exploring in summer. The sea

The cliffs at South Stack have a wonderful range of breeding seabirds.

cliffs have breeding Puffins, Guillemots, Razorbills, Kittiwakes, and Fulmars. There are regularly a few Choughs around the area. Peregrines have long nested here. In spring and autumn, migrants are regular and occasionally include a scarce or rare bird or two: it is well worth spending time looking for migrants on misty days after southerly winds in spring. In autumn, too, Manx Shearwaters and other seabirds may be seen passing offshore, usually rather distant beyond the lighthouse island.

❹ Elan Valley

Autumn colours in the Elan Valley.

Location 6km (3½ miles) southwest of Rhayader in central Wales.
Access Take the turning off the B4518 southwest of Rhayader.
Contact Elan Valley Trust, Elan Estate Office, Elan Village, Rhayader, Powys LD6 5HP
Tel: 44 (0)1597 810449
Web: www.elanvalley.org.uk
or Radnorshire Wildlife Trust, Warwick House, High Street, Llandrindod Wells, Powys LD1 6AG

A vast area of open, largely grassy moor surrounds the Elan Valley with its big, deep, rather birdless reservoirs, crags, and valley-side oakwoods. This is bleak country in winter, with a few Red Grouse, Ravens, Buzzards, and the odd Peregrine, but in summer it comes alive with woodland birds, including the typical oakwood trio of Redstart, Pied Flycatcher, and Wood Warbler. Common Sandpipers and Grey Wagtails may be seen, as can waders on the moors, including Golden Plovers and a few Dunlins. Red Kites are regular. There are also some feeding centres where many kites and other species can be seen closely in winter.

❺ Cors Caron, Tregaron

Location An area of moorland and bog 20km (12½ miles) southeast of Aberystwyth.
Access Take the B4343 north from Tregaron and explore minor roads in the area, east and west of the bog.
Contact Countryside Council for Wales, Neuaddlar, Tregaron, Ceredigion SY25 6LG
Tel: 01974 298480
Web: www.ccw.gov.uk

This is a large peat bog, very colourful in autumn and winter with bleached grasses, brown heather, purple willows, blue streams, and intensely coloured

mosses. The surrounding hills, typical of central Wales, may reveal hunting Red Kites and Buzzards. In winter, there are Merlins, Hen Harriers, Peregrines, Short-eared and Barn Owls, Willow Tits, and Stonechats. In summer, the usual woodland species abound, such as Redstarts and warblers. Long walks here let you appreciate the numbers of birds – a stark contrast to the paucity of bird life in many other farmed areas.

❻ Ynys-hir

Location On the south side of the Dyfi estuary, about 20km (12½ miles) northeast of Aberystwyth.
Access Off the A487 Aberystwyth to Machynlleth road. There is a visitor centre, hides, and trails.
Contact The Warden, Ynys-hir RSPB Nature Reserve, Eglwys-fach, Machynlleth, Powys SY20 8TA
Tel: 01654 700222
Web: www.rspb.org.uk

A mixed area with estuary, salt-marsh, wet meadows, hills and woodland. In summer, Ynys-hir has breeding Lapwings, Snipe, Redshanks, Pied Flycatchers, Redstarts, Wood Warblers, Whinchats, Stonechats, and Wheatears; Red Kites and Buzzards are always likely. At other times, the estuary has many passage waders and wildfowl, including Wigeon and small numbers of Greenland White-fronted Geese. Hen Harriers, Peregrines, and other birds of prey are possibilities.

Reedbeds bordering the tranquil waters of the estuary at Ynys-hir.

Storm Petrel

❼ Skomer Island

Location Off the Pembrokeshire coast, about 20km (12½ miles) west of Milford Haven.
Access By boat from Martins Haven, west of Haverfordwest.
Contact The Wildlife Trust West Wales, Welsh Wildlife Centre, Cilgerran, Cardigan, Ceredigion SA43 2TB
Tel: 01239 621212
Web: www.wtww.co.uk

This magical island is superbly colourful, with varied cliffs and swathes of vivid bluebells and red campions in early summer. It is dotted by thousands of Lesser Black-backed and Herring Gulls. The cliffs have Guillemots, Razorbills, Kittiwakes, and a few Puffins. The island surface is riddled with burrows, where tens of thousands of Manx Shearwaters breed and Storm Petrels nest in the many rocky cavities.

❽ Burry Inlet

Location A large estuary just west of Swansea.
Access Via minor roads on the north side of the Gower Peninsula, especially from Penclawdd, Llanrhidian, and Cwm Ivy. Several footpaths run across the dune and marsh systems.

Contact Countryside Council for Wales, Unit 4, Castelton Court, St. Mellon's, Cardiff CF30LT
Tel: 02920 772400

The Burry Inlet has expansive marshes and mudflats, and is especially good for Oystercatchers, Knots, Dunlins, Pintails, Wigeon, and, at its western end, a variety of birds on the rising tide that include Black-necked and Slavonian Grebes, Eiders, and occasional divers. Brent Geese have recently greatly increased here. In winter, Hen Harriers, Peregrines, and Merlins are regular, while Buzzards and Ravens are seen all year. To the west, Carmarthen Bay has a large flock of Common Scoters, often far offshore.

❾ Dinas and Gwenffrwd

Oakwoods at Dinas and Gwenffrwd.

Location 45km (28 miles) north of Swansea, in south Wales.
Access Off the minor road from Llandovery to Llyn Brianne, 16km (10 miles) north of Llandovery.
Contact The Warden, Troedrhiwgelynen, Rhandirmwyn, Llandovery SA20 0PN
Tel: 01654 700222
Web: www.rspb.org.uk

Central Wales once had the remnant population of Red Kites in the UK; these birds have now recovered, but seeing a kite in this hilly, well-wooded location is still exciting. Red Kites, Buzzards, and Ravens are year-round birds, as are Dippers, Treecreepers, Nuthatches, and Great Spotted Woodpeckers. Summer brings Wheatears, Ring Ouzels, Redstarts, Pied Flycatchers, Wood, Garden, and Willow Warblers, Blackcaps, and other migrants, making this whole area particularly rich in small birds. The rivers have Common Sandpipers and Grey Wagtails.

Ireland and Northern Ireland

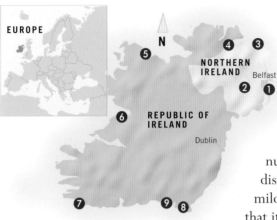

EUROPE

N

NORTHERN
IRELAND
Belfast

4 3

5

2 1

REPUBLIC OF
IRELAND

Dublin

6

7

9 8

THE EMERALD ISLE is, in large part, brighter green than ever before because of the chemical "improvement" of its farmland. Although the Corncrake and other farmland birds have declined as a result, it remains a wonderful place for seeing birds in exquisite surroundings. The coasts are alive with seabirds and, in the autumn, enriched by huge numbers of migrants passing offshore in Europe's finest display of seabird movements. Wildfowl relish Ireland's mild winters and the country's westerly position means that it receives rare vagrants from North America.

❶ Belfast Harbour

Wetlands at Belfast Harbour.

Location Belfast Lough is on the northeast coast of Northern Ireland, with the city of Belfast at its head.
Access Go through the Belfast Harbour estate off the A2 between Belfast and Holywood, taking the Airport Road for 3km (2 miles) to the car park and observation room.
Contact The RSPB
Tel: 02890 461458
Web: www.rspb.org.uk

Shallow wetlands, a lagoon, wet grassland, and mudflats create a peaceful haven against the city backdrop. Views of wildfowl, waders, gulls, and terns are excellent from the observation centre. High tide is best when waders flock to the reserve, from the main mudflats, to roost. Redshanks, Black-tailed Godwits, and Oystercatchers are numerous. From autumn to early spring there are also many Wigeon and chances of scarce or rare birds from time to time.

❷ Lough Neagh

View from the shores of Lough Neagh.

Location About 20km (12½ miles) west of Belfast, Northern Ireland.
Access A good area is around the Lough Neagh Discovery Centre near Kinnegoe Harbour on the south shore, in Oxford Island Nature Reserve. The RSPB's Portmore Lough reserve is on the east side. Leave the M1 at junction 9 to Aghalee, then follow road signs to the reserve.
Contact The RSPB
Tel: 02890 491547
Web: www.rspb.org.uk

Lough Neagh has up to 80,000 waders and wildfowl, but it is a big lake and getting close can be difficult. From the hides at Oxford Island, you can see Pochards, Goldeneyes, Scaup, Tufted Ducks, and other ducks in winter. There are ususaly Bewick's and Whooper Swans. In summer, there are Sedge and Grasshopper Warblers and many pairs of Great Crested Grebes, Black-headed Gulls, and Common Terns.

❸ Rathlin Island

Location This small island lies about 8km (5 miles) off the north coast of Northern Ireland.
Access By ferry from Ballycastle all year round. There is a minibus service on the island, and many small roads from which to explore. The best seabird cliffs are overlooked by a platform at the West Light.
Contact Caledonian MacBrayne Ferries
Tel: 02820 769299
or The RSPB warden
Tel: 02820 760062
Web: www.rspb.org.uk

Magnificent bird colonies on the cliffs at Rathlin Island.

Rathlin is an excellent site, notable for its spectacular cliffs and hay meadows, in which there may be a pair or two of Corncrakes. The chief interest, however, lies in the thousands of nesting seabirds; from March to July, these include Guillemots, Razorbills, Puffins, Kittiwakes, and Fulmars. The West Light area gives the best views. The island has potential for watching seabird migration offshore, including Manx Shearwaters, and attracts many small migrants in autumn, when the odd rarity is possible.

Sunset over Lough Foyle.

❹ Lough Foyle

Location This sea lough is 13km (8 miles) northeast of Londonderry.
Access Take the A2 between Limavady and Londonderry and use minor roads to explore the shores, mudflats, and surrounding damp fields and floods. Good spots are Magilligan Point at the northern end, Roe Estuary on the eastern shore, and Ballykelly Marsh and Longfield Point on the southern shore.
Contact The RSPB
Tel: 02890 491547
Web: www.rspb.org.uk

This site is outstanding in winter for its wildfowl, which include thousands of Wigeon, big herds of Whooper Swans, a few Bewick's Swans, Greenland White-fronted Geese, and Brent Geese. The Londonderry side of the lough is best, with big flocks of waders at high tide. On the sea, there may be divers and grebes, including a few Slavonian Grebes. In autumn, skuas and terns enter the lough close by Magilligan Point. Snow Buntings and Twites may be found near Roe Estuary in winter. The whole area attracts birds of prey, including Merlins, Peregrines, and Sparrowhawks.

❺ Kilcummin Head

Location About 25km (16 miles) north of Ballina.
Access From Ballina, take the R314 to Killala, head for Ballycastle then turn right towards the headland.
Contact Birdwatch Ireland, Ruttledge House, 8 Longford Place, Monkstown, Co. Dublin, Ireland
Tel: (01) 2804322
Email: info@birdwatchireland.org
Web: www.birdwatchireland.ie

This is one of many superb Irish headlands on the coast of County Mayo. It is usually good in spring, summer, and autumn for passing seabirds, including Gannets, Manx Shearwaters, Fulmars, Guillemots, Puffins, Razorbills, and Kittiwakes. In less clement autumn weather, it can be sensational, especially after a strong northwesterly wind when seabirds swept into Donegal Bay move out again to open sea. They can include Sabine's Gulls, Leach's Petrels in remarkable numbers, Storm Petrels by the hundred or thousand, Long-tailed, Pomarine, Arctic, and Great Skuas, Sooty and thousands of Manx Shearwaters, as well as rarer birds. They often seem to come by closer to the headland here than at most seawatching sites, giving extraordinarily good views. Observing these birds requires constant attention and concentration, however, as they fly by once and are gone.

❻ Cliffs of Moher

Location 40km (25 miles) northwest of Limerick on the County Clare coast.
Access Turn off the N67, 30km (19 miles) northeast of Kilkee, on to the R478; the visitor centre is off this road.
Contact BirdWatch Ireland, Ruttledge House, 8 Longford Place, Monkstown, Co. Dublin, Ireland
Email: info@birdwatchireland.org
Web: www.shannonheritage.com/CliffsofMoher

The Cliffs of Moher are wonderful to look at, but at 200m (650ft) high, really too big for good views of breeding birds. A thousand pairs of Puffins nest on an offshore islet, Goat Island, and many other seabirds breed alongside Peregrines, Choughs, Ravens, Twites, and Rock Doves – wild, handsome birds that put town pigeons to shame. Corncrakes were once regular in the region's hayfields, but have now mostly disappeared.

❼ Cape Clear Island

Cape Clear is famous for its birds.

Location A small island off the southwest coast of Ireland.
Access From Cork take the N71 as far west as Skibbereen, then take the R595 to Baltimore harbour. From here, a ferry crosses to Cape Clear island. There is a bird observatory with accommodation on the island.
Contact BirdWatch Ireland, Ruttledge House, 8 Longford Place, Monkstown, Co. Dublin, Ireland
Email: info@birdwatchireland.org

Cape Clear is a piece of old Ireland with small farms, drystone walls, small fields, and rocky headlands. The whole island deserves thorough exploration. In July and August, an abundance of Manx Shearwaters pass by, and, later in the autumn, Cory's, Great, and Sooty Shearwaters are possible. Storm Petrels are extremely numerous and often close inshore, and Gannets, Kittiwakes, skuas, and Fulmars are always about.

Buff-breasted Sandpiper

❽ Wexford Slobs

Location 15km (9½ miles) north of Rosslare at the southeastern tip of Ireland.
Access Wexford is set in a round bay; to the north are North Slob and the Wexford Wildfowl Reserve, off the Gorey road.
Contact BirdWatch Ireland, Ruttledge House, 8 Longford Place, Monkstown, Co. Dublin, Ireland
Email: info@birdwatchireland.org

The Slobs are wide, open expanses of damp grassland, pools, ditches, and floods on reclaimed farmland. Winter and early spring are the best times to visit, with Bewick's Swans outnumbering Whoopers. There are thousands of Greenland White-fronted Geese, some Pink-footed Geese, and sometimes a Snow Goose or two. Lapwings, Curlews, and Golden Plovers are widespread and numerous.

❾ Tacumshin

Location A wetland in the extreme southeastern corner of Ireland.
Access Turn off the N25 Wexford to Rosslare road, just west of Tagoat on to the R736. Take the minor road that leads to the lake shore around Tomhaggard and Tacumshin villages.
Contact BirdWatch Ireland, Ruttledge House, 8 Longford Place, Monkstown, Co. Dublin, Ireland
Email: info@birdwatchireland.org

A mixture of habitats surrounds a large lagoon, cut off from the sea by a sand bank. It has high water levels in winter but often drains in summer; the variable state of its shores affects its attraction to waders. Autumn, however, usually sees at least a couple of rarities, typically waders or ducks from North America, such as Buff-breasted, Pectoral, and White-rumped Sandpipers, and Blue-winged Teal.

Denmark

EUROPE

DENMARK

JUTLAND

Arhus

Copenhagen

FYN ZEALAND

N

GERMANY

THE DANISH MAINLAND is mostly low-lying and agricultural, and its birds are – for the most part – those that can adapt to a managed, disturbed environment. The country's real treasures are coasts, dunes, beaches, and wild islands – 483 of them. Little surprise, then, that its birds include great numbers of ducks (including many marine species such as Eiders, scoters, and Long-tailed Ducks), geese, swans, and waders. It is also well placed to receive migrants from and to the north.

❶ Gilleleje

Location The northern tip of Zealand, about 60km (37 miles) north of Copenhagen.
Access About an hour's drive north of Copenhagen, Gilleleje is the centre for exploring the Gilberghoved and Nakkehoved Fyr areas. There are many footpaths from the roads to the north coast between Gilbjerghoved and Gilleleje village and harbour.
Contact Dansk Ornitologisk Forening, Vesterbrogade 138-140, DK-1620, Copenhagen V
Web: www.dof.dk

Agricultural land, woods, gardens, and suburban areas combine to make an interesting area for migrants; the coast, in particular, is wonderful in spring and autumn, both for landbirds and seabirds offshore. There may be 100,000 small birds in spring, principally Meadow Pipits, Chaffinches, Bramblings, and Fieldfares, as well as massive numbers of Woodpigeons, Jackdaws, Barnacle Geese, Buzzards and Rough-legged Buzzards, Ospreys, and Cranes. Ring Ouzels pass through in April. Autumn migration includes Fulmars, a few Manx Shearwaters and Long-tailed Skuas, and thousands of Kittiwakes. In winter, there are many Eiders to be seen and the harbour usually has a Glaucous Gull or two.

❷ Djursland

Location On the east coast of Jutland, 40km (25 miles) east of Randers.
Access From Randers, drive east on road 16 to Grenaa; take a minor road north to Gjerrild and Gjerrild Nordstrand. The lighthouse is the best place to watch passing seabirds.
Contact Dansk Ornitologisk Forening, Vesterbrogade 138-140, DK-1620, Copenhagen V
Web: www.dof.dk

Djursland has mixed farmland, reeds and lakes, coastal scrub, and good seawatching spots. Spring and autumn migration periods are good for small landbirds and birds of prey; Greylag Geese, Marsh Warblers, Penduline Tits, and Scarlet Rosefinches breed. Seabirds pass by in autumn and early winter, with remarkable numbers of Razorbills in some years, but also gulls, terns, and skuas.

Scarlet Rosefinch

View across the Tofte Sø lake.

❸ Lille Vildmose and Tofte Sø

Location About 20km (12½ miles) southeast of Ålborg in north Jutland.
Access From Ålborg, take the 507 southeast to Hadsund. Explore the Lille Vildmose area on minor roads to the southeast of Kongerslev and the coast at Øster Hurup. 15km (9½ miles) north of Hadsund is the artificial lake of Tofte Sø.
Contact Dansk Ornitologisk Forening, Vesterbrogade 138-140, DK-1620, Copenhagen V
Web: www.dof.dk

This is one of the finest lowland peat bogs in Europe and the largest in Denmark. It is a private reserve with no general access, but the observation tower is good and roads give adequate views of most parts. In the breeding season, there are Red-necked and Black-necked Grebes, a Cormorant colony, Greylag Geese, Garganeys, and many birds of prey including Honey Buzzards and Goshawks. Cranes breed in some years. In autumn and winter, there are more birds of prey, (including Golden and White-tailed Eagles) and a good flock of Bean Geese. Small birds are interesting, too, with Great Grey Shrikes and Twites especially good if you can find them. If the water level of the lake falls in late summer, migrant waders can be numerous and varied.

④ Skagen

Location The northernmost tip of Jutland, about 100km (62 miles) northeast of Ålborg.
Access From Ålborg, take the E45 to Frederikshavn, then route 40 to Skagen.
Contact Dansk Ornitologisk Forening, Vesterbrogade 138-140, DK-1620, Copenhagen V
Web: www.dof.dk

Around the city is a large area of low-lying dunes, heathland, and plantations. The area is good for migrants, but sightings depend on the winds. Flagbakken, southwest of Skagen, is excellent for raptors, including Marsh Harriers, Rough-legged Buzzards, Ospreys, Peregrines, Hobbies, Merlins, and Kestrels. Grenen – the far northeastern tip – is good in westerly winds for autumn seabirds and small migrants. In autumn, seabirds include Arctic, Pomarine, and Long-tailed Skuas, Gannets, petrels, and odd rarities. Arctic Redpolls and Parrot Crossbills are likely in winter.

⑤ Vejlerne

Location The northwest coast of Jutland, 60km (37 miles) west of Ålborg.
Access The largest nature reserve in Denmark; much is visible from paths and roads. The best areas are close to route 11 around Bygholm Vejle, Kærup Holme, Østerild Fjord, and Bulbjerg on the coast where there is Denmark's only Fulmar colony.
Contact National Forest and Nature Agency, Skov- og Naturstyrelsen, Haraldsgade 53, 2100 Copenhagen Ø
Email: sns@sns.dk

An area of partly-drained fjords, lakes, reedy swamps, meadows, and salt-marsh, this is a good year-round site. In the breeding season, there are Red-necked Grebes, Bitterns, White Storks, hundreds of Greylag Geese, Montagu's Harriers, Spotted Crakes, 200 pairs of Avocets, and Black Terns. In winter, there are many Bewick's and Whooper Swans, Bean, Pink-footed, and Greylag Geese, and thousands of Wigeon, Teal, Red-breasted Mergansers and other ducks.

View from the observation tower at the Vejlerne reserve.

Ruff

⑥ Harboør and Agger Peninsulas

Location The west coast of Jutland, 60km (37 miles) northwest of Holstebro.
Access From Holstebro, take the 11 then the 513 to Lemvig, then the 181 to Harboør and Thyborøn. Ferries cross from Thyborøn to the north peninsula and Agger. View the dunes, shallow lagoons, and bays to the north of Harboør and around Agger.
Contact Dansk Ornitologisk Forening, Vesterbrogade 138-140, DK-1620, Copenhagen V
Web: www.dof.dk

This region – peninsulas around an open fjord – is excellent all year round. Spring migrant waders include thousands of Dunlins, Bar-tailed Godwits, and Pink-footed Geese. There are also breeding waders including Ruffs, Avocets, Black-tailed Godwits, Sandwich, Little, Common, and Arctic Terns, and Black-necked Grebes. Autumn is good for Bewick's Swans, Brent Geese, Shore Larks, and Lapland Buntings. The Pink-footed Geese return too, many staying over in mild winters. It is worth searching for rarer geese, such as Red-breasted and Lesser White-fronted, present in some years. Brent Geese are numerous in winter and Glaucous Gulls should be looked for in the harbours.

⑦ Vind Hede

Location About 100km (62 miles) north of Esbjerg in western Jutland.
Access 10km (6 miles) south of Holstebro, turn west off route 11 to the village of Vind. Explore the heathland area to the northwest.
Contact Dansk Ornitologisk Forening, Vesterbrogade 138-140, DK-1620, Copenhagen V
Web: www.dof.dk

This is an area of plantation and heath mixed with farmland. A tiny handful of Black Grouse survive on the heath and may be seen at dawn in spring; take care not to disturb them. Buzzards, Goshawks, and Crested Tits are all around in summer. At dusk, you might find Long-eared Owls; you are more likely to spot Nightjars, which churr in the gathering gloom, and hawk moths over the open heath.

⑧ Ringkøbing Fjord

Wetlands adjacent to Ringkøbing Fjord.

Location A large enclosed fjord about 50km (31 miles) north of Esbjerg.
Access The 181 between Nørre Nebel and Hvide Sande along the Tipperne peninsula gives good views.
Contact Dansk Ornitologisk Forening, Vesterbrogade 138-140, DK-1620, Copenhagen V
Web: www.dof.dk

This inlet in western Jutland has excellent coastal meadows, marshes, and pools. There is an interesting harbour at Hvide Sand, worth exploring for gulls in winter. Thousands of Mute and Bewick's Swans, Pink-footed, Brent, and Barnacle Geese, tens of thousands of Wigeon, Teal, Mallards, Pintails, and other ducks make it a good area for the wildfowl enthusiast in winter, while birds of prey include Rough-legged Buzzards and an occasional White-tailed Eagle. Peregrines and Merlins are also seen on migration; Dotterels appear in May.

9 Blåvands Huk/ Skallingen

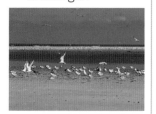

Beach at Blåvands Huk.

Location The most westerly point of Jutland, northwest of Esbjerg.
Access Take the 463 from Esbjerg; turn west at Billum and follow the 431 to Blåvand, where there is a bird observatory, and the point itself at Blåvands Huk. 8km (5 miles) before Blåvand at Ho, a minor road leads south to Skallingen.
Contact Dansk Ornitologisk Forening, Vesterbrogade 138-140, DK-1620, Copenhagen V

Dunes, marshes, wet meadows, and low, sandy ground overlook the open sea at this sheltered bay. It is a great migration point: thousands of geese, ducks, and waders move through in spring, while in autumn there are seabirds off Blåvands Huk and many migrant songbirds in the fields and golf course area of Skallingen. The best conditions for the seabirds are in west or southwesterly gales.

10 Romodaemningen and Ballum Enge

Location On the island of Rømø, around 30km (19 miles) south of Esbjerg.
Access Turn west off route 11, 2km (1¼ miles) north of Skærbæk, on to route 175. This becomes a causeway which leads on to the island. Lakolk Lake lies to the west of the 175. There are meadows along the 175 on the eastern side of the island.
Contact Dansk Ornitologisk Forening, Vesterbrogade 138-140, DK-1620, Copenhagen V

Narrowly separated from the Jutland mainland, this island has meadows (at Ballum), a reedy lake, heathland, and woodland to add variety to its coastal habitats. Spring and early summer see breeding Red-necked Grebes, Bitterns, Marsh and Montagu's Harriers, Spotted Crakes, and various waders and terns including

A large flock of Barnacle Geese at Ballum Enge.

Gull-billed Terns. Migration is good for waders and wildfowl, including many passing Brent, Barnacle, and Pink-footed Geese, as well as Rough-legged Buzzards, and Snow and Lapland Buntings. The area is large and reedbed birds often elusive, but it is always worth a visit.

11 Langeland

Location A narrow island about 50km (31 miles) southeast of Odense.
Access From Odense, drive south on route 9 to Rudkøbing. Turn towards Bagenkop on the 305 and just before reaching it, take the minor road to Gulstav and Dovns Klint.
Contact Dansk Ornitologisk Forening, Vesterbrogade 138-140, DK-1620, Copenhagen V

The southern end of the island has reed-fringed lakes with observation towers. Visit in March to June or July for Red-necked Grebes, Bitterns, Marsh Harriers, Marsh and Savi's Warblers, Golden Orioles, and Bearded Tits. Migrants in spring and autumn include Brent and Barnacle Geese, Eiders, and a selection of birds of prey, with regular Ospreys, Honey Buzzards, and Red Kites.

12 Gedser

Location The southern tip of the island of Falster, about 150km (93 miles) south of Copenhagen.
Access Gedser is at the end of the main E55 road.
Contact Dansk Ornitologisk Forening, Vesterbrogade 138-140, DK-1620, Copenhagen V

Greylag Geese and Marsh Harriers breed at this site, but it is primarily an autumn migration spot. You can see good numbers of passing Brent and Barnacle Geese, tens of thousands of Eiders, many Scaup and Wigeon, and fine bird of prey movements. On some days, there may be hundreds of Rough-legged Buzzards, as well as Buzzards, Honey Buzzards, and Sparrowhawks, and an occasional White-tailed Eagle. Rarities may turn up among the small bird flocks, too. In westerly winds, there are seabirds, with Pomarine Skuas and Little Gulls quite frequent. Spring migration is much less interesting.

Pomarine Skua

13 Møn

Clifftops at Møn.

Location A small island off southeast Zealand, about 100km (62 miles) south of Copenhagen.
Access From the E4, turn off east at either junction 41 or 42 to Stege. Concentrate on the headland area east of Stege, including Klintholm Havn, Jydelejet, Liselund, and the northwestern islet at Nyord.
Contact Dansk Ornitologisk Forening, Vesterbrogade 138-140, DK-1620, Copenhagen V

This low, flat island rises to tall cliffs on its well-wooded eastern side. The woods are good for Golden Orioles, Red-breasted Flycatchers, Greenish Warblers, and Wrynecks in summer. In spring and autumn, migrants include Black and White Storks, Red-footed Falcons and Hobbies, Ortolan Buntings, and some rarities. Small migrants can number hundreds on the best days.

Sweden

EUROPE

SWEDEN

N

15

14 Stockholm

7 9 10 13

6 11 8

12

5 1

2 3

4

SWEDEN FORMS the overwhelming bulk of peninsular Scandinavia – far bigger than Norway, with much less of its area north of the Arctic Circle. It includes extensive mountainous areas, from which rivers run southeast into the Baltic Sea and Gulf of Bothnia. Rivers, coasts, wetlands, and forests are the dominant habitats for birdlife in this country. Its spectacular species, including Cranes, Black-throated Divers, White-tailed Eagles, and large numbers of geese, vie for the birdwatcher's attention with less dramatic but rare or local birds, such as Collared Flycatchers, Thrush Nightingales, and several kinds of owls and woodpeckers.

❶ Lake Åsnen

Location A large natural lake situated approximately 25km (16 miles) south of Växjö in southern Sweden.
Access The lake is served by bus from Växjö, but a car is better for dealing with the whole lake region. Views are often rather distant from roads and footpaths but there are good spots with excellent birds.
Contact Swedish Ornithology Society, Stenhusa Gård, SE-380 62 Mörbylånga
Tel: +46 (0)485-444 40/
+46 (0)485-444 48
Email: info@sofnet.org
Web: www.sofnet.org

The lake is shallow and extremely fragmented, with innumerable headlands and bays, many of them protected in a string of nature reserves. In winter, there are good numbers of Goosanders, many Smews, White-tailed Eagles, and Waxwings. Migrants include swans and geese, Nutcrackers, pipits, and buntings. Breeding birds are superb, with Black-throated Divers, Ospreys, Honey Buzzards, Marsh Harriers and Goshawks, Capercaillies, Black Grouse and Hazel Hens, and Pygmy and Tengmalm's Owls.

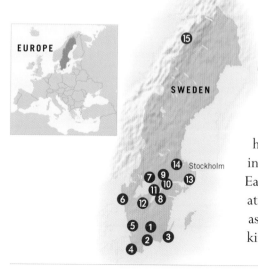

Pygmy Owl

❷ River Helge/Hammarsjön

Location The lower reaches of the River Helge and its associated lakes are just south of Kristianstad in southern Sweden.
Access By bus or car towards Åhus and Yngsjö, via Asum and Skånes Viby. The area is well served by roads and tracks, but is too large to cover easily on foot. A day on a bicycle is a good way to work the region.
Contact Swedish Ornithology Society, Stenhusa Gård, SE-380 62 Mörbylånga
Tel: +46 (0)485-444 40/
+46 (0)485-444 48
Email: info@sofnet.org
Web: www.sofnet.org

The lakes, drained lakes, reedy swamps, wet grassland, and meadows are all good for breeding birds and migrants. In winter, there are many Whooper Swans, White-tailed Eagles, Rough-legged Buzzards, and geese including Bean Geese, although they are much more numerous in October. In summer, you might find Bitterns, Garganeys, Marsh Harriers, Red Kites, Ospreys, Quails, Ruffs, Black-tailed Godwits, Black Terns, Woodlarks, Marsh and Icterine Warblers, and Penduline and Bearded Tits.

Ottenby, on the island of Öland, is one of Europe's top migration spots.

❸ Ottenby

Location Ottenby is at the southern tip of the island of Öland, in the Baltic, off the southeast coast of Sweden.
Access Take the 6km (3½ mile) bridge from the mainland at Kalmar. Head south to Ottenby. The best bird areas are widely dispersed.
Contact Ottenby fågelstation
Tel: 0485 661093
Email: ottenby@post.utfors.se
Web: www.sofnet.org

The south of the island has meadows, inlets, sandy beaches, and a large wood. It has long been famous as a migration watchpoint and has an enviable list of well over 300 species, including many "firsts" for Sweden. In summer, you may find Greylag Geese, Velvet Scoters, Montagu's Harriers, Avocets, Ruffs, Sandwich Terns, Barred Warblers, Red-breasted and Collared Flycatchers, and Thrush Nightingales. In winter, there are occasional King Eiders, White-tailed and Golden Eagles, Shore Larks, and Snow Buntings. Spring and autumn bring many more wildfowl and waders, including Broad-billed Sandpipers, pipits including Red-throated, and all kinds of warblers, flycatchers, chats, and finches.

Waxwing

❹ Falsterbo

Location At the southeastern tip of Sweden, southwest of Malmö.
Access Approached via the E6 to Vellinge and then road 100. There is a bus service most of the way.
Contact Falsterbo Bird Observatory, Fyrvägen 35, SE-239 40 Falsterbo
Tel: +46 40 470688
Email: birdobs@fbo.pp.se
Web: www.falsterbofagelstation.se

Falsterbo is at the end of a long peninsula with a hammer-headed western end. There is a mixture of woodland, beaches, heaths, lagoons, marshes, and meadows. It is exciting for migrating birds, especially in autumn, as well as for northern breeding birds such as Waxwings. The southern tip of the "hammer" is probably the best starting point.

❺ Mellbystrand/ Laholm Bay

Location On the west coast of Sweden in the province of Halland; the bay is just south of Halmstad.
Access Take the E20 south of Halmstad; the coast road leads north and south each side of the RV24; both directions are interesting.
Contact Swedish Ornithology Society, Stenhusa Gård, SE-380 62 Mörbylånga
Tel: +46 (0)485-444 40/
+46 (0)485-444 48
Email: info@sofnet.org
Web: www.sofnet.org

A long sandy beach is backed by dunes and fields. Most of the bird interest lies offshore, although there are interesting breeding birds and migrants at times. Look over the sea for Red-throated Divers, Red-necked and Slavonian Grebes, Sooty and Manx Shearwaters, Leach's petrels in autumn, Gannets, geese, scoters, and all four European skuas.

❻ Svartedalen

Location A large woodland area about 40km (25 miles) north of Göteborg.
Access Roads branching off the E6 at Järlanda and Stora Höga reach this large reserve.
Contact Swedish Ornithology Society, Stenhusa Gård, SE-380 62 Mörbylånga
Tel: +46 (0)485-444 40/
+46 (0)485-444 48
Email: info@sofnet.org
Web: www.sofnet.org

Late winter and early spring are the best times to hear and see woodland birds such as Capercaillies, Black Grouse, Black Woodpeckers, Pygmy, Tengmalm's, and Eagle Owls, Goshawks, and Nutcrackers. There are also breeding Red-backed Shrikes, Crossbills, Black-bellied Dippers, Icterine Warblers, Black-throated Divers, and Honey Buzzards.

❼ Kilsviken and Mariestad, Lake Vänern

Location Lake Vänern is 70km (43 miles) west of Örebro; Kilsviken and Mariestad lie on the eastern shore.
Access South of Kristinehamn, on road 64. There are tracks through the Nötön-Åråsviken reserve.
Contact Swedish Ornithology Society, Stenhusa Gård, SE-380 62 Mörbylånga
Tel: +46 (0)485-444 40/
+46 (0)485-444 48
Web: www.sofnet.org

Lake Vänern hosts a variety of wildfowl in winter.

This is a large wetland at the northeastern edge of Lake Vänern, with several bays and islands, reedbeds, and woodlands. Hazel Hens, Black Woodpeckers, Black-throated Divers, Cranes, Ospreys, Scarlet Rosefinches, and Red-breasted Flycatchers head a good spring and summer list. Migration brings a few thousand Cranes, Ruffs, Rough-legged Buzzards, Red-throated Pipits, and Lapland Buntings.

❽ Lake Tåkern

Reedbeds bordering Lake Tåkern.

Location 40km (25 miles) west of Linköping in south-central Sweden.
Access Turn from the E4 towards Kyleberg. The reserve has observation hides and towers and marked trails.
Contact Tåkern Field Station, PO Box 204, 595 22 Mjölby
Email: lars.gezelius@lansstyrelsen.se
Web: www.takern.se/

A national nature reserve, this lake has been partly drained in the past but remains of great interest. April to June are the best months, followed by July and August when swans, geese, and ducks seek safe refuge when moulting and many other migrants arrive. Red-necked Grebes breed here. There are big herds of Mute Swans, many Bean, White-fronted, and Pink-footed Geese and some Lesser White-fronted Geese, thousands of Bearded Tits, and some White-tailed Eagles in autumn.

❾ Oset

Location 20km (12½ miles) east of Örebro in south-central Sweden.
Access East of Örebro, signposted from the city along the south side of the river Svartån.
Contact Swedish Ornithology Society, Stenhusa Gård, SE-380 62 Mörbylånga
Tel: +46 (0)485-444 40/
+46 (0)485-444 48
Email: info@sofnet.org
Web: www.sofnet.org

The Svartån estuary with its surrounding wetlands and woodland is a national nature reserve. It is good in spring and early summer for its breeding birds and migrants. Look for Bitterns, wildfowl, birds of prey including Honey Buzzards, Ospreys, and Goshawks, Great Snipe if you can find them, Temminck's Stints, a few River Warblers, and Marsh Warblers. In winter, there are Smews, Goosanders, and Great Grey Shrikes. Ducks and geese on migration return in September and October.

⑩ Lake Kvismaren

Location 20km (12½ miles) southeast of Örebro in southern Sweden.
Access Reached from the 207 road south towards Odensbacken, then a road signposted to Kvismaren.
Contact Kvismare Bird Observatory, Kvismare fågelstation, Norrbyås 421, SE-705 95 Örebro
Tel: +46 19 238031
Web: www.kvismaren.org/en

The lakeland has been partly drained, but recent management has recreated excellent habitats: flood meadows, fields, woodland, and reed-fringed pools. White-tailed and Golden Eagles are especially tempting in winter, along with Rough-legged Buzzards and many wildfowl. Migration periods see more Bean, White-fronted, and Pink-footed Geese, among which you should search diligently for Lesser White-fronts. Bean Geese reach 6,000 in the spring but 25,000 in the autumn. In summer, the breeding birds are magnificent, with many grebes, Bitterns, Gadwalls and Garganeys, and Marsh Harriers.

⑪ Tivedens

Conifers in Tivedens National Park.

Location On the shores of Lake Vättern 80km (50 miles) southwest of Örebro.
Access Follow highway 49 between Askersund and Karlsborg, then take the road north to Bocksjö.
Contact Swedish Ornithology Society, Stenhusa Gård, SE-380 62 Mörbylånga
Tel: +46 (0)485-444 40/
+46 (0)485-444 48
Email: info@sofnet.org
Web: www.sofnet.org

A huge area of conifer forest, bog, and lakeland. March and April are best for displaying Goshawks, Capercaillies, Hazel Hens, Pygmy and Tengmalm's Owls, as well as Black-throated Divers, Goldeneyes, Ospreys, Honey Buzzards, Cranes, and

The shores of Lake Hornborgasjön.

Woodlarks. Mid-summer is usually a rather quiet period.

⑫ Lake Hornborgasjön

Location 20km (12½ miles) southwest of Skövde in south-central Sweden.
Access Reached by bus or car to the village of Varnhem. There are several observation towers near Broddetorp.
Contact Hornborga Naturum, Hornborgasjön, 521 98 Broddetorp
Tel: 0500 491450
Email: hornborga.naturum@o.lst.se
Web: www.hornborga.com

A large rehabilitated lake surrounded by farmland and reedy marshes, this is a good area for spring migration. The spectacular influx of Cranes in late March and April is one of Sweden's most popular birdwatching events, and is well worth the trip. At the southern tip of the lake, the Trandansen observation centre is a popular Crane viewing area where you can also see Red-necked, Slavonian, and Black-necked Grebes, Bitterns and harriers, and Great Reed Warblers. In winter, a few White-tailed Eagles are in the area.

⑬ Stockholm Ekoparken

Location Situated in the centre of Sweden's capital city, Stockholm.
Access Well served by public transport.
Contact Förbundet för Ekoparken, Stora Skuggans väg 30, 115 42 Stockholm
Tel: 802017-3533
Email: info@ekoparken.org
Web: www.ekoparken.org

This is a remarkable city centre national park, where 100 species of birds breed and more than 250 have been recorded: not bad for a region surrounded by urban development. It includes islands, woodlands, lakes, and meadows. A visit in spring or early summer will likely reveal Barnacle Geese, Gadwalls, Goldeneyes, Goshawks, Eagle Owls, River and Marsh Warblers, and Thrush Nightingales – a good list for a visitor from farther south in Europe. Migrant waders include Wood Sandpipers and Temminck's Stints, and there is always the chance of a surprise or two. In winter, the chief interest is the wildfowl.

⑭ Farnebofjärden

Location A large area of wetlands and forest, 60km (37 miles) northwest of Uppsala in central Sweden.
Access Forest roads lead into the Tinas Area nature reserve; there is a tourist information centre at Tyttbo.
Contact Swedish Ornithology Society, Stenhusa Gård, SE-380 62 Mörbylånga, Sweden
Tel: +46 (0)485-444 40/
+46 (0)485-444 48
Email: info@sofnet.org
Web: www.sofnet.org

The river Dalälven here spreads into a highly irregular lake, with many islets, sheltered, secluded bays, and swampy forests. The area is rich in good woodland birds, including Capercaillies, Hazel Hens, Black, White-backed, and Three-toed Woodpeckers, Ural, Pygmy, and Tengmalm's Owls, Cranes, Ospreys, Hobbies, Wood and Green Sandpipers, and a host of common

woodland birds. There are several thousand Whooper Swans during spring migration and Waxwings are often around. Birds of prey, waders, and wildfowl can be very varied during autumn migration.

⑮ Padjelanta national park

Location On the border with Norway in the far north of Sweden, 450km (280 miles) northwest of Umeå.
Access A vast region reached via Kvikkjokk. There are numerous marked footpaths and places to stay.
Contact Swedish Environmental Protection Agency (Naturvårdsverket), Blekholmsterrassen 36, SE-106 48 Stockholm
Tel: 08 6981000,
Email: natur@naturvardsverket.se
Web: www.naturvardsverket.se

This huge complex of tundra and forest reserves is best visited early or late in the year to avoid the mosquito season. You will be rewarded by breeding Black-throated Divers, Smews, Velvet Scoters, White-tailed Eagles, Rough-legged Buzzards, Long-tailed Skuas, and Lapland Buntings. Siberian Jays, Pine Grosbeaks, Hazel Hens, and Three-toed Woodpeckers are exciting residents.

Siberian Jay

Norway

SWEDEN

NORWAY

Oslo

N

NORWAY IS A SMALL, elongated country that encompasses a variety of habitats. It extends north beyond the Arctic Circle and has large, cold, barren, mountainous areas above the tree line, yet boasts lowlands with extensive lakes and forests. Norway's southern tip is at the latitude of northern Scotland and much of the country is an Arctic environment with few birds – but those present are very exciting. Lowland forests are home to owls, woodpeckers, and other typically northern species. The coastline is exceptionally convoluted and includes Europe's best populations of White-tailed Eagles and a few dramatic seabird colonies.

The Lofoten archipelago is wonderful for observing seabirds.

❶ Lofoten

Location The Lofoten archipelago is a mixture of islands, including Røst, Værøy, and Vestågøy, lying off the northwest coast of Norway.
Access Visited by air and boat from Bodø. Boat trips to seabird islands are available in summer, when most important colonies are otherwise not open to visitors.
Contact Norsk Ornitologisk Forening, Sandgata 30 B, N-7012 Trondheim
Tel: 73 526040
Email: nof@birdlife.no

Røst itself is a group of islands with excellent seabird colonies. The once-vast Puffin colony has suffered a dramatic decline but is still worth a visit, and you will see breeding Storm Petrels,

Leach's Petrels, Guillemots, Brunnich's Guillemots, Razorbills, Kittiwakes, Fulmars, and Shags. The cliffs are at their best from the beginning of March to late July. Other islands have lesser numbers of seabirds, as well as White-tailed Eagles, Peregrines, Eiders, and Slavonian Grebes. In winter, when daylight is short, Long-tailed Ducks, Gyrfalcons, and Glaucous Gulls are likely. Autumn migration brings a sprinkling of diverse songbird migrants.

❷ Vega

Location An archipelago northwest of Brønnøysund (central Norway).
Access Take the Rv 17 to Horn, from where you can catch a ferry.
Contact Norsk Ornitologisk Forening, Sandgata 30 B, N-7012 Trondheim
Tel: 73 526040
Email: nof@birdlife.no

This is a great area in winter, with vast numbers of Eiders, thousands of King Eiders, Long-tailed Ducks, and Velvet Scoters. Spring may be better; the days lengthen and many of the above birds remain, and are joined by Barnacle, Pink-footed, and Greylag Geese, and large numbers of commoner waders. The Barnacle Goose movements are impressive, with most of the Svalbard breeding birds moving through the area. In summer, you might see Red-throated Divers, Greylag Geese, Whimbrels, Ruffs, and charming Black Guillemots swimming around the islets.

Velvet Scoter

❸ Dovrefjell

Remote, wild Dovrefjell national park.

Location This national park is between Hjerkinn and Oppdal, 110km (68 miles) south of Trondheim.
Access You reach this region via the E6 and Kongsvold Fjellsture, where marked trails lead into the mountains.
Contact Directorate for Nature Management, 7485 Trondheim
Tel: 73 580500
Email: postmottak@dirnat.no
Web: http://english.dirnat.no/

The Dovrefjell and Rondane mountain plateaux are only suitable for visits between late May and July. Breeding birds are typical of such mountainous ground; there are Golden Eagles, Rough-legged Buzzards, Merlins, Gyrfalcons, Long-tailed Ducks, Ptarmigan, Golden Plovers, Dotterels, Dunlins, Purple Sandpipers, and Temminck's Stints. Shore Larks, Lapland Buntings, and Snow Buntings breed on the high, exposed ground.

❹ Hardangerfjord

Hardangerfjord offers stunning views.

Location In the heart of the stunning fjordland region of southeast Norway, near Bergen.
Access A popular tourist region, the best sites are visible from main roads north of Odda on the Rv 550. Picnic sites offer the simplest, safest access.
Contact Norsk Ornitologisk Forening, Sandgata 30 B, N-7012 Trondheim
Tel: 73 526040
Email: nof@birdlife.no

This fjord is magnificent, with thick woodland on surrounding steep slopes. The best birds are found breeding in May and June. Golden Eagles, Rough-legged Buzzards, a range of woodpeckers including White-backed and Grey-headed, Wrynecks, Nutcrackers, Icterine Warblers, flycatchers, thrushes, warblers, and finches are to be found here.

❺ Akersvika

Location A large delta on Lake Mjøsa, near Hamar, 110km (68 miles) north of Oslo.
Access The E6 road between Oslo and Trondheim crosses over the site. There is an observation tower on the south side.
Contact Norsk Ornitologisk Forening, Sandgata 30 B, N-7012 Trondheim
Tel: 73 526040
Email: nof@birdlife.no

A sedgy and grassy wilderness around a double river delta, this reserve is good in spring, late summer, and autumn when many migrants are about. Birds include Black- and Red-throated Divers, Teal, Wigeon, Garganeys, Shovelers and Goldeneyes, waders such as Ringed and Golden Plovers, Ruffs, Whimbrels, Temminck's Stints, Greenshanks, and Common and Wood Sandpipers. Smaller birds include Bluethroats, Yellow Wagtails, and Icterine Warblers.

❻ Kurefjorden

Location A small fjord 60km (37 miles) south of Oslo.
Access From the E6, take the Rv 119 to Larkollen and Kureskjær. The reserve is easily viewed from roadsides.
Contact Norsk Ornitologisk Forening, Sandgata 30 B, N-7012 Trondheim
Tel: 73 526040
Email: nof@birdlife.no

This is a wetland area with islets, weedy shorelines, some freshwater marsh, and a small woodland. It is good for migrants, including Wigeon, Mallards, Teal, Shovelers, Goldeneyes, Red-breasted Mergansers, Goosanders, and waders such as godwits, Whimbrels, Spotted Redshanks, and Ruffs. Cranes also pass through. In winter, there are many Mute Swans, Goosanders, and Goldeneyes if the area remains free of ice.

❼ Hardangervidda

Location An area south of Geilo, 200km (124 miles) northwest of Oslo.
Access The area is crossed by the Rv 7 in the north and approached by the Rv 8 from Geilo to Skare.
Contact Directorate for Nature Management, 7485 Trondheim
Tel: 73 580500
Email: postmottak@dirnat.no

Rising to 1,500m above sea level, this vast mountain area is cold, exposed, and largely

A tranquil lake in the Hardangervidda mountain plateau.

treeless, with many scattered lakes. Curiously, bird numbers fluctuate in step with the lemming population, so a "lemming year" is the best time to visit. Late May and June are ideal because birds concentrate where snow is melting. Black-throated Divers, Scaup, Common and Velvet Scoters, Long-tailed Ducks, Rough-legged Buzzards, Cranes, Dunlins, occasional Gyrfalcons, Purple Sandpipers, Temminck's Stints, Red-necked Phalaropes, Willow Grouse, Long-tailed Skuas, and Bluethroats breed in the area. In some years, there may also be Snowy Owls.

❽ Utsira

Location An island off Haugesund on the southwest coast of Norway.
Access Reached by boat from Haugesund. The bird observatory is open in spring and autumn.
Contact Bird Observatory
Tel: 91 828380
Web: www.utsirafuglestasjon.no

This small island has farmland at its centre and rocky shores and open heaths around its perimeter. It is best in spring, and again in August/September when migration is at its height, bringing big numbers of birds to a small area. Fulmars, Shags, and Puffins breed and Fulmars, Manx, and Sooty Shearwaters and some auks pass by offshore. Fulmars can be especially abundant, with thousands on many days in autumn.

Marsh Warbler

❾ Lista

Location A peninsula 20km (12½ miles) west of Farsund near the most southerly tip of Norway.
Access There is a bird observatory at Gunnarsmyra – also the best place to stay in the area.
Contact Norsk Ornitologisk Forening, Sandgata 30 B, N-7012 Trondheim
Tel: 73 526040
Email: nof@birdlife.no

The heath, grassland, woodland, and wetlands of the peninsula are best visited in spring and autumn, when migrants are often numerous and rarities may crop up. Migrants include Brent and Greylag Geese, Common Scoters and Long-tailed Ducks, and an occasional Gyrfalcon. Breeding birds are less exciting, but include Marsh Warblers.

Finland

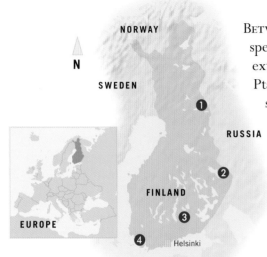

NORWAY

N

SWEDEN

RUSSIA

①

②

FINLAND

③

EUROPE

④

Helsinki

BETWEEN SWEDEN AND NORWAY in size, Finland is a spectacular and diverse country. In the north, it is an extension of Siberia, with species including the Dotterel, Ptarmigan, and Gyrfalcon on the treeless tundra. Further south, much of the area is covered by untouched forests of pine, spruce, and birch. Lakes and rivers make up ten per cent of Finland's surface area, and much of the land is bog, which provides ideal habitats for arctic waders, taiga Bean Geese, Common Cranes, and Whooper Swans. The abundance of special birds makes Finland a great draw to the birdwatcher from the south who wishes to sample northern species.

① Kuusamo (Valtavarra ridge)

Location 30km (19 miles) north of Kuusamo in central eastern Finland.
Access Drive north of Kuusamo on road 5; after 30km (19 miles) turn right on to the 8694 towards Ruka ski centre and stop after 4km (2½ miles) on Valtavarra Ridge. Walk uphill through the forest on a rough track.
Contact BirdLife SUOMI-FINLAND, Annankatu 29A, P.O. Box 1285, FIN-00101, Helsinki
Tel: (09) 4135 3300
Web: www.birdlife.fi

Here you can experience an old, undamaged "taiga" forest. May is the best time to visit for Capercaillies, Black Grouse, Hazel Hens, woodpeckers, Siberian Jays, Collared Flycatchers, Arctic and Greenish Warblers, Two-barred Crossbills, and Pine Grosbeaks. You may even be lucky enough to sight a Red-flanked Bluetail.

Pine Grosbeak

② Patvinsuo national park

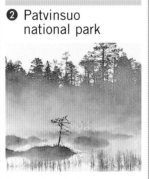

Morning mist at Patvinsuo.

Location About 80km (50 miles) northeast of Joensuu in southeastern Finland.
Access From Joensuu take road 73 to Eno, then roads 516 and 520 and finally the 5202 to Kitsi before the national park is signposted. There is an information centre at Suomu.
Contact Via national park website
Web: www.luontoon.fi

This is a vast area of moorland and undisturbed forest. There are also two large lakes with Red- and Black-throated Divers but little else. From April onwards, the snow melts and access is easier, and then you might find Whooper Swans, Bean Geese, Golden Eagles, Ospreys, Cranes, Capercaillies, Willow Grouse, Hazel Hens, and Broad-billed Sandpipers.

③ Heinola

Location 140km (87 miles) northeast of Helsinki.
Access Turn to Heinola town centre off route 4 between Lahti and Mikkeli.
Contact BirdLife SUOMI-FINLAND, Annankatu 29A, P.O. Box 1285, FIN-00101, Helsinki
Email: office@birdlife.fi

Wildfowl and waders are attracted to the Kymijoki river but the town itself has parks that take in some good habitats. In summer, there are Black Woodpeckers, best seen early in the season and early in the day. Wrynecks also breed and there are Dippers on the river. Golden Orioles make the woodland patches ring to their fluty calls in summer. In winter, there may be divers and Smews.

Heinola has varied habitats, walkways, and a bird sanctuary.

④ Turku Ruissalo

Location 7km (4½ miles) west of Turku in southwestern Finland.
Access Take the local bus from Turku, and then walk the nature trail across the island, covering the central woodland and the western shore.
Contact BirdLife SUOMI-FINLAND, Annankatu 29A, P.O. Box 1285, FIN-00101, Helsinki
Email: office@birdlife.fi

This is a wooded area with oak forest in the east and meadows and shallow water areas elsewhere. It has a remarkable variety of breeding birds – almost 100 species, including Black and Grey-headed Woodpeckers and Thrush Nightingales. Migrants include Barnacle Geese, many ducks, waders, and small birds, but it is the woodpeckers that seem to be the main attraction here from February to April.

Iceland

N

ICELAND

Reykjavik

EUROPE

ONE OF THE MOST northerly countries in Europe, and the most westerly, Iceland is thinly populated by people even in its low-lying, grassy southern region. Elsewhere, it is harsh, rocky, and high, with snow and glaciers on its inland plateau. Many rivers and lakes attract huge numbers of waterfowl and wading birds, which thrive on a brief abundance of insect life in summer. Few species remain in the short, cold days of winter. The coasts have high cliffs and islands with many breeding seabirds – among the greatest spectacles of European wildlife.

Dramatic landscape at Snæfells.

① Myvatn

Location 40km (25 miles) from the north coast of Iceland.
Access A short flight or an eight hour bus journey from Reykjavík to Akureyri, just west of Myvatn. Cars and bikes can be hired in Reykjahlid.
Contact Icelandic Society for the Protection of Birds, Fuglaverndarfélag Islands, PO Box 5069, IS-125, Reykjavík
Email: fuglavernd@fuglavernd.is
Web: www.fuglavernd.is

Myvatn is a large, shallow lake that abounds in wildfowl. There are up to 50,000 breeding pairs of 15 species of ducks, the main attractions being Harlequin Ducks and Barrow's Goldeneyes – two species found nowhere else in Europe – together with good numbers of Long-tailed Ducks, Scaup, and Common Scoters. Huge numbers of Red-necked Phalaropes can be seen; Black-tailed Godwits and Purple Sandpipers also breed here.

② Snæfells peninsula

Location 120km (74 miles) northwest of Reykjavík as the crow flies.
Access By road, head west from route 1 towards Ólafsvík. Explore the coastal cliffs around Arnastapi on the south side and Ólafsvík on the north.
Contact Icelandic Society for the Protection of Birds, Fuglaverndarfélag Islands, PO Box 5069, IS-125, Reykjavík
Email: fuglavernd@fuglavernd.is

The peninsula offers a chance to see White-tailed Eagles, Great Skuas, Glaucous Gulls, Ptarmigan, Black-tailed Godwits, and Whooper Swans. On the cliffs, there are Guillemots, Razorbills, Puffins, and Fulmars. Red-necked Phalaropes are regular and often numerous offshore and in the sheltered bays in autumn.

③ Reykjavík

Location Iceland's captial, on the southwestern side of the island.
Access The harbour area and Lake Tjörnin near the town centre are always worth a look. Try the Botanical Gardens for migrants and look at nearby headlands, especially the golf course area on Seltjarnar Peninsula.
Contact Icelandic Society for the Protection of Birds, Fuglaverndarfélag Islands, PO Box 5069, IS-125, Reykjavík
Email: fuglavernd@fuglavernd.is

Autumn is a good time to visit the capital: wildfowl have moved to the sea or lake and diverse migrants appear – even occasional rarities from North America. There are breeding Red-necked Phalaropes (and perhaps a Grey Phalarope or two) on pools in the area, Arctic Terns on the town lake, and breeding Scaup and Eiders. By late summer, there are usually Barrow's Goldeneyes on the lake and many Eiders in the harbour area. Glaucous Gulls are regular year-round and can be watched closely.

Red-necked Phalarope

④ Northwest Peninsula

The bleak, beautiful northwest coast.

Location The northwestern corner of Iceland.
Access Ísafjördur can be reached by bus and flights from Reykjavík. The area is rugged, exposed, and isolated, and only for the adventurous.
Contact Icelandic Society for the Protection of Birds, Fuglaverndarfélag Islands, PO Box 5069, IS-125, Reykjavík, Iceland
Email: fuglavernd@fuglavernd.is

Gigantic cliffs on the peninsula are home to countless breeding seabirds. Hælavíkurgbjarg and Hornbjarg can be reached only by boat, but the cliffs at Látrabjarg can be accessed on foot. The long hike is worthwhile because this is Europe's biggest seabird colony, with around a million birds, including no fewer than 400,000 pairs of Razorbills, and many other special species often in great numbers.

177

The Netherlands

EUROPE

Amsterdam

EUROPE

NETHERLANDS

BELGIUM   GERMANY

N

THIS LOW-LYING COUNTRY has numerous stunning islands and areas reclaimed from the sea (polders). These coastal wetlands, as well as inland lakes and marshes, old woodlands, and sandy heaths make for varied birdwatching year-round. There are huge flocks of geese from autumn to late spring and equally dramatic flocks of ducks in winter. Black Woodpeckers, Goshawks, and Crested Tits are resident in the woodlands, and the country hosts many wintering birds of prey from the north and east.

Marshes on Texel, an excellent island for birds in any season.

❶ Texel

Location A large island in the Frisian chain, 1km (⅔ mile) north of Den Helder.
Access By ferry from Den Helder.
Contact Natuurmonumenten, Schaep and Burgh, Noordereinde 60, 1243 JJ 's-Graveland
Tel: (035) 655 99 33
Web: www.natuurmonumenten.nl

Texel has a host of nature reserves. Mokbai to the south has a reedy mere with breeding Spoonbills and many waders in winter. The east side of the island has a number of lagoons and interesting inland sites, as well as a great sweep of tidal flats in the Waddenzee. In winter, look for huge flocks of Eiders and other wildfowl, such as Red-breasted

Mergansers, as well as divers, grebes, and waders. Inland in winter are Brent Geese and good numbers of Golden Plovers, Fieldfares, and Redwings. Twites and Snow Buntings are likely around De Cocksdorp. In spring and summer, the low fields and marshes have breeding Avocets and Black-tailed Godwits. A marshy area in the centre of the island, Waal en Burg, is full of winter waders (including hundreds of Ruffs) and wildfowl. Pine forests in the west have Long-eared Owls and Short-toed Treecreepers.

❷ Vlieland

Location Just northeast of Texel in the Frisian chain (see site 1).
Access Reached from Harlingen and, in summer, from Texel. At 19km (12 miles) long, it is better to explore by bicycle than on foot.
Contact Vogelbescherming Nederland, PO Box 925, 3700 AX Zeist
Tel: 030 6937700
Email: birdlife@vogelbescherming.nl
Web: www.vogelbescherming.nl

This island is best in spring, summer, or late autumn. Breeding birds include Cormorants, Spoonbills, Shelducks, Eiders, Marsh and Hen Harriers, Buzzards, Hobbies, Avocets, Kentish Plovers, Nightingales, and Icterine Warblers. In autumn, there are good numbers of waders and wildfowl, and sometimes interesting and rare migrants. It is well worth exploring wetlands, beaches, woodland, and gardens at any time of year.

Cormorant

❸ Ameland

The sandy shoreline of Ameland.

Location One of the Frisian Islands, Ameland lies between the islands of Terschelling and Schiermonnikoog.
Access Reached by ferry from Holwerd, Friesland. Try Langeduinen in the northwest (cycle tracks and boardwalks) and Hollum in the west for waterfowl and waders.
Contact Nes Nature Centre
Tel: 0519 542737

At 24km (15 miles) long and 4km (2½ miles) wide, Ameland is principally open grassland and dunes with a few patches of forest. Hen Harriers, Short-eared Owls, Bitterns, Shelducks, Eiders, Avocets, plovers and Black-tailed Godwits, four species of terns, Bluethroats, Icterine Warblers, and Scarlet Rosefinches breed here. In autumn, there are good numbers of small migrants with a few rarities and a large passage of ducks and geese. In winter, the area is exceptionally good for waders and wildfowl.

④ Bildtpollen

Location A long coastal area between the Holwerd ferry pier and Zwarte Haan in the north of the Netherlands.
Access Reached from the N357 road between Hallum and Holwerd.
Contact Vogelbescherming Nederland, PO Box 925, 3700 AX Zeist
Tel: 030 6937700
Web: www.vogelbescherming.nl

In summer, this reserve is alive with birds, such as breeding Oystercatchers, Avocets (around 2,000 pairs), Black-tailed Godwits, Redshanks, Common Terns, wagtails, larks, and pipits. In spring and autumn, the area is full of migrating waders. Winter is exceptional, with thousands of Bean, Barnacle, and Brent Geese, tens of thousands of Wigeon, Curlews, Oystercatchers, Redshanks, and other waders, and a good chance of Shore Larks and Snow Buntings.

Shore Lark

⑤ Lauwersmeer

Location Between Anjum and Lauwersoog, about 35km (22 miles) northwest of Groningen.
Access Explore the Pampusplat area south of Lauwersoog on the N361, Lauwersoog harbour in winter, and the complex of roads to the west.
Contact Vogelbescherming Nederland, PO Box 925, 3700 AX Zeist
Tel: 030 6937700
Web: www.vogelbescherming.nl
www.lauwersmeer.com/eng/

This vast area is good in spring and autumn for migrant waders, Spoonbills, Little Gulls and terns, and in summer for Avocets, Common and Arctic Terns, and other breeding wetland birds. In winter, the chief interest is the wildfowl: tens of thousands of Barnacle and White-fronted Geese, with lesser numbers of Bean, Pink-footed, and Brent Geese, and the chance of a Red-breasted Goose or two.

Great White Egret

⑥ Dollard estuary

Location At the mouth of the River Ems on the German border.
Access View from Punt van Reide east of Termunterzijl; at Nieuw Statenzijl on the Westerwoldsche river mouth; and on the Oldambt polders near Schmeeda and Winschoten.
Contact Vogelbescherming Nederland, PO Box 925, 3700 AX Zeist
Tel: 030 6937700
Web: www.vogelbescherming.nl

In summer, this is a great place for breeding waders, especially vast numbers of Redshanks. Big colonies of Avocets are another attraction. Corncrakes still nest on the polders, as do Marsh and Montagu's Harriers, Short-eared Owls, and Quails. Reedbeds hold Bluethroats and Spotted Crakes. In winter, there are great numbers of wildfowl and waders, with famously large concentrations of Spotted Redshanks (5,000) and Avocets. For geese, the area is best in spring when vast numbers of several species can be seen on migration.

⑦ Friesland – Zuidwest

Location The swathe of wetlands and wet grassland around Sneek and west to the IJsselmeer coast.
Access Best watched from the network of roads accessed via the N359 and N354.
Contact Vogelbescherming Nederland, PO Box 925, 3700 AX Zeist
Tel: 030 6937700
Web: www.vogelbescherming.nl

Winter brings vast numbers of Smews, Goosanders, Pochards, Tufted Ducks, and huge flocks of White-fronted and Barnacle Geese. The Kornwerderzand dam in the north is a good area, as are the Heegermeer and Fluessen lakes and their hinterlands. In spring and summer, look for Spoonbills, occasional Caspian Terns, and Great White Egrets, Black-tailed Godwits, Penduline Tits, Bluethroats, and a good variety of other waders, gulls, terns, and warblers. Ruffs are sometimes abundant in spring at Workumerwaard.

⑧ IJsselmeer

Location The IJsselmeer (once a tidal waterbody connected to the North Sea) dominates the coastline of The Netherlands.
Access This huge area has roads around the southern and eastern sides and along the great dam.
Contact Vogelbescherming Nederland, PO Box 925, 3700 AX Zeist
Tel: 030 6937700
Web: www.vogelbescherming.nl

This is a fabulous place in winter, although conditions may be extraordinarily harsh. Vast numbers of wildfowl flock on the open areas, often merging into one huge belt of birds. Great numbers of Tufted Ducks, Pochards, and Coots can be seen almost anywhere; among them are smaller flocks of Scaup, Red-breasted Mergansers, other ducks, and the occasional Red-necked Grebe or diver. In sheltered spots and harbours on the south side by the IJmeerdijk road (such as Pampushaven), there are marvellous flocks of Goosanders and Smews – hundreds or sometimes thousands together. Buzzards, occasional Rough-legged Buzzards and Goshawks, Hooded Crows, Barn and Short-eared Owls, and flocks of geese keep the interest levels high at all times.

Extensive icing of the IJsselmeer is common in the bitter winters.

⑨ De Wieden, Overijssel

Location 10km (6 miles) west of Meppel.
Access The reserve is close to the N762, just west of Meppel.
Contact The Wieden, Beulakerpad 1, 8326 AH St. Jansklooster
Tel: (0527) 24 66 44
Web: natuurmonumenten.nl/dewieden

This is the largest peat moor area in northwest Europe. Spring sees a great variety of warblers, including Icterine, Grasshopper, and Savi's, Bluethroats, Pied Flycatchers, and Penduline Tits, as well as Black Terns and migrating waders, Bitterns, Purple Herons, Greylag Geese, and Spotted Crakes. Nearby woodland has Goshawks, Hobbies, and Golden Orioles. White Storks breed around De Wieden and adjacent villages but are more numerous in autumn.

Savi's Warbler

⑩ Wieringen

Location A former island, now connected with the mainland east of Den Helder.
Access Reached from the N99.
Contact Vogelbescherming Nederland, PO Box 925, 3700 AX Zeist
Tel: 030 6937700
Web: www.vogelbescherming.nl

The real interest here begins in autumn; Black Terns are abundant – more than 200,000 have been counted at Balgzand. In winter, tens of thousands of Oystercatchers and Knots mix with lesser numbers of other waders and wildfowl. Scaup may be present in tens of thousands, with equal numbers of Tufted Ducks and Pochards adding to a magnificent spectacle. Brent Geese, Hooded Crows, and Coots are common and Twites and Snow Buntings likely along the shores.

⑪ Oostvaarders-plassen

Location Just west of Lelystad on Flevoland, the reclaimed province east of Amsterdam.
Access Reached from the south (Harderwijk) on the N302 and an associated grid of small roads. The Oostvaardesdijk runs along the northern edge of the reserve.
Contact Staatsbosbeheer, Princenhof Park 1, PO Box 1300, NL - 3970 BH Driebergen
Tel: 030 692 6111
Email: info@staatsbosbeheer.nl

This is a vast area of reedbeds and lagoons, with scattered willow scrub and open mud. Spoonbills and Cormorants breed, along with Bitterns, Great White Egrets, Greylag Geese, Marsh, Hen and Montagu's Harriers, Goshawks, Avocets, Barn Owls, Bluethroats, Marsh and Icterine Warblers, and Bearded and Penduline Tits. Spring and autumn migrants include many more wildfowl, waders, Hobbies, Little Gulls, Black and occasional White-winged Black Terns, and various wagtails, pipits, and warblers. In winter, the area has great numbers of common wildfowl.

Spoonbill Lake in Oostvaarders-plassen nature reserve.

⑫ East Flevoland

Location An island of land reclaimed from the sea, situated just to the east of Amsterdam.
Access Drive on to the Flevoland polders from Harderwijk; explore the coastal belt and north to Lelystad.
Contact Vogelbescherming Nederland, PO Box 925, 3700 AX Zeist
Tel: 030 6937700
Web: www.vogelbescherming.nl

This is a magnificent winter birdwatching venue. There are birds of prey practically everywhere, with many Buzzards and a sprinkling of Rough-legged Buzzards and Hen Harriers. Geese vary according to weather conditions, but expect to see good numbers of Bean and White-fronted Geese.

⑬ Harderbroek

Location Opposite Harderwijk on the southern edge of Flevoland.
Access From Harderwijk, go north on the N302 towards Lelystad. As you cross the channel, Harderbroek is to your left.
Contact Vogelbescherming Nederland, PO Box 925, 3700 AX Zeist
Tel: 030 6937700
Web: www.vogelbescherming.nl

One of many polderland reserves, this superb area has a magic of its own. In spring and summer, there are Bitterns, Nightingales, Bluethroats, Savi's Warblers, and Bearded Tits. Marsh and Hen Harriers are frequent from autumn to spring; White-fronted, Bean, and Brent Geese are commonly seen. Wigeon, Gadwalls, Pintails, Pochards, Tufted Ducks, Goldeneyes, and other ducks are common in winter.

Rough-legged Buzzard

⑭ Naardermeer

Location A wetland and forest area 20km (12½ miles) southeast of Amsterdam.
Access The reserve is reached via the A1 and Muiden, then east on a road parallel with the A1, turning south towards Ankeveen. Take the De Goog road and follow signs to Naardermeer where you can join a guided boat trip or take tracks to hides.
Contact Natuurmonumenten, Postbus 9955, 1243 ZS's-Graveland
Tel: 035 655 99 11
web: www.natuurmonumenten.nl

Naardermeer is best seen from a boat between April and September. It has old forests around a big lake with extensive reedbeds. You can also hire a bike and ride around the outside of the reserve, looking in, which gives a good chance of seeing birds such as Purple Herons, Goshawks, Black-tailed Godwits, and Black Terns. The boat provides a chance of better views of Cormorants (there is a massive colony), Greylag Geese, ducks, Marsh Harriers, Bluethroats, Savi's Warblers, and Bearded Tits.

⑮ Hoge Veluwe

Location Between Arnhem and Apeldoorn.
Access On the A1 from Amsterdam take exit 17 onto the N310 for Otterlo, then follow signs to Hoge Veluwe. There is also an entrance at Schaarsbergen from the N311. Bus services link the various reserve entrances and also come to the reserve from Arnhem in summer.
Contact Veluws Bureau voor Toerisme, Deventerstraat 19B, 7311 BH Apeldoorn
Tel: 026 4951023
Email: info@theveluwe.com
Web: www.theveluwe.com

There are several large nature reserves in southern Veluwe of which the Veluwezoom national park is the easternmost. It has forests and heaths with birds of prey including Honey Buzzards in summer, as well as Black Woodpeckers, Wrynecks, Short-toed Treecreepers, Crested Tits, Firecrests, Hawfinches, and usually a few Crossbills. The Hoog-Buurlo heath is good for Red-backed Shrikes, Woodlarks, Nightjars, and Hobbies. Kootwijkerzand dunes have Tawny Pipits.

⑯ Zeeland

Location A complex of islands and channels south of the Brouwersdam around Middelburg, Goes, Bergen op Zoom, and Vlissingen.
Access The area can be explored from several main roads, including the N57, A58, and N61.
Contact Vogelbescherming Nederland, PO Box 925, 3700 AX Zeist
Tel: 030 6937700
Web: www.vogelbescherming.nl

Zeeland is a fantastic spot for birds in winter, especially if exceptionally cold weather pushes geese and ducks south from their strongholds in the north. Brent Geese are commonly sighted, while Barnacle, Greylag, and White-fronted Geese can be abundant and widespread. Bewick's and Whooper Swans are frequent. Occasional Lesser White-fronted and Red-breasted Geese will test your powers of observation and patience. On the numerous waterways around the island, there are big numbers of Little, Great Crested (15,000), and Black-necked

Crested Tit

Mud flats and marshland at Zeeland, in the southwest Netherlands.

Grebes, Wigeon, Gadwalls, Goldeneyes, and Red-breasted Mergansers. In spring and summer, look out for Avocets, Ringed and Kentish Plovers, as well as Sandwich and Little Terns.

⑰ Biesboch

Biesboch marshlands in spring.

Location A big sandy heath and forest area with wetlands 20km (12½ miles) southeast of Rotterdam.
Access Take exit 23 from the A27 to get to Werkendam. There is a visitor centre at nearby Hollandse Biesboche and viewpoints over Petrusplaat.
Contact Mijl-op-Zeven Visitor Centre, Groote Peel National Park
Tel: 0495 641497
Web: www.nationaal-parkdegrootepeel.nl

The Groote Peel and De Peel reserves in the Biesboch area have high numbers of breeding Bluethroats, as well as Bean and White-fronted Geese in winter. Strabrechtse Heide, 10km (6 miles) southeast of Eindhoven along the A67,

is a heath and fen with breeding Black-necked Grebes, Bitterns, Shovelers, Hobbies, Water Rails, Bluethroats, and Stonechats. Black Woodpeckers, Nightjars, Woodlarks, and Crested Tits nest locally. In winter, look out for Hen Harriers and Great Grey Shrikes. Soerendonks Goor, west of the A2, to the south of Eindhoven, has nesting Black Terns, while the Budel-Dorplein reserve a little to the south has an abundance of Mediterranean Gulls, Marsh Harriers, Marsh Warblers, and Bearded Tits.

⑱ Brouwersdam and Haringvleit

Location The Brouwersdam crosses from Goeree-Overflakkee, Voorne, and the intervening Haringvleit in the north to Schouwen in the south, between the Rhine and the Scheldt.
Access Look from the main road (the N59), and check low-lying fields inland for geese. Den Bommel (north of the N59 and just east of Oude Tonge) is an excellent centre.
Contact Vogelbescherming Nederland, PO Box 925, 3700 AX Zeist
Tel: 030 6937700
Web: www.vogelbescherming.nl

In autumn, there are often plentiful waders and terns in this area. In winter, you are likely to see a few Guillemots and Razorbills, wildfowl, including Long-tailed Ducks, Scaup, and Smews, grebes including many Red-necked, as well as numerous other divers and gulls. The area immediately inland is good for geese, including Barnacle Geese, as well as Twites, Buzzards, and other birds of prey, and winter thrushes and finch flocks.

Barnacle Goose

181

Belgium

NETHERLANDS

N

Brussels

GERMANY

BELGIUM

EUROPE

LUXEMBURG

FRANCE

EXTENDING FROM low-lying North Sea coasts to high inland forests, Belgium's small size belies its variey of birds. It shares some of the winter wildfowl and birds of prey that enliven the Netherlands in the flatter, lower parts of Flanders and Antwerp, while its summer woodland and farmland birds are similar to those of northern France. The Ardennes in the south is not high enough for Alpine species, but has typical European forest birds. Coniferous woods support such characteristic birds as Goshawks, Crested Tits, and Crossbills.

❶ Blankaart Reserve

Hide at the Blankaart Reserve.

Location Part of the Ijzer valley complex of reserves.
Access Reached from the N369 between Diksmuide and Ieper, south of Woumen. The car park is near a castle, from which a footpath leads to the "Vogelkijkhut" hide.
Contact BirdLife Belgium, Kardinaal Mercierplein 1, 2800 Mechelen
Tel: 015-29 72 20
Email: info@natuurpunt.be
Web: www.natuurpunt.be

This wetland area is worth a look if you are in the vicinity: in summer, you might see Little Bitterns and Great Reed Warblers, and hear their remarkable song. Look in surrounding woodland for commoner breeding birds, such as Crested Tits and Short-toed Treecreepers, and perhaps woodpeckers. It is easy to reach flooded areas nearby in winter, where there will be Bewick's Swans, wildfowl, waders, and birds of prey.

❷ Oostende

Location The coastal area to the northeast of the port of Oostende.
Access Take the N34 coast road northeast towards Zeebrugge; turn left towards the Oostende lighthouse. Walk to the pier area and beaches.
Contact BirdLife Belgium, Kardinaal Mercierplein 1, 2800 Mechelen
Tel: 015-29 72 20
Email: info@natuurpunt.be
Web: www.natuurpunt.be

The waste ground, beaches, breakwaters, and harbours here are especially good in autumn. The eastern pier is superb after a northwesterly gale, although birdwatching conditions can fall flat in calm weather. You may see divers, grebes, Fulmars, Manx and Sooty Shearwaters, Leach's Petrels, Gannets, Brent Geese, Long-tailed Ducks, scoters, and Grey Phalaropes. Pomarine, Arctic, Long-tailed, and Great Skuas are all likely. Little Gulls are common, Sabine's Gulls rare but possible, with Kittiwakes and a variety of terns (including Gull-billed and Caspian) and Little Auks adding to the fun. In winter, you should see Purple Sandpipers and various wildfowl on the sea. There may even be a distinguished visitor from the north in the form of a Glaucous Gull on the beach.

Flooded meadows in the Zwin Reserve host many wetland birds.

❸ Zwin Reserve

Location About 10km (6 miles) northeast of Zeebrugge ferry terminal at the mouth of the river Zwin.
Access Take the N34 to Knokke-Heist, from where the reserve is well signposted.
Contact BirdLife Belgium, Kardinaal Mercierplein 1, 2800 Mechelen
Tel: 015-29 72 20
Email: info@natuurpunt.be
Web: www.natuurpunt.be

This dammed, silted-up estuary has some meadows, flooded with salt water, mudflats, and dunes, all easily seen from the main dam and associated footpaths. In winter, the area is good for Hen Harriers, Merlins, and Short-eared Owls. Shore Larks, Lapland Buntings, Snow Buntings, and Twites form a characteristic proportion of the salt-marsh and beach birds. Migrants include Purple Herons and Spoonbills. In summer, there are breeding Cormorants, Little Egrets, Night Herons, introduced White Storks, Shelducks, Avocets, Kentish Plovers, Mediterranean Gulls, Common Terns, Icterine Warblers, and Serins. This list of distinctive birds emphasizes the difference between a continental coastal reserve and a British one; despite the relative proximity of the two, this area has an obvious continental character.

❹ Antwerp and the Zegge reserve

Wetlands at the Zegge reserve.

Location Zegge reserve is near Geel, northern Belgium, 35km (22 miles) east of the Antwerp.
Access Antwerp harbour is best reached from the Haven road parallel to the N49 towards Zelzate from Antwerp centre. The A13 leads from Antwerp to Geel.
Contact Zegge Reserve, Groene Wandeling 9, 2970 Gravenwezel

The complicated area of river, docks, reedbeds, and wasteland near Antwerp itself is worth a visit, as are the wetlands, woods, and polders farther afield. From autumn to spring, there are many species of waders and wildfowl, and a variety of other birds, including grebes and Smews, turn up in the docks area. The Zegge reserve to the east of Antwerp is a good spot for Bluethroats.

❺ Kalmthoutse Heath

Location 20km (12½ miles) north of Antwerp.
Access From Antwerp take the N11 to Putte then the N111 to Kalmthout and the reserve entrance.
Contact Tourist office
Tel: 03 666 61 01
Email: toeisme@kalmthont.be
Web: www.kalmthout.be

The best time to visit this small heath is in spring and summer, when Gadwalls and other wildfowl breed. There are nesting Curlews, Black-tailed Godwits, Nightjars, Stonechats, and Woodlarks. In the forest, there are Long-eared Owls, Black Woodpeckers, Redstarts, and Crested Tits. Honey Buzzards may also be seen. In winter, the pools have Smews and Goldeneyes.

Honey Buzzard

The delightful Schwalm river valley.

❻ Schwalm Valley

Location A river valley in the Ardennes, about 35km (22 miles) from Liège.
Access From Robertville, take the N676 then the N647 towards Elsenborn and the N658 towards Harperschied. This road is sometimes closed because of military exercises.
Contact BirdLife Belgium, Kardinaal Mercierplein 1, 2800 Mechelen
Tel: 015-29 72 20
Email: info@natuurpunt.be
Web: www.natuurpunt.be

The valley is a beautiful area – in part kept that way by the proximity of a military camp and training ground. If you can get along the valley, in summer you may find Wrynecks and both Great Grey and Red-backed Shrikes. There are Tengmalm's Owls and Black Woodpeckers in the woodland hereabouts and, in winter, Nutcrackers around the conifer forests. Birds of prey can include Red Kites.

❼ Hautes-Fagnes

Winter landscape at Hautes-Fagnes.

Location The plateau is in the east, about 30km (19 miles) east of Liège.
Access Take the A3 from Liège, turn south on to the N68. Between Eupen and Malmedy, take the N676 southeast towards Robertville where there is an information centre and trails.
Contact BirdLife Belgium, Kardinaal Mercierplein 1, 2800 Mechelen
Tel: 015-29 72 20
Email: info@natuurpunt.be
Web: www.natuurpunt.be

Woods, heaths, and bogs fill this region. The heaths have a small number of Black Grouse that may be seen from the paths in spring. In summer, you could see (or hear) Tengmalm's Owls and there is a chance of Honey Buzzards, woodpeckers, Woodlarks, and Crossbills. Tengmalm's Owls have increased with the recent provision of nest boxes here.

❽ Anlier Forest and Belgian Lorraine

Location The far southeast corner of Belgium.
Access The town of Arlon just off the E411 makes a good base to explore the area around the villages of Irton, Ethe, Vance, and Habay.
Contact BirdLife Belgium, Kardinaal Mercierplein 1, 2800 Mechelen
Tel: 015-29 72 20
Email: info@natuurpunt.be
Web: www.natuurpunt.be

This is a large, diverse region where beech forests alternate with farmland. Very early spring is the best time for some elusive woodland specialities, such as Black and Middle Spotted Woodpeckers, Goshawks, and Hazel Hens (rare even in this location). Later in the breeding season is better for Black Storks, Honey Buzzards, Black and Red Kites, Hobbies, Nightjars, Woodlarks, Nightingales, Melodious Warblers, Firecrests, both species of treecreepers (try to hear their special song), Golden Orioles, and Red-backed and Great Grey Shrikes. Some areas also have Middle Spotted and Grey-headed Woodpeckers. Like most woodland sites, it demands time and patience, but you can see a lot of birds if you search for the best locations.

183

France

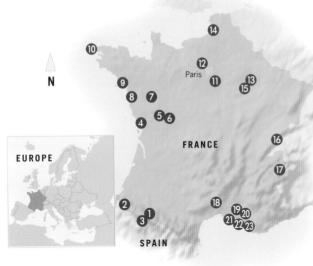

Paris

FRANCE

EUROPE

SPAIN

FRANCE IS ALMOST a microcosm of Europe. It has seabird islands and migration watch points in Brittany, concentrations of geese, ducks, and waders in the estuaries and bays of its north and west coasts, and exciting woodland birds inland. Many of its agricultural areas remain rich in birds, while the high Alps, the Jura, and the Cevennes ranges add still more bird interest. In the south, it has some of the most famous bird areas in Europe around the Camargue.

❶ Col du Tourmalet

Cloud in the valley below the Col.

Location About 15km (9½ miles) east of Luz-St-Sauveur in the Haute Pyrénées.
Access The Col is accessible on the N918 from June onwards, via Luz-St-Sauveur; adjacent forests can be watched from the road or paths.
Contact Ligue pour la Protection des Oiseaux (LPO), La Corderie Royale, BP 263, 17305 Rochefort Cedex
Tel: 05 46 821234
Web: www.lpo.fr

As well as fabulous mountain scenery, the beautiful Col du Tourmalet has nesting Snowfinches and Rock Thrushes, and is generally good for Alpine Accentors, Alpine Choughs, Alpine Swifts, Crag Martins, and other high-altitude species. The forests on the way up have Black Woodpeckers, Crested Tits, and Firecrests. Other nearby roads, for example to the Cirque de Troumouse above Gèdre, are all worth trying too.

❷ Col d'Orgambideska

Location A pass on the Spain–France border, about 60km (37 miles) southwest of Oloron-Sainte-Marie.
Access Take the D919 from Oloron-Sainte-Marie, then the D918 and D26 to Larrau; then, travel west to Saint-Jean-Pied-de-Port, Bayonne, and Orthez for 10km (6 miles).
Contact OCL 11, rue Bourgneuf, F-64100 Bayonne
Tel: 05 59 25 62 03.

This is the best migration watch point across the Pyrenees. Black Kites and Honey Buzzards are early (August) migrants, but September is the best time for Black Storks, Ospreys, Hobbies and Marsh Harriers, Swallows, and martins. Later, there are Red Kites, Buzzards, and Sparrowhawks. Finches, Woodpigeons, larks, and thrushes come later, often in huge numbers.

Woodpigeon

Pine woodland surrounding the dramatic Cirque de Gavarnie.

❸ Gavarnie

Location 60km (37 miles) south of Lourdes in the Haute Pyrénées.
Access From Lourdes, take the N21 to Argelès-Gazost, the N918 to Luz-St-Sauveur, then the N921 to Gavarnie (only accessible in summer).
Contact Ligue pour la Protection des Oiseaux (LPO), La Corderie Royale, BP 263, 17305 Rochefort Cedex
Tel: 05 46 821234
Web: www.lpo.fr

The Pyrenees are dramatic mountains, truly Alpine in scale, although many of the best birds can be seen in the gorges and foothills lower down. Gavarnie has a superb "cirque" or corrie – a rounded hollow among the high peaks, some of which are covered with forest, others bare. By walking up towards the peaks in summer (in winter the whole valley is closed), you may be lucky enough to see a wide range of Pyrenean birds, including Griffon Vultures, Golden Eagles, and other raptors. The top birds at the site are the Lammergeier and Wallcreeper, but you are more likely to see Choughs, Alpine Choughs, Snowfinches, Citril Finches, Crested Tits, and Firecrests. Alpine Accentors are regular visitors to the car park. Black Woodpeckers breed in the woods nearby and Black Redstarts are found on the cliffs and in the villages lower down.

❹ Baie d'Aiguillon

Location A large bay to the north of La Rochelle on the Biscay coast.
Access Visible from several roads and villages on its north shore; from Triaize take the D746 to Vignaud and turn south towards the shore.
Contact Ligue pour la Protection des Oiseaux (LPO), La Corderie Royale, BP 263, 17305 Rochefort Cedex
Tel: 05 46 821234
Web: www.lpo.fr

At low tide, the bay has extensive mudflats populated by waders and wildfowl; high tide brings them to roosts on the higher marshes, where they can be watched from the sea walls. It has the largest numbers of coastal waders in France. Montagu's Harriers, Hobbies, Red-legged Partridges, Quail, and Bluethroats breed in the area. Spring and autumn may bring migrant Spoonbills, Little Egrets, and Black Storks.

Quail

❺ Pinail National Nature Reserve

Location About 30km (19 miles) northeast of Poitiers, in central western France.
Access From Poitiers, turn right off the N10 on to the D15 towards Dissay. Turn left just before Dissay, then right shortly afterwards to Bondilly. After the Château du Fou, take a track to the Pinail reserve car park.
Contact Reserves naturelle Pinail, Ferme du Château du Fou, 86210, Vouneuil-sur-Vienne
Tel: 05 49 02 33 47
Email: pinail@espaces-naturels.fr
Web: www.reserve-pinail.org

Public paths cut through this superb forest reserve. Spring and summer are best for breeding birds, but observation is easier in winter (but avoid the boar hunting season); Short-toed Treecreepers, Black and Middle Spotted Woodpeckers, and Goshawks are all hard to spot in summer. Breeding birds include Hobbies, Montagu's and Hen Harriers, Honey Buzzards, Short-toed Eagles, Grasshopper Warblers, Woodlarks, Nightjars, and Hawfinches. Dartford Warblers and Stonechats also breed on the heaths.

❻ La Brenne

Location Just west of Châteauroux, about 80km (50 miles) southeast of Tours.
Access From Tours, take the N143 to Châtillon-sur-Indre, then to Mézières-en-Brenne. Interesting areas lie between here and the village of Rosnay, about 25km (16 miles) to the south.
Contact Ligue pour la Protection des Oiseaux (LPO), La Corderie Royale, BP 263, 17305 Rochefort Cedex
Tel: 05 46 821234
Web: www.lpo.fr

This is a tranquil area of lakes, reedbeds, forests, meadows, and heaths. Gabriere Lake is best in autumn and winter. In spring, you can find plentiful nesting Black-necked Grebes, Purple Herons, Little Bitterns,

The lakes of La Brenne remain largely undiscovered by tourists.

ducks, Marsh Harriers, Black Kites, Short-toed Eagles, Honey Buzzards, Whiskered and Black Terns, and Savi's and Great Reed Warblers. In winter, there are large concentrations of Smews and Greylag and Bean Geese.

❼ Rille Lake

Location A reservoir on the Lathan River, 40km (25 miles) northwest of Tours.
Access From Noyant on the D766, take the D141 southeastwards through Breil. At the junction with the D62, turn east towards Rille.
Contact Ligue pour la Protection des Oiseaux (LPO), La Corderie Royale, BP 263, 17305 Rochefort Cedex
Tel: 05 46 821234
Web: www.lpo.fr

This lake fluctuates in level, sometimes revealing sand bars, at other times flooding nearby meadows. The land is private but is criss-crossed by public paths. In spring and summer, there are many common wetland birds and waders on migration. Autumn sees a good influx of waders and ducks, as well as Black-necked Grebes, Spoonbills, Black Storks, Honey Buzzards, and Whiskered Terns on the move through the region.

Black-necked Grebe

❽ Guérande/Le Croisic

Location On the Biscay coast, about 30km (19 miles) west of St Nazaire.
Access From Guérande, take the D774 and then the N171 to Le Croisic. Explore the marsh roads and footpaths wherever possible.
Contact Ligue pour la Protection des Oiseaux (LPO), La Corderie Royale, BP 263, 17305 Rochefort Cedex
Tel: 05 46 821234
Web: www.lpo.fr

The mudflats and marshes of Guérande are bordered by sand bars to the north and southeast and rocky shores to the southwest. There are harbours and jetties, all giving good views of bird flocks. In summer, there are breeding Black-winged Stilts, Avocets, Bluethroats, and Common Terns. Spring and autumn migrations bring many waders, Spoonbills, and large numbers of seabirds offshore in autumn. In winter, look out for Black-necked Grebes.

❾ Gulf of Morbihan

Location On the south coast of Brittany immediately south of Vannes, about 180km (112 miles) northwest of Nantes.
Access The D780 Sarzeau road encircles the eastern and southern sides of the inlet.
Contact Ligue pour la Protection des Oiseaux (LPO), La Corderie Royale, BP 263, 17305 Rochefort Cedex
Tel: 05 46 821234
Web: www.lpo.fr

This almost enclosed inlet is studded with 40 islands. In winter, large areas of uncovered mud at low tide attract huge numbers of waders and wildfowl, especially Brent Geese, Wigeon, Mallards, Teal, Pintails, Grey Plovers, Shovelers, Shelducks, Redshanks, Curlews, and Dunlins. Avocets are numerous and Little Egrets have increased dramatically in the area.

❿ Ile d'Ouessant

Location The most westerly island in France, 20km (12½ miles) off the Brittany coast.
Access By boat from Brest or Conquet, or by air from Brest-Guipavas; rent a bike on the island.
Contact Ligue pour la Protection des Oiseaux (LPO), La Corderie Royale, BP 263, 17305 Rochefort Cedex
Tel: 0546 821234, or Centre Ornithologique, F-29242 Ile d'Ouessant, Finistère
Tel: 098 48 8265
Web: www.lpo.fr

Rocky cliffs topped with heathland at the Ile d'Ouessant.

This is a gem: an island with lovely seabird colonies, Dartford Warblers, Choughs, and the chance to see fabulous migration in spring and autumn. Much depends on the weather; given a good westerly wind there can be huge numbers of Manx, Mediterranean, and Sooty Shearwaters, occasional Cory's, Great, and Little Shearwaters, many Fulmars, Storm Petrels, Grey Phalaropes, Arctic, Great, and Pomarine Skuas, Kittiwakes, and Sabine's Gulls.

⓫ Forêt de Fontainebleau

The Fontainebleau Forest in autumn.

Location 60km (37 miles) southeast of Paris.
Access Leave Paris on the A6/E15. Take the Ury junction, then the N152 to Fontainebleau; northwest are the La Tillaie and Le Gros-Fouteau reserves.
Contact Ligue pour la Protection des Oiseaux (LPO), La Corderie Royale, BP 263, 17305 Rochefort Cedex
Tel: 05 46 821234
Web: www.lpo.fr

Middle Spotted Woodpecker

This big, forested area in the valley of the Seine is a popular and attractive region, with plenty of commoner woodland birds. There are all the typical warblers, tits, Nuthatches, finches, and thrushes of northwest European woodland in summer, as well as Pied Flycatchers, Redstarts, Buzzards, Honey Buzzards, Sparrowhawks, and Hobbies in spring and summer. The real interest lies in woodpeckers, best seen and heard in spring, with Grey-headed, Green, Black, Great, Middle, and Lesser Spotted all possible. The well-marked "Route Ronde" just 5km (3 miles) from the town encloses many good spots for woodpeckers.

⓬ Bois de Boulogne

Location A small woodland in the northwestern suburbs of Paris.
Access Take the Paris Metro to Port Maillot; follow the well-marked routes.
Contact Ligue pour la Protection des Oiseaux (LPO), La Corderie Royale, BP 263, 17305 Rochefort Cedex
Tel: 05 46 821234
Web: www.lpo.fr

This is a remnant of the once vast Rouvray Forest, with a number of lakes and streams. You can see or hear woodland species, such as Willow, Wood, and Garden Warblers, Redstarts, Chiffchaffs, Blackcaps, Short-toed Treecreepers, and Crested and Long-tailed Tits. Black Redstarts are common around the buildings. In winter, the lakes have Pochards and Tufted Ducks and the woods are good for Fieldfares, Redwings, Siskins, Redpolls, and Bramblings.

⓭ Lac du Chantecoq

A bay in the Lac du Chantecoq.

Location About 170km (105 miles) east of Paris, 15km (9½ miles) southwest of St Dizier.
Access Take the D384 from St Dizier; the lake is well signposted.
Contact Ligue pour la Protection des Oiseaux (LPO), La Corderie Royale, BP 263, 17305 Rochefort Cedex
Tel: 05 46 821234
Web: www.lpo.fr

This reservoir is surrounded by woods, open fields, reedbeds, and flooded willows. It is principally a spring, autumn, or winter venue. In winter, there are Bean and Greylag Geese, many ducks and sometimes White-tailed Eagles. In autumn, more waders appear if water levels are low. Migration brings large numbers of Cranes in November; their spring return is perhaps more spectacular, with as many as 25,000 Cranes in March, best seen as they come to roost in the evenings.

⑭ The Somme Bay

Location About 70km (43 miles) south of Boulogne in northwest France.
Access The D940 runs along the shores of the bay.
Contact Ligue pour la Protection des Oiseaux (LPO), La Corderie Royale, BP 263, 17305 Rochefort Cedex
Tel: 05 46 821234
Web: www.lpo.fr

This estuarine area is backed by a private reserve. In winter, there are many ducks, including Pintails, Wigeon, and Shovelers, and thousands of waders. Hooded Crows are winter regulars, and there are often Rough-legged Buzzards, Peregrines, and Merlins. Look for Twites in the marsh. In spring, Spoonbills appear on migration. In autumn, wader numbers are vastly increased and there are many more gulls, terns, and some Arctic Skuas, an occasional Osprey, and excellent numbers of finches, thrushes, larks, and pipits.

⑮ Foret d'Orient Lake

Location Just east of Troyes, about 150km (93 miles) east of Paris.
Access Take the N19 from Troyes. Turn off north at Lusigny-sur-Barse. At Géaudot, take the D43 to Mesnil-Saint-Père.
Contact Ligue pour la Protection des Oiseaux (LPO), La Corderie Royale, BP 263, 17305 Rochefort Cedex
Tel: 05 46 821234
Web: www.lpo.fr

This reservoir, which controls the flow of the Seine, is surrounded by forest. Bean Geese and Cranes migrate through here in spring; Ospreys, Cranes, Black Terns, and many waders in autumn. In winter, there is a good chance of seeing Greylag and Bean Geese, Smews, and White-tailed Eagles. There are still birds in summer; woodpeckers and Goshawks breed in the surrounding woods, and there are good numbers of commoner woodland birds.

⑯ French Jura

Location The area between Morez in the southwest and Pontarlier in the north, about 50km (31 miles) north of Geneva.
Access In the north, the area is best accessed along the Mont d'Or road, off the N57; in the south, use the D415 Bois D'Amont road.
Contact Ligue pour la Protection des Oiseaux (LPO), La Corderie Royale, BP 263, 17305 Rochefort Cedex
Tel: 05 46 821234
Web: www.lpo.fr

This sharp range of mountains is almost as good as the Alps for mountain and forest birds. Of the rarer or more difficult species, there are Hazel Grouse, Pygmy, Tengmalm's, and Eagle Owls, Wallcreepers, and Citril Finches, plus woodpeckers in the forests. Goshawks, Sparrowhawks, and Peregrines add spice. Look out for Crag Martins, Bonelli's and Wood Warblers, Fieldfares, Crossbills, and Nutcrackers. In autumn, Mont d'Or has Dotterels on migration;

White-tailed Eagle

they rest on alpine meadows and can be viewed from well-marked trails from the high car park.

⑰ Haute-Savoie and the Vanoise National Park

Pine-clad slopes in the Haute-Savoie.

Location Straddling the Italian border, 100km (62 miles) east of Grenoble.
Access The information centre for the National Park is at Lanslebourg-Mont Cenis on the N6.
Contact Ligue pour la Protection des Oiseaux (LPO), La Corderie Royale, BP 263, 17305 Rochefort Cedex
Tel: 05 46 821234
Web: www.lpo.fr

The Haute-Savoie area is good for Rock Partridges, although they are hard to find; there is also the possiblity of a reintroduced Lammergeier. Snowfinches, Alpine Choughs, Alpine Accentors, Citril Finches, Nutcrackers, and Golden Eagles are all present. The Vanoise National Park is a high area with Snowfinches and Wallcreepers; the best view is from the Col de L'Iséran on the D902 road.

View of Cévennes national park.

⑱ Cévennes national park and the Gorges du Jonte

Location About 60km (37 miles) north of Montpellier, the Cévennes sweep up to the west of the Rhône valley.
Access There is an information centre at Florac on the N106. A viewing platform on this road 10km (6 miles) east of Le Rozier, near Le Truel, overlooks the Gorges du Jonte. The Causse Méjean grassland at the southwestern end is best accessed from Le Rozier, along the D996.
Contact Ligue pour la Protection des Oiseaux (LPO), La Corderie Royale, BP 263, 17305 Rochefort Cedex
Tel: 05 46 821234
Web: www.lpo.fr

The Cévennes offers excellent birdwatching in the good, clear weather of summer, when birds of prey are especially numerous and easy to see. Griffon Vultures have been reintroduced and can be seen with Black and Egyptian Vultures in the gorges. Alpine Accentors and Rock Buntings are found on higher slopes, while Golden and Short-toed Eagles, Goshawks, Buzzards, Black and Red Kites, Ravens, Choughs, Peregrines, Red-legged Partridges, Alpine Swifts, and Crag Martins are likely. Ring Ouzels, Rock Thrushes, and Subalpine Warblers are summer birds, and Wallcreepers are possible in winter.

187

Magnificent view across the Les Alpilles range of limestone hills

⑲ Les Alpilles

Location The hills immediately to the east of Arles.
Access From Arles take the D17 east and then turn north onto the D27 to Les Baux-de-Provence.
Contact Ligue pour la Protection des Oiseaux (LPO), La Corderie Royale, BP 263, 17305 Rochefort Cedex
Tel: 05 46 821234
Web: www.lpo.fr

This range of hills is good in any season, with excellent views afforded by the roads and paths running through the area. In winter and very early spring, look and listen around the gorges and cliffs for elusive Wallcreepers by day and Eagle Owls at dusk. Both are hard to pinpoint, but this is probably as good a place for Eagle Owls as any in Europe. There may be some wintering Alpine Accentors, Rock Sparrows, and Rock Buntings on the very tops of the crags. In summer, you may find Short-toed and Bonelli's Eagles, Alpine Swifts, Blue Rock Thrushes, Crag Martins, and Sardinian and Subalpine Warblers.

Eagle Owl

⑳ La Crau

Location About 25km (16 miles) southeast of Arles, just east of the Camargue.
Access Take the N113 from Arles. The best areas are the disused aerodrome at Piste de Vallon, south of the N113-D5 intersection, Croix de Crau, and the area east of the D5.
Contact Ligue pour la Protection des Oiseaux (LPO), La Corderie Royale, BP 263, 17305 Rochefort Cedex
Tel: 05 46 821234
Web: www.lpo.fr

Thousands of years ago, this area was a huge delta. Now it is a dry, stony plain intermittently dotted with short, aromatic herbs. The steppe, locally called Coussous, is grazed by sheep in summer and partly occupied by the military, so keep to tracks. In winter, you may stumble across nomadic flocks of Pin-tailed Sandgrouse and Little Bustards. In spring, these are dispersed and easier to find as they display. This remarkable habitat also has Stone-curlews, Little Owls, Egyptian Vultures, Short-toed Eagles, Black Kites, Great Spotted Cuckoos, Skylarks, and Short-toed Larks. Rollers breed here and flock in summer.

㉑ La Camargue: Étang de Vaccares

The Camargue wetlands.

Location The huge wetland area between Montpellier and Marseille.
Access Étang de Vaccares is a permanent lake. Take the D570 south of Arles then the D36 and D36D towards the lake (beyond Gageron and Villeneuve).
Contact Ligue pour la Protection des Oiseaux (LPO), La Corderie Royale, BP 263, 17305 Rochefort Cedex
Tel: 05 46 821234
Web: www.lpo.fr

This large lake with reedy edges is good for Bitterns, Great White, Little, and Cattle Egrets, Marsh Harriers, Black-winged Stilts, Black and Whiskered Terns, Moustached and Sedge Warblers, and Bearded and Penduline Tits. The whole area has typical Mediterranean summer birds, such as Hoopoes, Bee-eaters, a few Rollers, Calandra Larks, and various warblers. In winter, there are big numbers of Coots, Red-crested Pochards, Pochards, Tufted Ducks, and Goldeneyes, and tens of thousands of dabbling ducks. Great White Egrets are numerous.

㉒ La Camargue: Tour de Vallat

Location On the eastern edge of Étang de Vaccares (see site 21).
Access The centre of the Camargue Reserve Authority, Tor de Vallat is reached from Villeneuve on the D36D south towards Salin-de-Badon.
Contact Ligue pour la Protection des Oiseaux (LPO), La Corderie Royale, BP 263, 17305 Rochefort Cedex
Tel: 05 46 821234
Web: www.lpo.fr

This is a good area for views over the lake, with special facilities for birdwatchers. Typical wetland and reedbed birds in spring and summer are Squacco, Night and Purple Herons, Little Bitterns, Marsh Harriers, Great Spotted Cuckoos, ducks, and a few Greater Spotted Eagles. It is set within a great area for birds, with marshes, salinas, beaches, dunes, and woods and bushy areas, justifying the Camargue's international reputation.

㉓ La Camargue: Étang du Fangassier

Location The main salt pan area of the Camargue, south of the Étang de Vaccares (see site 21).
Access Take the D36B south of Étang de Vaccares, then turn right on a minor road towards the salt lake.
Contact Ligue pour la Protection des Oiseaux (LPO), La Corderie Royale, BP 263, 17305 Rochefort Cedex
Tel: 05 46 821234
Web: www.lpo.fr

This is the site of the magnificent and justly famed colony of Greater Flamingos – one of a mere handful in Europe. Numbers vary from year to year, but you should prepare yourself to see thousands of these majestic pink birds. In spring and summer, look out too for Mediterranean and Slender-billed Gulls, Sandwich, Common, Little, and Whiskered Terns, and nesting Avocets. Short, scrubby vegetation in the salty areas has a few Spectacled Warblers, very much restricted to such habitats in southern Europe. In spring and autumn, migrating waders of many kinds are common.

Switzerland

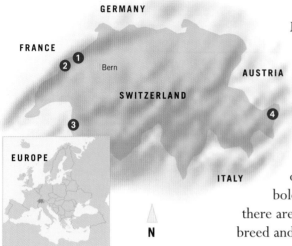

GERMANY

FRANCE

Bern

SWITZERLAND

AUSTRIA

ITALY

EUROPE

❶ ❷ ❸ ❹

N

Mountains dominate the Swiss scenery and bird life. Many Alpine birds are best seen on the pastures and rocky slopes below the snow line. High woods too are good for birds, but many take a lot of finding – Tengmalm's Owls, for example, are strictly nocturnal, while Three-toed Woodpeckers and Hazel Grouse are scarce and shy. Nutcrackers, Alpine Choughs, and others make up for these elusive birds by their bolder nature. Switzerland is not all about the Alps: there are good wetlands too, where interesting species breed and many more appear on migration.

❶ Lac de Neuchâtel

Wetlands beside the Lac de Neuchâtel.

Location About 35km (22 miles) west of Bern.
Access The lake has many marshy areas around it, the best on the northeastern side between Neuchâtel and Portalban. The Cham-Pittet reserve, with a visitor centre, is just east of Yverdon at Cheseaux Noréaz.
Contact SVS-BirdLife Suisse, Wiedingstrasse 78, PO Box 8521, CH-8036, Zurich
Tel: +41 (0)44 457 70 20
Email: svs@birdlife.ch
Web: www.birdlife.ch

This is the best wetland area in Switzerland. In spring, Marsh Sandpipers, Temminck's Stints, and Red-necked Phalaropes are typically observed by the lake. The marshes attract the usual range of reedbed birds, and Great White Egrets have been seen here. Sadly, most of Switzerland's wetlands have suffered drainage and development, making sites such as Neuchâtel all the more important.

❷ Swiss Jura

Location Along the Swiss/French border, west of Bern.
Access Easily reached by road. Try the Col de Chasseral region in the north; Col du Monllendruz and Col de Crozet, Montoiseau in the south; and Creux-du-Van and nearby gorges in the centre of the area.
Contact SVS-BirdLife Suisse, Wiedingstrasse 78, PO Box 8521, CH-8036, Zurich
Tel: +41 (0)44 457 70 20
Email: svs@birdlife.ch
Web: www.birdlife.ch

This scenic area has high mountains and thickly wooded slopes, dissected by gorges and punctuated by patches of high meadow. Birds to seek out include Hazel Hens, Black Woodpeckers, and Nutcrackers in the forests. Citril Finches may be seen where the forest meets high pastures. Scan the gorges for Wallcreepers – a good view is an unmissable experience – and look out for mountain species such as Alpine Choughs and Swifts.

Citril Finch

❸ Col de Bretolet

Location South of Montreux and Champéry on the border with France.
Access From the end of the Val d'Illiez railway line at Champéry, follow signposts to Barme and walk along a track beside a stream: after 3km (2 miles) head up for the pass.
Contact SVS-BirdLife Suisse, Wiedingstrasse 78, PO Box 8521, CH-8036, Zurich
Tel: +41 (0)44 457 70 20
Email: svs@birdlife.ch
Web: www.birdlife.ch

This region is excellent for Alpine birds, including Rock Partridges, Ptarmigan, Nutcrackers, Alpine Choughs, Alpine Accentors, Water Pipits, Rock Thrushes, Crag Martins, Snowfinches, and Citril Finches. The bridge at Feschelbach Gorge, east of Leuk, is said to be good for Wallcreepers.

The Col de Bretolet hosts impressive numbers of migrating birds of prey.

❹ Swiss national park

Location On the border with Italy, about 180km (112 miles) southwest of Zürich.
Access A big area in eastern Switzerland. The visitor centre at Zernez is accessible from Route 28.
Contact National Park House, CH-7530 Zernez
Tel: +41 (0)44 457 70 20
Email: info@nationalpark.ch
Web: www.birdlife.ch

This remarkable area of forests, meadows, and pasture rising to mountain peaks, is the centre of a Lammergeier reintroduction programme. Other birds include occasional Wallcreepers, owls (including Pygmy and Tengmalm's), and woodpeckers (including Black), but these species are extremely elusive in the forests, and more easily heard than seen. Citril Finches are likely on forest edges.

Germany

NETHERLANDS

N

EUROPE

GERMANY

Berlin

Frankfurt

Munich

POLAND

CZECH
REPUBLIC

SWITZERLAND   AUSTRIA

Northern middle europe south of the Baltic is strangely unexplored by most birdwatchers, but there is enough of interest to attract the most discerning enthusiasts. Germany is a large country with a wide sweep from the northern coastal plain to the mountainous south, so it offers a great range of birds and striking seasonal changes. There are exciting wetlands along the Baltic and North Sea coasts, as well as agricultural land that retains its traditional character; species such as Corncrakes, White-tailed Eagles, and Aquatic Warblers hang on here.

❶ Bodensee, Mindelsee, and Wollmatinger Ried

Location The area around Konstanz on the Swiss border.
Access Bodensee (Lake Constance) is easily watched from the E54 road along its north shore. The Mindelsee lies to the west, near the village of Moggingen, where there is a bird observatory. Wollmatinger Ried reserve, west of Konstanz, can be visited only on guided tours booked in advance through NABU.
Contact Naturschutzbund Deutschland (NABU), Herbert-Rabius-Str. 26, D-53225 Bonn
Email: NABU@NABU.de
Web: www.nabu.de

In summer, it is a good plan to combine a visit to the lakes with a walk around the nearby woodland; in winter, the lake itself is the main attraction. White Storks and Red-crested Pochards breed here, and Great Crested Grebes are abundant in summer. Where the lake discharges into the Rhine, wintering Pochards, Tufted Ducks, and Coots are seen in their tens of

Great Crested Grebe

thousands; equally large flocks are found at the Wollmatinger Ried reserve and at Konstanzer Bucht bay, which remains ice-free in winter. Red-crested Pochards winter in some hundreds at the eastern end of the lake. Nearby castles may attract Wallcreepers in winter.

❷ Munich

Location The city lies 70km (43 miles) north of the Austrian border.
Access Visit the canals and the Speichersee reservoir about 5km (3 miles) northeast of the city.
Contact Naturschutzbund Deutschland (NABU), Herbert-Rabius-Str. 26, D-53225 Bonn
Email: NABU@NABU.de
Web: www.nabu.de

Munich's Speichersee reservoir has large numbers of breeding Cormorants, Black-necked Grebes, and wildfowl, and a few Red-crested Pochards, Great Reed Warblers, and Night Herons. In winter, it attracts wildfowl; moulting flocks are worth a look in late summer and autumn, when you will see Tufted Ducks, Pochards, many Shovelers and Gadwalls, and a thousand or more Red-crested Pochards. If nothing else, it will test your identification skills of "brown ducks" in summer plumage.

Wind-felled trees in an Alpine forest.

❸ Karwendel and the Bavarian Alps

Location Straddling the Austrian border, south of Munich.
Access There are several roads and ski-lifts into higher areas, for example near Oberammergau and Grainau.
Contact Naturschutzbund Deutschland (NABU), Herbert-Rabius-Str. 26, D-53225 Bonn
Email: NABU@NABU.de
Web: www.nabu.de

Access is made easy by the presence of winter sports and other tourist centres, but the area has undoubtedly been

damaged by development. It is a region of limestone mountains with open meadows, mixed forest, high crags, and open slopes. Golden Eagles and Peregrines nest here, and in the forest you may see Hazel Hens, Black Grouse, and Capercaillies – all of which are shy and locally in decline. Eagle, Pygmy, and Tengmalm's Owls are similarly elusive; you are far more likely to see Black, White-backed, and Three-toed Woodpeckers, many Bonelli's Warblers, and Serins in the forest areas. Ring Ouzels, Ptarmigan, Snowfinches, and Alpine Choughs are present at higher altitudes.

A spectacular view at Berchtesgaden.

Visit this part of the Danube while you can: the whole system is likely, at some time, to be "upgraded" to carry ever-larger ships. The areas that remain more or less natural should be explored for Little Bitterns, White Storks, various ducks, commoner birds of prey, Spotted Crakes, Black-tailed Godwits, many Curlews, Sand Martins, and Bluethroats, which breed in the wetter parts. The forested areas are good for woodpeckers, Collared Flycatchers, and Red-backed Shrikes. Large numbers of ducks winter here, depending on the extent of the flooding.

❹ Berchtesgaden national park

Location 30km (19 miles) south of Salzburg on the Austrian border.
Access From Salzburg, take the B158 south to Berchtesgaden, from where a minor road leads to the park.
Contact Naturschutzbund Deutschland (NABU), Herbert-Rabius-Str. 26, D-53225 Bonn
Email: NABU@NABU.de
Web: www.nabu.de

In common with many Alpine areas, Berchtesgaden suffers from the over-development of winter sports facilities. It is, however, an accessible region with interesting high-altitude birds, such as Alpine Choughs and Ptarmigan. The forests are good for Honey Buzzards, Golden Eagles, Black Grouse, Capercaillies, Eagle, Pygmy, and Tengmalm's Owls, Black, White-backed, and Three-toed Woodpeckers, Bonelli's Warblers, and Serins. Summer is the best time to visit the mountains, although early spring is better for forest birds.

❺ Bayerischer Wald national park

Light penetrates the summer canopy.

Location 50km (31 miles) north of Passau, on the Czech border.
Access From Passau, drive north on the B85 then the B533 to Grafenau. The park lies just to the north on minor roads. There is an information centre at Neuschönau, about 10km (6 miles) northeast of Grafenau.
Contact Naturschutzbund Deutschland (NABU), Herbert-Rabius-Str. 26, D-53225 Bonn
Email: NABU@NABU.de
Web: www.nabu.de

The Bayerischer Wald and the higher Böhmer Wald along the border make an interesting region for birds. Spring is probably the best time to visit, when forest birds are easier to spot. There are good numbers of Hazel Hens, a few Capercaillies, many pairs of Pygmy Owls, and a few Tengmalm's Owls. You may be lucky to see the small numbers of Grey-headed and White-backed Woodpeckers, but the populations of Black and Three-toed Woodpeckers are much larger. The mix of forest, peat bogs, lakes, alpine meadows, and cliffs presents opportunities for good, varied birdwatching.

❻ Danube Valley, Regensburg

Location In southeastern Germany, 125km (78 miles) northeast of Munich.
Access Constant, intensive development is changing the character of the valley as the river is canalized and its floodplain drained. Visit the best remaining undisturbed areas, which lie southeast of Regensburg and around Straubing.
Contact Naturschutzbund Deutschland (NABU), Herbert-Rabius-Str. 26, D-53225 Bonn
Email: NABU@NABU.de
Web: www.nabu.de

❼ Lampertheimer Altrhein

Location A lake by the Rhine close to Mannheim in southern Germany.
Access From Mannheim, take the B44 north to Lampertheim.
Contact Naturschutzbund Deutschland (NABU), Herbert-Rabius-Str. 26, D-53225 Bonn
Email: NABU@NABU.de
Web: www.nabu.de

One of a series of lakes that is a remnant of an old channel cut off by the straightening of the Rhine. This lake is shallow, surrounded by reedbeds and forest, and backed by damp meadows (increasingly dry as time goes by, due to agricultural drainage). Great Crested Grebes, Cormorants, Grey Herons, Little Bitterns, and other wetland species nest here, while in the woods there are Red Kites, Black and Middle Spotted Woodpeckers, and other more common woodland species.

Little Bittern

Bluethroat

❽ Kuhkopf-Knoblauchsaue

Location About 25km (16 miles) west of Darmstadt in the Rhine valley.
Access From Darmstadt, take the B26 west. Turn south on the B44 towards Stockstadt, then west on the K156 to Riedstadt-Erfelden.
Contact Naturschutzbund Deutschland (NABU), Herbert-Rabius-Str. 26, D-53225 Bonn
Email: NABU@NABU.de
Web: www.nabu.de

This lakeland area is surrounded by old forests and wet meadows that host a good variety of birds. When water levels are low, waders appear in spring and autumn. Red-necked Grebes, Little Bitterns, Kingfishers, and Bluethroats breed in the wetter areas, while the woods have Honey Buzzards, Black Kites, Black and Middle Spotted Woodpeckers, Red-backed, Great Grey, and Woodchat Shrikes, and five species of owls. The best time all-round is summer, but in autumn there may be Cranes about and a variety of migrant waders to see.

❾ Marburg

Location The city is about 100km (62 miles) north of Frankfurt.
Access Reached from Frankfurt first on the E451/A5 then the B3.
Contact Naturschutzbund Deutschland (NABU), Herbert-Rabius-Str. 26, D-53225 Bonn
Email: NABU@NABU.de
Web: www.nabu.de

Woodland birds abound in this area: the castle park and cemetery area offer open space from which to watch over the woods. There are also good and undemanding forest walks during which you can see the smaller species. Look out for soaring Buzzards and Black Kites in summer, as well as Red-backed Shrikes, Marsh Warblers, and Serins. The woods always have Short-toed Treecreepers, Crested, Marsh, and Willow Tits, Hawfinches, and several species of woodpeckers.

❿ Thüringer Wald

Location 50km (31 miles) southwest of Erfurt in central Germany.
Access From Suhl, drive south on the B247 towards Schleusingen Turn. Then, go northeast on the L2607 to Breitenbach, and walk upstream along the River Vesser to Vesser. Alternatively, head from Schleusingen on route 4 to Ilmenau, drive on route 88 to Bad Blankenburg, and explore the Schwarza valley.
Contact Naturschutzbund Deutschland (NABU), Herbert-Rabius-Str. 26, D-53225 Bonn
Email: NABU@NABU.de
Web: www.nabu.de

The Thüringer Wald is a broad upland area in central Germany running southeast to northwest. Its woods are good for Capercaillies, Nutcrackers, and the usual selection of rather difficult woodpeckers and owls, including Eagle, Pygmy, and Tengmalm's. They are also worth a leisurely wander for their commoner breeding birds in spring and summer.

⓫ Brandenburg and Berlin

Location Berlin and the city of Brandenberg (to the west) are in northeast Germany.
Access Berlin is in a lowland valley surrounded by many marshes and lakes. It is worth taking a trip to Schwedt in the Oder Valley, about 90km (56 miles) northeast of Berlin on the B2, and to Lübben, about 90km (56 miles) southeast of Berlin, on the E55/A13 then the B87.
Contact Naturschutzbund Deutschland (NABU), Herbert-Rabius-Str. 26, D-53225 Bonn
Email: NABU@NABU.de
Web: www.nabu.de

The region around Berlin, and the Oder valley farther north, has excellent marshes, flood meadows, and woodland. There are some very exciting birds: White-tailed Eagles and perhaps Great Bustards are possible around Lübben, just south of Berlin, while the Oder valley has Corncrakes, Little Crakes, Aquatic Warblers, Black and White Storks, White-tailed and Lesser Spotted Eagles, and some Cranes nesting. In winter, it is a good area for Smews, Whooper and Bewick's Swans, and birds of prey, including Rough-legged Buzzards. There is much to see, and the area certainly merits a longer trip.

⓬ Mecklenburg Lakes

Location A wide plain, 150km (93 miles) northwest of Berlin.
Access There are several lakes to visit in the area: try the Lewitzer Teiche reserve near Parchim, just off the E26 Hamburg-Berlin Autobahn; lakes by the Goldberg-Crivitz L15 road near Langenhagen; and the Dambecker See north of Schwerin.
Contact Naturschutzbund Deutschland (NABU), Herbert-Rabius-Str. 26, D-53225 Bonn
Email: NABU@NABU.de
Web: www.nabu.de

The North German Plain in the Schwerin and Neubrandenburg area is often superb for birds, especially in nature reserve areas where agricultural development is held at bay. Around 150 species breed here, with Cranes and White-tailed and Lesser Spotted Eagles among the highlights. You may find a pair or two of Ferruginous Ducks, which are declining in Europe. On the Dambecker See, variable numbers of Black-necked Grebes and Common and Black Terns breed, and several thousand Greylag, Bean, and White-fronted Geese appear in spring and autumn.

Recreation and wildlife draw visitors to the Mecklenburg Lakes.

⑬ Unteres Odertal

Embankments are good vantage points.

Location A wetland area near Eberswalde, about 60km (37 miles) northeast of Berlin.
Access A large area of winter floods and riverside meadows close to Eberswalde and Angermunde can be viewed from the B2.
Contact Naturschutzbund Deutschland (NABU), Herbert-Rabius-Str. 26, D-53225 Bonn
Email: NABU@NABU.de
Web: www.nabu.de

A river and canal pass through long-reclaimed agricultural land. Floods occur occasionally, and the area is full of reedbeds and marshy meadows. It has good summer birds, including storks, a selection of birds of prey including White-tailed Eagles, Red Kites, and three species of harriers, Spotted Crakes, Corncrakes in good numbers, Snipe, Black Terns, Bluethroats, and Black

Woodpeckers. Many more White Storks move through in spring, when thousands of Bean Geese and White-fronted Geese can be seen, along with large numbers of ducks, Lapwings, Ruffs, and Coots. White-tailed Eagles and occasional Peregrines are worth seeing in winter.

⑭ Peenatalmoor

Location 150km (93 miles) north of Berlin.
Access The river Peene flows into the Oder estuary near Anklam, 50km (31 miles) northeast of Neubrandenburg on the B109. Explore minor roads from here for good wetland sites.
Contact Naturschutzbund Deutschland (NABU), Herbert-Rabius-Str. 26, D-53225 Bonn
Email: NABU@NABU.de
Web: www.nabu.de

This stretch of peat bog and flood plain has reedy marshes and willow thickets that provide habitat for breeding Bitterns, White Storks, Greylag Geese, Red and Black Kites, harriers, crakes, Cranes, waders, and woodpeckers. There are River Warblers, Nightingales and Bluethroats, Penduline Tits, and Scarlet Rosefinches in the damp bushy areas, and Woodlarks in drier clearings in nearby forests.

Eroded cliffs on Rügen Island.

⑮ Rügen Island

Location A large island joined to the mainland by a road bridge, about 250km (155 miles) north of Berlin.
Access By road from Stralsund, northeast of Rostock on the E251. The Wittow area in the north has access to interesting shoreline sites.
Contact Naturschutzbund Deutschland (NABU), Herbert-Rabius-Str. 26, D-53225 Bonn
Email: NABU@NABU.de
Web: www.nabu.de

This island forms part of a vast South Baltic complex of wetlands that is vital for wildfowl, waders, and Cranes from autumn to spring. The bay immediately to the east – Greifswalder Bodden – has a nuclear power station that keeps the sea ice-free in winter, attracting large numbers of ducks. Thousands of Mute Swans and Cormorants are notable, while Bewick's Swans pass through in the autumn. The vast majority of the geese here are White-fronted, while Wigeon, Teal, Scaup, Tufted Ducks, Long-tailed Ducks, and Goldeneyes all appear in their thousands.

⑯ Westrugen and Zingst

Location The area 30km (19 miles) northwest of Stralsund, west of Rügen island (see above).
Access The small town of Zingst overlooks the western part of the bay; Hiddensee is a long island forming the bay's eastern side.
Contact Naturschutzbund Deutschland (NABU), Herbert-Rabius-Str. 26, D-53225 Bonn
Email: NABU@NABU.de
Web: www.nabu.de

This is a large area of shallow sea, marsh, reedbeds, and meadows. In summer, there are numerous breeding waterfowl and colonies of Sandwich, Common, and Little Terns, and Sand Martins. Numbers swell in autumn and winter, with thousands of Mute Swans, Bean, White-fronted, and Greylag Geese, Teal, Tufted Ducks, and Goldeneyes. The area is excellent for Crane migration, too, with 25,000 in autumn.

Goldeneyes and Smews may be seen in the Zingst area.

The vast Schleswig-Holstein region.

⑰ Schleswig-Holstein Wattenmeer

Location The large region at the base of the Jutland peninsula, north of Hamburg.
Access Husum off the B5 on the west coast makes a good base from which to explore the many inlets and islands in the area.
Contact Naturschutzbund Deutschland (NABU), Herbert-Rabius-Str. 26, D-53225 Bonn
Email: NABU@NABU.de
Web: www.nabu.de

This vast area of mudflats, salt-marshes, estuaries, and lagoons, backed by meadows and freshwater marsh, is wonderful for birds: just explore and find your own best spots. Breeding birds include Marsh Harriers, thousands of pairs of Avocets, and Gull-billed, Sandwich, Common, Arctic, and Little Terns. Migrant waders are numerous, with tens of thousands of Oystercatchers, Grey Plovers, Curlews, Redshanks, and Spotted Redshanks, and hundreds of thousands of Knots and Dunlins. Wintering, migrating, and moulting wildfowl include tens of thousands of Barnacle and Brent Geese, Wigeon, Shelducks, Teal, and Eiders: this is where nearly all northwest Europe's Shelducks come to moult. The area can be enormously rewarding.

⑱ Helgoland

Location Two small islands off the north coast, 180km (112 miles) northwest of Hamburg.
Access By ferry from Cuxhaven, Wilhelmshaven, Bremerhaven, or Hamburg.
Contact Naturschutzbund Deutschland (NABU), Herbert-Rabius-Str. 26, D-53225 Bonn
Email: NABU@NABU.de
Web: www.nabu.de

Helgoland (Heligoland) has a place in the history of migration study and, like Fair Isle in Scotland, is a place of pilgrimage as well as an exciting spot to visit in spring or autumn.

Breeding birds include a few Fulmars and Razorbills and many more Kittiwakes and Guillemots. Migrants are the main attraction, however, with a remarkable list of around 400 species in all. Spring migrants include Thrush Nightingales, Bluethroats, shrikes, and chats. In autumn, there are greater numbers and variety, with regular "Siberian" birds such as Yellow-browed Warblers, Olive-backed and Richard's Pipits, and northern species including Rustic and Little Buntings, Arctic Warblers, and huge numbers of commoner Wheatears, Garden Warblers, Whitethroats, Redstarts, and Pied Flycatchers. There is a Bird Observatory on Oberland which is the better of the two islands; the other, Düne, is a flashy and fleshy tourist resort in the main.

Fulmar

⑲ Niedersachisches national park

Location A huge stretch of the Wattenmeer between the Ems and the Elbe in northwest Germany.
Access Best explored from Emden, Norden, Minsen, and Wilhelmshaven.
Contact Naturschutzbund Deutschland (NABU), Herbert-Rabius-Str. 26, D-53225 Bonn
Email: NABU@NABU.de
Web: www.nabu.de

This area of shallow sea and intertidal flats, sheltered by the East Frisian Islands, is fantastic for birds despite constant pressures from development and pollution. It is an important area for breeding terns and Avocets, but bird numbers are hugely increased in autumn and winter. Pink-footed, Greylag, Barnacle, and Brent Geese are numerous, but are put in the shade by tens of thousands of Shelducks and Eiders. Wigeon, Pintails, Teal, and other wildfowl are abundant, while waders include thousands of Oystercatchers, Avocets, Grey Plovers, Knots, and Dunlins reach six figures. Kentish Plovers, Spotted Redshanks, Sanderlings, and other species are also common on passage.

⑳ Zwillbrocker Venn

Location About 50km (31 miles) west of Münster, in northwest Germany, along the Dutch border.
Access The area around Ahaus and Stadtlohn on the Netherlands border is best explored from minor roads.
Contact Naturschutzbund Deutschland (NABU), Herbert-Rabius-Str. 26, D-53225 Bonn
Email: NABU@NABU.de
Web: www.nabu.de

The River Berkel flows northwest from near Münster, through a flat area of wet meadows, moors, and patches of heathland. Bird interest is diminishing as the fields are being drained for intensive agriculture, but ducks, Honey Buzzards, the odd pair of both Red and Black Kites, Marsh Harriers, Oystercatchers, Snipe, many Black-tailed Godwits, Curlews, a handful of Nightjars, and Black Woodpeckers breed, making a varied selection for a spring or summer visit. Curiously, a population of Flamingos – probably zoo escapees – has established here, with 20–40 breeding adults; in winter, they migrate to Zealand, in the southwest of the Netherlands.

Austria

BIRDWATCHING IS MADE SIMPLE in Austria because many of the choicest Alpine habitats are within year-round reach of developed ski resorts, with easy access to a good transport network. The country also has extensive, internationally significant wetlands, including the great Neusiedler See – a vast, shallow, lake with a concentration of herons, egrets, geese, ducks, waders, and terns. Lower Austria is rich in woodlands mixed with agricultural land, where there are good birds of prey, shrikes, flycatchers, owls, and woodpeckers.

❶ Neusiedler See

Reedbeds bordering Neusiedler See.

Location On the Hungarian border in the province of Burgenland, an hour's drive southeast of Vienna.
Access The best approaches are from Neusiedl am See and Weidem am See in the north, Podersdorf am See on the east shore, and Oggau and Rust in the west.
Contact BirdLife Austria, Museumsplatz 1/10/8, A-1070 Wien
Email: birdlife@blackbox.at
Web: www.birdlife.at
or National Park Information Centre
Tel: 02175 3442

One of Europe's famed bird areas, the lake is 30km (19 miles) long and mostly very shallow. It is fringed by a wide reedbed that reduces views of the open water but holds exciting birds itself. It is a good migration spot, as shown by its almost 300-strong bird list. Late spring and summer are the best times to visit: explore the reedbeds, surrounding marshy areas, and adjacent farmland and woods for a great variety of birds. Highlights include about one hundred pairs of breeding Great White Egrets, as well as Little Crakes, Sakers, Great Bustards, Black and White Storks, Night Herons, Ferruginous Ducks, Syrian Woodpeckers (by Esterhazy Castle), Collared Flycatchers, Nutcrackers, Bluethroats, and Moustached, River, and Barred Warblers. Birds of prey include Lesser and Greater Spotted Eagles at times and Red-footed Falcons in spring. Many waders, gulls, and terns appear here on their annual migration.

❷ Seewinkel

Location A complex of small lakes east of Neusiedler See (see site 1).
Access Explore either side of the B51. Walk along the Einser Canal near Pamhagen in the south, look at the plains east of Pamhagen, and try the Waasen-Hansag Reserve to the east.
Contact BirdLife Austria, Museumsplatz 1/10/8, A-1070 Wien
Email: birdlife@blackbox.at
Web: www.birdlife.at
or National Park Information Centre
Tel: 02175 3442

The Seewinkel wetlands are easier for birdwatching than the huge Neusiedler See itself. In the open plains south of Andau, you may see Great Bustards and Sakers. The Canal area is good for migrating storks and birds of prey, and for River and Barred Warblers in spring. The lakes have some of the Neusiedler See species, with breeding Black-necked Grebes, White Storks, Garganeys, Avocets, and Black-tailed Godwits. There are many herons, egrets, Little Bitterns, terns, and wildfowl, and breeding warblers and Bearded Tits. Bee-eaters are widespread in the area.

Sunrise is a wonderful time to visit the Seewinkel wetlands.

Ptarmigan, Black Grouse, Capercaillies, Pygmy Owls, Tengmalm's Owls, Black, White-backed, and Three-toed Woodpeckers, and Red-backed Shrikes. With luck you may find Rock Partridge, but this species is rather elusive and is best sought early in spring when birds are calling or displaying.

❼ Rheindelta, Bodensee

Location The southeast corner of Bodensee (Lake Constance), in the province of Vorarlberg.
Access The best area is between the Rhine (Old Rhein) and a new channel (the New Rhein). This is accessible via Fussach village, reached from Bregenz on the B202, or Gaissau, reached by turning off the B202 at Höchst.
Contact BirdLife Austria, Museumsplatz 1/10/8, A-1070 Wien
Email: birdlife@blackbox.at
Web: www.birdlife.at

Passage migrants heading south in autumn are frequently grounded by low cloud over the Alps and pause here, waiting for good weather. At such times, there may be 100 species, including Caspian and Whiskered Terns, waders, wildfowl, birds of prey, and small birds, such as Red-throated Pipits. Waders include many rarities, so it is worth exploring thoroughly. The Seerestaurant, on the lake shore on a road from Gaissau, is a good spot from which to access Fussacher Bucht, a good bay for waders and terns. A few pairs of Little Bitterns, Purple Herons, Red-crested Pochards, and Black-tailed Godwits breed here too.

Black-tailed Godwit

❸ Marchauen-Marchegg Reserve, River March

Location 40km (25 miles) east of Vienna, close to the Slovakian border.
Access Drive east from Vienna. At the northern edge of the village of Marchegg on the B49, take a track east to the reserve car park.
Contact WWF Österreich, Ottakringer Straße 114–116, A-1160 Wien
Tel: 01 488 170
Email: wwf@wwf.at
Web: www.wwf.at

The River March floods its valley in winter, creating an extensive wetland area with damp fields and low bushy growth in summer. This attracts River Warblers and storks, including the rarer Black Stork, a few Corncrakes, Red Kites, and Marsh Harriers. The patches of woodland near the reserve entrance have breeding Collared Flycatchers. In winter, White-tailed Eagles frequent this and neighbouring valleys, which have the best remaining flood-plain forests of central Europe.

River Warbler

View over the Schneeberg Mountains.

❹ Schneeberg Mountains

Location A mountain range about 50km (31 miles) southwest of Vienna.
Access Head south from Vienna on the A2 and turn west at Wiener Neustadt (jn 44). Minor roads lead to Puchberg; take the rack-and-pinion railway to the top of Schneeberg.
Contact BirdLife Austria, Museumsplatz 1/10/8, A-1070 Wien
Email: birdlife@blackbox.at
Web: www.birdlife.at

This area has many typical Alpine species – Ptarmigan, Golden Eagles, Alpine Accentors, Snowfinches, and Citril Finches. Look for Alpine Choughs and Crag Martins and, lower down, Nutcrackers and Black Woodpeckers. Many of these demand time and effort, but the scenery is fantastic wherever you wander.

❺ Hohe Tauern national park, Innsbruck

Location 60km (37 miles) east of Innsbruck and southwest of Salzburg.
Access Explore the minor roads in the park. There are administration centres at: Neukirchen am Großvenediger, Salzburg; Matrei in Osttirol, Tyrol; and Großkirchheim, Carinthia. All are reached via Mittersill on the B165, B168, and B108 respectively.
Contact BirdLife Austria, Museumsplatz 1/10/8, A-1070 Wien
Email: birdlife@blackbox.at
Web: www.birdlife.at

You may be lucky enough to see Lammergeiers here, thanks to a reintroduction scheme. More likely sightings include Griffon Vultures (in summer) and Golden Eagles. The area has many Alpine species, from Nutcrackers, Alpine Swifts, and Black Woodpeckers, to Bluethroats and Red-backed Shrikes lower down, and Ptarmigan, Alpine Choughs, Alpine Accentors, and Snowfinches higher up. The whole sweep of the Alps is in fact one vast bird area that can be explored over a long period; eventually you will discover your own favourite spots.

❻ Karwendel Reserve, West Austrian Alps

Location In the Tirol region, north of Innsbruck in western Austria.
Access Direct access from Innsbruck to the skiing centres and their associated roads provides the easiest routes to the high mountains. There is an information centre at Hinterriss, close to the German border.
Contact BirdLife Austria, Museumsplatz 1/10/8, A-1070 Wien
Email: birdlife@blackbox.at
Web: www.birdlife.at

This whole area is beautiful, with deciduous forest in the lower valleys merging upwards into conifer forest that then peters out into high, rocky slopes and peaks. In summer, there are breeding Honey Buzzards, Golden Eagles, Peregrines, Hazel Hens,

Hungary

SLOVAKIA

N

Budapest

HUNGARY

Debrecen

YUGOSLAVIA

EUROPE

RELATIVELY UNEXPLORED by most birdwatchers, Hungary has a great deal to offer. Enclosed by the Carpathians and the Alps and bordered in part by the Danube, it has mountain, wetland, and lowland birds in equal measure. Wetland and grassland reserves, in particular, are full of good birds. Hungary's agriculture and transport systems are fast being developed along western European lines and birds such as the Great Bustard will find it increasingly difficult to survive the large-scale habitat changes; visit soon for a glimpse of birds in traditional farmland.

❶ Hortobágy

Bundles of cut reeds at Hortobágy.

Location Close to Debrecen, about 250km (155 miles) east of Budapest.
Access A large area, with Hortobágy village at its centre. There are good views from route 33 between Tiszafüred and Debrecen.
Contact Hungarian Ornithological and Nature Conservation Society (MME), 1121 Költo utca 21, 391, H-1536, Budapest
Tel: +36 1 275 62 47
Email: mme@mme.hu
Web: www.mme.hu

The habitat here is largely steppe grassland, with scattered ponds and marshes. The grasslands have breeding Great Bustards, Montagu's Harriers, Stone-curlews, Rollers, Lesser Grey Shrikes, and Short-toed Larks. The ponds are good for grebes, Purple, Night, and Squacco Herons, Great White and Little Egrets, Little Bitterns, Spoonbills, Red-footed Falcons, Little Crakes, Whiskered Terns, Moustached and Aquatic Warblers, and Bluethroats. Glossy Ibises and Pygmy Cormorants may be seen from a hide at Hortobágy-halastó. In winter, White-tailed Eagles can be found and hundreds of Lesser White-fronted Geese are star birds.

❷ Pilisi and Budai Hills, Budapest

Location The hills 20km (12½ miles) to the north and west of Budapest.
Access For the Pilisi Hills take road 10 or 11 north from Budapest. The Budai Hills to the west are easily reached by local bus.
Contact Hungarian Ornithological and Nature Conservation Society (MME), 1121 Költo utca 21, 391, H-1536, Budapest
Tel: +36 1 275 62 47
Email: mme@mme.hu
Web: www.mme.hu

These forested hills, mingled with meadowland, river valleys, farmland, and crags, make a good day trip from the capital. Their birds are common in Hungary but may be new to western visitors. They include various woodpeckers (including Grey-headed and Syrian), Red-backed Shrikes, Barred Warblers, Short-toed Treecreepers, Golden Orioles, Collared and Red-breasted Flycatchers, Honey Buzzards, Sakers, Short-toed eagles, and both storks. Bee-eaters add colour and characteristic calls.

❸ Kiskunság national park

Location Around Kecskemét, 70km (43 miles) southeast of Budapest.
Access The best area is 30km (19 miles) west of Kecskemét, where road 52 crosses a railway south of Szabadszállás. To the north are lakes and marshes, to the south, salt lakes.
Contact Kiskunság national park, 6001, Kecskemét, Liszt F utca 19 or Hungarian Ornithological and Nature Conservation Society (MME), 1121 Költo utca 21, 391, H-1536, Budapest
Tel: +36 1 275 62 47
Email: mme@mme.hu
Web: www.mme.hu

Four shallow lakes in this area of steppe and salty marsh attract a wide range of birds, from Great White Egrets, Avocets, Spoonbills, and Marsh Harriers, to Black and Whiskered Terns, Red-footed Falcons, Rollers, Mediterranean Gulls, Bee-eaters, and shrikes. Satisfaction is guaranteed with such striking and colourful birds on offer. In the surrounding area, you may see a Great Bustard. October sees a large crane and wildfowl passage in the area. If you visit in winter, expect many thousands of Bean Geese among other wildfowl. There is an observation tower in the south of the park.

Kiskunság national park has a variety of habitats and exciting birds.

197

Poland

GERMANY

N

POLAND

Warsaw

EUROPE

SLOVAKIA

At present, much of Poland is underdeveloped, its agriculture less intensive than in the west. Birds like the Corncrake, lost to most of Europe, still thrive here along with several other rare species. The Great Snipe and Aquatic Warbler, for example, survive in its marshes and grasslands and attract increasing numbers of birdwatching visitors from the north and west. Poland's easterly position means severe winters, when many birds simply move out, but warm, dry summers attract a number of "southern" species to breed surprisingly far north.

❶ Lake Drużno, Elbląg and Gdańsk

Location Midway between Gdańsk and Kaliningrad in northern Poland.
Access The lake is situated south of Elbląg (south of Gdańsk Bay).
Contact Polish Society for the Protection of Birds, Odrowaza 24, 05-270 Marki k. Warszawy
Tel: +48 22 761 82 05,
+48 22 188 50 81
Email: office@otop.most.org.pl
Web: www.otop.org.pl

This large, shallow lake is rather polluted but nevertheless has good nesting wetland birds including Ferruginous Ducks, Little Gulls, and Black Terns. Many Greylag Geese, Gadwalls, Pochards, Marsh Harriers, Montagu's Harriers, Spotted Crakes, Little Crakes, Corncrakes, Cranes, Black-headed Gulls, Common Terns, and Bluethroats also breed here. Migrants are often good, with a few hundred Greylag Geese and Cranes regularly seen.

Little Crake

❷ River Vistula, Gdańsk

Location Between Gdańsk, Tczew, and Elbląg in northern Poland.
Access The River Vistula divides into several streams as it flows into Gdańsk Bay. The nearby Vistula Lagoon to the east is separated from the Baltic Sea by a long, narrow spit. There is good access to all parts of the wetland.
Contact Polish Society for the Protection of Birds, Odrowaza 24, 05-270 Marki k. Warszawy
Tel: +48 22 761 82 05,
+48 22 188 50 81
Email: office@otop.most.org.pl
Web: www.otop.org.pl

The mouth of the main river is an excellent site for waders, with its shallow estuary, sandbanks, offshore islets, lagoons, and coastal freshwater lakes. Large numbers of waders pass through, and on a good day in spring or autumn there may be a thousand or more to view. Sandwich, Common, and Little Terns breed and there are large flocks of non-breeding Little Gulls and Common Gulls. To the north of Elbląg, a smaller channel expands into the huge Vistula Lagoon where many more birds breed, including Great Crested Grebes, a big Cormorant colony, Grey Herons, ducks, harriers, crakes, Black-tailed Godwits, and Common Terns.

The Biebrza Puszcza marshes are wonderful for Aquatic Warblers.

❸ Biebrza Puszcza marshes

Location 45km (28 miles) northwest of Białystock in northeast Poland.
Access The marshes can be viewed from roads east of Biebrza around Wizna, Dobarz, and Goniądz.
Contact Polish Society for the Protection of Birds, Odrowaza 24, 05-270 Marki k. Warszawy
Tel: +48 22 761 82 05,
+48 22 188 50 81
Email: office@otop.most.org.pl
Web: www.otop.org.pl

The Polish marshes, threatened by agriculture and development, remain some of the finest in Europe: the Biebrza floodplain is an international treasure, scenically and in wildlife terms. Here, in summer, there are still hundreds of calling Corncrakes, a few hundred Great Snipes, 1,000 pairs of White-winged Black Terns, and thousands of Aquatic Warblers in their remaining stronghold. You may see Greater Spotted, Lesser Spotted, and Short-toed Eagles, Red Kites, White (and perhaps Black) Storks, Cranes, Whiskered and Black Terns, Bluethroats, Thrush Nightingales, River Warblers, and Black Woodpeckers. The Great Snipe trail is on private land generously made available to the public: please do not abuse this gesture by leaving the trail. It is best at dusk when the birds display and Aquatic Warblers are singing.

❹ Siemianówka Reservoir

Location On the border with Belarus, just to the north of the Puszcza Białowieska (see site 5).
Access From the village of Siemianówka, 20km (12½ miles) north of the Puszcza Białowieska, take a track eastwards and then north to the south shore of the lake.
Contact Polish Society for the Protection of Birds, Odrowaza 24, 05-270 Marki k. Warszawy
Tel: +48 22 761 82 05,
+48 22 188 50 81
Email: office@otop.most.org.pl
Web: www.otop.org.pl

Fish ponds and damp meadows around the reservoir create a good birdwatching area. There are wetland species, such as Bitterns, Little Bitterns, White Storks, Ferruginous Ducks, Black-tailed Godwits, Common and sometimes White-winged Black Terns, and Spotted Crakes in small numbers. White-tailed Eagles may be in the area and Marsh Harriers are frequent. Migrant waders and terns may be seen, depending on weather and water levels. The surrounding area is also good for birds: Lesser Grey Shrikes and Rollers can be seen locally. A highlight is the Citrine Wagtail, a rare breeder here.

❺ Puszcza Białowieska

Location The national park is on the border with Belarus about 70km (43 miles) south of Białystock.
Access There are good trails to the west and south, including the Linia Kurdzimowskego track and Droga Olemburska track, reached from Czerlonka.
Contact Polish Society for the Protection of Birds, Odrowaza 24, 05-270 Marki k. Warszawy
Tel: +48 22 761 82 05,
+48 22 188 50 81
Email: office@otop.most.org.pl
Web: www.otop.org.pl

This national park includes the largest tract of ancient mixed forest in Europe. It can only be visited with a permit and a guide from the authorities, but there are unregulated areas nearby that are worth trying too. The forest is a magical one, famous for its reintroduced European Bison, and it has a remarkable 159 breeding bird species including

Dense vegetation in the Bialowiesha Forest is best explored with a guide.

15 birds of prey, eight owls, all of the European woodpeckers except Syrian, and 18 different warblers. Expert guides will lead you to elusive owls and woodpeckers, and you are sure to see a range of special birds.

❻ Chełm

Location This province is 70km (43 miles) east of Lublin, in southeastern Poland, near the Ukrainian border.
Access Chełm and Brzeżno are the main centres with tracks leading north and south; also look at the Zamość and Gotówka areas.
Contact Polish Society for the Protection of Birds, Odrowaza 24, 05-270 Marki k. Warszawy
Tel: +48 22 761 82 05,
+48 22 188 50 81
Email: office@otop.most.org.pl
Web: www.otop.org.pl

This large region is studded with good marshes; the best are protected as nature reserves and have breeding Bitterns, White Storks, many Marsh and Montagu's Harriers, Spotted Crakes, an occasional pair of Cranes, Black-tailed Godwits, and White-winged Black Terns. There are some Bluethroats and good numbers of Aquatic Warblers. With luck, you might chance upon some Great Snipes. There are still Corncrakes in the meadows and good birds in nearby forests, making the region a good one for a lengthy stay.

❼ High Tatra: Tatrzański national park

Striking views in the High Tatra.

Location Part of the Carpathian range that sweeps westwards across the southern tip of Poland. The national park lies 100km (62 miles) south of Kraków.
Access Zakopane is the nearest town; go east to Bystre, then take a cable car from nearby Kuźnice to the peaks.
Contact Polish Society for the Protection of Birds, Odrowaza 24, 05-270 Marki k. Warszawy
Tel: +48 22 761 82 05,
+48 22 188 50 81
Email: office@otop.most.org.pl
Web: www.otop.org.pl

Excessive tourist development has caused some deterioration in the wildlife here, but there are still many interesting birds, including Golden Eagles, Black, White-backed, and Three-toed Woodpeckers, Pygmy and Tengmalm's Owls, Hazel Hens, Bluethroats, and Capercaillies. High summits have Alpine specialists, such as Alpine Accentors and Alpine Choughs.

With a little luck, you may also see a Wallcreeper.

❽ Szczecin Bay

Location A large estuary at the mouth of the River Odra, in northwest Poland on the German border.
Access Several points of access on the east and north sides of the bay, and from Szczecin itself, provide viewing possibilities.
Contact Polish Society for the Protection of Birds, Odrowaza 24, 05-270 Marki k. Warszawy
Tel: +48 22 761 82 05,
+48 22 188 50 81
Email: office@otop.most.org.pl
Web: www.otop.org.pl

The River Odra expands into a large bay, almost closed off from the Baltic. It is highly developed and polluted, yet has striking numbers of waterfowl. Red Kites frequent the area in summer and White-tailed Eagles feed over the estuary all year. The migrant and wintering birds provide most interest: there are hundreds of Great Crested Grebes and Cormorants, and tens of thousands of ducks, including Tufted Ducks, Pochards, Goldeneyes, Smews, and Red-breasted Mergansers, and thousands of Coots.

Smew

199

Romania

EXTENDING EAST as far as the Black Sea, Romania has one of Europe's great bird areas – the Danube Delta. This alone has a list of rare and special birds that would fill the page, but there is far more on offer. High mountain ranges have Alpine birds, and eastern specialities, such as Pied Wheatears and Long-legged Buzzards, are seen on rocky outcrops. Forests are host to a range of woodpeckers and owls, and open farmland sees shrikes and Rollers in summer.

❶ Gurghiu Mountains, Transylvanian Alps

Location 32km (20 miles) from Cluj-Napoca in Northwest Romania.
Access The nearest big town is Târgu Mureş, on road 15, 35km (22 miles) east of the mountains. There are good footpaths, but be warned that reliable maps and petrol stations are hard to find.
Contact Romanian Ornithological Society, Bd. M. Kogalniceanu nr. 49, sc. A, ap. 8, 050108 Sector 5, Bucuresti
Tel: 031 4255657
Email: office@sor.ro
Web: www.sor.ro

There are exciting and beautiful places throughout this area and plenty of time is needed to do it justice. The best time to visit is mid-summer, when you might find Long-legged Buzzards, Honey Buzzards, Lesser Spotted Eagles, Black, Grey-headed, Syrian, White-backed, and Three-toed Woodpeckers, Ural, Eagle, Pygmy, and Tengmalm's Owls, Wallcreepers (difficult), Rock Thrushes, Red-breasted Flycatchers, Sombre Tits, Lesser Grey Shrikes, Barred Warblers, and Rock Buntings. The list of excellent birds goes on and on, and any birdwatching visitor from western Europe can hardly fail to be enthralled by the bird diversity of this site.

❷ Retezat national park

Location At the west end of the Transylvanian Alps, north of Dobreta-Turnu Severin and 300km (185 miles) northwest of Bucharest.
Access From Bucharest, approach on roads 68 and 66 along the northern edge of the mountain range.
Contact Retezat National Park
Tel: 0372 742024
Email: office@retezat.ro
Web: www.retezat.ro
www.panparks.org/source/rete.html

This mountainous area has beech and spruce forest and, higher up, pines, alpine meadows, and glacial lakes. You might come upon Golden and Lesser Spotted Eagles, a whole range of exciting owls and woodpeckers, Hazel Hens, Capercaillies, Red-breasted and Collared Flycatchers, Ring Ouzels, Water Pipits, Alpine Accentors, Firecrests, Nutcrackers, and Wallcreepers.

Capercaillie

Wetlands created by the Danube river.

❸ Danube Delta

Location The Danube enters the Black Sea just south of the Ukraine border.
Access The gateway to the delta is Tulcea, 290km (180 miles) from Bucharest by road. From there, it is best to explore by road or boat.
Contact The Danube Delta Biosphere Reserve Authority, The Department of Environment, The Ministry of Environment, 820243 – Tulcea, Str. 34A PORT, OP3 PO Box 32
Tel: +40 240 51 89 45
Email: arbdd@ddbra.ro
Web: www.ddbra.ro

The Danube Delta is really a patchwork of first-class sites, and even a week's visit is hardly enough to break the surface. Summer wetland birds are truly exceptional, and some, such as the Dalmatian Pelican, are globally threatened. Expect to see an abundance of Night Herons, Purple Herons, Little Bitterns, Pygmy Cormorants, and spectacular White Pelicans. There are Whiskered Terns and Little and Great White Egrets, Glossy Ibises, Ferruginous Ducks, Spoonbills, Red-crested Pochards, and Red-necked Grebes. Add in Penduline Tits, White-tailed and Lesser Spotted Eagles, Red-footed Falcons, Marsh Harriers, Rollers, Lesser Grey Shrikes, and Black and Grey-headed Woodpeckers, and your notebook will be bursting with great experiences. Bee-eaters are commonplace. In winter, there are vast numbers of wildfowl, including huge flocks of Red-breasted Geese.

Spain and Portugal

EUROPE

FRANCE

PORTUGAL

Lisbon ⑫   Madrid

SPAIN

Valencia

Seville

N

SPAIN IS ARGUABLY the finest birdwatching destination in Europe. Its physical variety, often within a small area, makes it possible to experience the snowy peaks of the Sierra Nevada on the same day as Mediterranean scrub and sizzling wetlands. It is unparalleled in Europe for its breeding birds of prey, including the rare Spanish Imperial Eagle. Though less explored, Portugal has most of the Iberian birds including some, such as the Black-shouldered Kite, that are its own specialities.

❶ Picos de Europa

Location 85km (53 miles) southwest of Santander in northern Spain.
Access By road from Arenas and Leon. Try the Cares gorge on the Cabrales to Poncebos road. Fuente De off the C621 is a must; a good base is nearby Espinama.
Contact Sociedad Española de Ornitología (SEO), Melquiades Biencinto 34, E-28053 Madrid, Spain
Tel: 91 434 0910
Email: seo@seo.org
Web: www.seo.org

This is a limestone block, deeply cut by valleys, leaving spectacular peaks and outcrops towering above dramatic gorges. It is often rather damp and misty but good days in summer are sublime. Birds of prey in particular are excellent: you could see Golden and Bonelli's Eagles, Griffon and Egyptian Vultures, Peregrines, kites, and Honey Buzzards, amongst others.

Egyptian Vulture

❷ Hecho valley

Location At the western end of the Pyrenees, 70km (43 miles) east of Pamplona.
Access From Jaca, take the N240 west to Puente la Reina then turn north towards Hecho and beyond.
Contact Sociedad Española de Ornitología (SEO), Melquiades Biencinto 34, E-28053 Madrid, Spain
Tel: 91 434 0910
Email: seo@seo.org
Web: www.seo.org

This valley is beautiful in summer, starting from low-lying farmland and a stony river, and quickly rising into high, forested hills, then big crags, gorges, and mountains. As you drive up in summer, expect to see Crag Martins, Dippers, Red and Black Kites, Buzzards, perhaps Bee-eaters, and increasing numbers of Griffon and Egyptian Vultures in the hills. Stop often and look out for Golden, Booted, and Short-toed Eagles; you may also see Lammergeiers. Choughs and Alpine Choughs are in large numbers in the valley if the conditions are harsh higher up. Forests near the top have Black Woodpeckers, Crested Tits, Firecrests, Short-toed Treecreepers, and Citril Finches. There are Wallcreepers in the area in most years.

Cliffs and scrubland near Riglos.

❸ Riglos

Location The foothills of the Pyrenees, about 90km (56 miles) north of Zaragoza.
Access From the A132 road northwest of Huesca, turn off east to Riglos on Hu310. Walk along the foot of the spectacular cliffs.
Contact Sociedad Española de Ornitología (SEO), Melquiades Biencinto 34, E-28053 Madrid, Spain
Tel: 91 434 0910
Email: seo@seo.org
Web: www.seo.org

Riglos is a deservedly popular spot: looking up at its overhanging cliffs is an awesome experience. The slopes at the foot of the cliffs have Black Wheatears, Black Redstarts, and Dartford Warblers. The orchards and woods lower down are awash with Nightingale song and there are Orphean Warblers, Short-toed Treecreepers, Serins, Woodchat Shrikes, Bee-eaters, Golden Orioles, and Rock Buntings. Around the cliffs are many Crag Martins and Choughs. In winter, you might be lucky and see a Wallcreeper. Birds of prey are always in view, with stunning views of Red Kites and Griffon Vultures, often also Egyptian Vultures, Peregrines, and other species. Keep a look out at all times for the magnificent Lammergeier; over the cliffs to the west towards Aguero, as well as above Riglos are the most likely sites.

201

Dramatic landscape at Belchite.

❼ Belchite

Location A small village 40km (25 miles) south of Zaragoza.
Access From Zaragoza take the N232; after 20km (12½ miles) turn onto the C222 for Belchite.
Contact Sociedad Española de Ornitología (SEO), Melquiades Biencinto 34, E-28053 Madrid, Spain
Tel: 91 434 0910
Email: seo@seo.org
Web: www.seo.org

This area of arid steppe and agricultural land with withered crops can sometimes resemble a moonscape. The area has Stone Curlews, Black-bellied and Pin-tailed Sandgrouse, Calandra, Lesser Short-toed, and Dupont's Larks (a speciality here), Black and Black-eared Wheatears, Little Bustards, and Spectacled Warblers. On summer mornings, sandgrouse flock to drink at Balsa de Planeron in their thousands, visible from the road running northeast from the village.

❹ Ordesa national park

Location In the central Pyrenees, about 130km (81 miles) west of Andorra.
Access From Torla on the C140, 27km (17 miles) from Biescas, a small road runs to Ordesa.
Contact Sociedad Española de Ornitología (SEO), Melquiades Biencinto 34, E-28053 Madrid, Spain
Tel: 91 434 0910
Email: seo@seo.org
Web: www.seo.org
or Ordesa National Park
Web: www.ordesa.net

Giant cliffs above forested slopes are home to Lammergeiers and Griffon Vultures. You could see Golden Eagles, Black Woodpeckers, Dippers, Crag Martins, Red-backed Shrikes, and Ortolan Buntings. At higher altitudes, look for Choughs, Alpine Choughs, Alpine Accentors, and Ptarmigan. Water Pipits breed on the higher pastures.

Ptarmigan

❺ Aiguamolls de L'Emporda

Wetlands at Aiguamolls de L'Emporda.

Location Just to the east of Figueres in northeast Spain.
Access Easily reached from the A7 or N11 between Barcelona and La Jonquera. There is an information centre at the natural park.
Contact Sociedad Española de Ornitología (SEO), Melquiades Biencinto 34, E-28053 Madrid, Spain
Tel: 91 434 0910
Email: seo@seo.org
Web: www.seo.org

This big wetland is second only to the Ebro Delta (see below). The site covers coastal marshlands around the mouths of the Fluvia and Muga rivers, and has freshwater and brackish pools, salt-marshes, grassland, farmland, and some riverine woodland. About 300 species have been recorded here. Birds are mostly wetland species and include all the usual kinds, from Bitterns, Little Bitterns, Cattle and Little Egrets, and Purple Herons to Marsh Harriers, Moustached Warblers, and Penduline Tits. Purple Gallinules are also found here. Look out for Great Spotted Cuckoos, Short-toed Eagles, Bee-eaters, Rollers, and shrikes.

❻ Ebro Delta

Location On the east coast of Spain between Barcelona and Valencia.
Access Start at the visitor centre at Deltebre off the N340. Try around Deltebre and La Marquesa beach, El Fangar, El Garxal, La Noria, the Sant Antoni saltpans, La Tancada lagoon, and the L'Encanyissada lagoon.
Contact Sociedad Española de Ornitología (SEO), Melquiades Biencinto 34, E-28053 Madrid, Spain
Tel: 91 434 0910
Email: seo@seo.org
Web: www.seo.org

This huge delta, threatened with drainage and development, is magnificent for birds. At any time, you can find Cattle Egrets, Greater Flamingos, Red-crested Pochards, Avocets, Slender-billed Gulls, Lesser Short-toed Larks, and Moustached Warblers. In summer, there are Little Bitterns, Night and Squacco Herons, Black-winged Stilts, Collared Pratincoles, and Audouin's Gulls. Winter brings Great White Egrets and huge numbers of Grey Herons, Marsh and Hen Harriers, and many wildfowl and waders.

❽ Laguna de Gallocanta

View over the Laguna de Gallocanta.

Location A natural lake 90km (56 miles) southwest of Zaragoza.
Access From Daroca, take the C211 towards Cillas and then a minor road, the Cv633, to Gallocanta village. Many small roads and tracks give good views of the lake. Explore from Las Cuerlas village to the west.
Contact Sociedad Española de Ornitología (SEO), Melquiades Biencinto 34, E-28053 Madrid, Spain
Tel: 91 434 0910
Email: seo@seo.org
Web: www.seo.org

This is the largest lake in Spain. It is excellent for wintering ducks, Coots (more than 200,000 individuals recorded) and Cranes (up to 54,000 recorded). It has many other interesting wetland birds, including Red-crested Pochards, Black-winged Stilts, and Avocets. The surrounding steppe landscape is home to Great and Little Bustards, Stone-curlews, Black-bellied Sandgrouse, and Tawny Pipits. Cranes come in at dusk in winter from the south and east, and are best seen from Bello and Tornos. They make a truly outstanding sight and sound.

❾ Sierra de Guadarrama

Location A large mountain range north of Madrid.
Access Heading northwest of Madrid on the A6, take the N601 from Collado Villalba to the Navacerrada and Cotos mountain passes. The route between the two is excellent.
Contact Sociedad Española de Ornitología (SEO), Melquiades Biencinto 34, E-28053 Madrid, Spain
Tel: 91 434 0910
Email: seo@seo.org
Web: www.seo.org

Part of the Sistema Central, the Guadarrama range is a wide, rolling landscape of granite hills with mixed forest and scrubland at higher levels. You can drive, walk, or use chair lifts to get to higher altitude. The birds are great: look for the two superstar raptors – Spanish Imperial Eagles and Black Vultures. There are also Griffon Vultures, Golden, Booted, and Short-toed Eagles, and both kites to keep you on your toes, plus White Storks, Black Redstarts, Rock Thrushes, Alpine

Accentors, Dartford and Bonelli's Warblers, Citril Finches, and Rock Buntings: an excellent selection of Iberian birds in fact. Spring and summer are best for a visit.

❿ Sierra de Gredos

The slopes of the Sierra de Gredos.

Location A large range of granitic mountains, 80km (50 miles) west of Madrid.
Access From Madrid use the C501.
Contact Sociedad Española de Ornitología (SEO), Melquiades Biencinto 34, E-28053 Madrid, Spain
Tel: 91 434 0910
Email: seo@seo.org
Web: www.seo.org

These mountains are deforested in the north, with a covering of broom and bushy scrub. The south side is steeper, with forest on the lower slopes. Follow roads to high altitudes to see Griffon Vultures, Golden, Short-toed, and Booted Eagles, Goshawks, Red and Black Kites, White Storks, Alpine Accentors, Choughs, and Rock Sparrows. Lower slopes have Great Spotted Cuckoos, Red-rumped Swallows, Crag Martins, Bee-eaters, Black Wheatears, and Ortolan Buntings.

⓫ Trujillo/Montfragüe

Location 75km (47 miles) northeast of Merida in the province of Extremadura.
Access The C524 from Plasencia to Trujillo crosses the area.
Contact Agencia de Medio Ambiente de Extremadura, Calle Enrique Diez Canedo s/n, 06800 Merida-Badajoz, Spain
or Sociedad Española de Ornitología (SEO), Melquiades Biencinto 34, E-28053 Madrid, Spain
Tel: 91 434 0910
Email: seo@seo.org
Web: www.seo.org

A large range of hills with extensive woodland, the Montfragüe region is especially good for birds of prey. All year round, there are Red and Black-shouldered Kites, Griffon Vultures, the largest colony of Black Vultures in Europe, Sparrowhawks, Goshawks, Spanish Imperial Eagles, Golden and Bonelli's Eagles, Peregrines, Eagle Owls, Crag Martins, Thekla Larks, Black Wheatears, Azure-winged Magpies, and Choughs. In summer, these are joined by Black Storks, Egyptian Vultures, Black Kites, Short-toed and Booted Eagles, as well as Red-rumped Swallows, Orphean Warblers, and Golden Orioles. There is a rare chance of seeing one of Europe's most localized breeding birds, the White-rumped Swift. This wonderful area has tremendous views from places such as the old Montfragüe castle.

The Montfragüe region offers the possibility of rare bird species.

Booted Eagle

⓬ Tejo Estuary

Location A large estuary just east of Lisbon, Portugal.
Access The reserve is reached via the N118 south from Porto Alto. A 10km (6 mile) track leads to the reserve.
Contact Sociedade Portuguesa para o Estudo das Aves, Avenue John Chrysostom, n. #18 - 4. ° Dto 1000-179 Lisboa, Portugal
Tel: (+351) 21 322 04 30
Email: spea@spea.pt
Web: www.spea.pt

The reserve covers salinas and the estuary edge. In spring and autumn, you could see many Curlew Sandpipers and Black-tailed Godwits; winter brings Avocets and Greater Flamingos. Collared Pratincoles on passage, Alpine and Pallid Swifts, White Storks, and Bonelli's and Booted Eagles offer a mouth-watering list of possibilities if you wander inland.

⓭ Faro marshes

Location In the Algarve, just west of Faro airport in southern Portugal.
Access Check out the salinas around Ludo Farm and the lagoons in the golf resort of Quinta do Largo.
Contact Sociedade Portuguesa para o Estudo das Aves, Avenue John Chrysostom, n. #18 - 4. ° Dto 1000-179 Lisboa, Portugal
Tel: (+351) 21 322 04 30
Email: spea@spea.pt
Web: www.spea.pt

The pools by the São Lourenco golf course are best for the extraordinary Purple Gallinule or Swamphen; there are also herons and egrets, warblers, and wildfowl here. The nearby pines often have Azure-winged Magpies. Hoopoes, Bee-eaters, Fan-tailed Warblers, Subalpine Warblers, and Woodchat Shrikes are likely; look out for White Storks flying over on migration.

⑭ Algarve

Location The entire southern coastal belt of Portugal from Cabo de São Vicente to the Spanish border.
Access Faro is the main resort and airport; explore widely around the coast (Cabo de São Vicente, Quinta da Rocha, Quinta do Lago, Tavira) and inland to Monchique, Castro Verde, Sabrana, and Penilhos.
Contact Sociedade Portuguesa para o Estudo das Aves, Avenue John Chrysostom, n. #18 - 4. ° Dto 1000-179 Lisboa, Portugal
Tel: (+351) 21 322 04 30
Email: spea@spea.pt
Web: www.spea.pt

The picturesque south coast of Portugal is worth investigating in any season. Offshore there are Cory's Shearwaters, while marshes and salinas have Greater Flamingos, Red-crested Pochards, Purple Herons, Little and Cattle Egrets, Night Herons, Little Bitterns, White Storks, and various gulls, terns, and waders. Inland, there are Little Bustards, Great Spotted Cuckoos, Azure-winged Magpies in the woods, Lesser Short-toed, Thekla, and Crested Larks, Short-toed and Booted Eagles, Lesser Kestrels, Stone Curlews, Alpine Swifts, Bee-eaters, Hoopoes, Choughs, Red-rumped Swallows, and a good selection of warblers.

The dreamily picturesque Algarve is wonderful for Iberian birds.

⑮ Coto Doñana

Majestic pines in Coto Doñana.

Location A large delta wetland in the coastal triangle formed by the towns of Cádiz, Seville, and Huelva in Southern Spain.
Access West of Seville, on the El Rocio to Matalascañas road. Entry to the reserve is from the visitor centre at La Rocina but many birds can be seen from roads and tracks nearby.
Contact Sociedad Española de Ornitología (SEO), Melquiades Biencinto 34, E-28053 Madrid, Spain
Tel: 91 434 0910
Email: seo@seo.org
Web: www.seo.org

This "must see" area is among Europe's most important sites. It varies from very wet to very dry, with isolated lagoons and salinas. Much of the surrounding land has been drained and farmed. Winter sees the area full of birds, with huge numbers of waders and wildfowl. Migrants include herons, egrets, storks, various birds of prey, Audouin's Gulls, Caspian Terns, and Glossy Ibises. In summer, there are Little Bitterns, Night, Purple, and Grey Herons, Little and Cattle Egrets, Spoonbills, White Storks, Whiskered and Gull-billed Terns, Great Spotted Cuckoos, shrikes, Rollers, and Hoopoes. Residents include some fantastic birds – Spanish Imperial Eagles, Purple Gallinules, and Greater Flamingos, as well as Marbled Teals, a few Crested Coots, and Azure-winged Magpies.

⑯ Laguna de Medina

Location 10km (6 miles) southeast of Jerez de la Frontera in Cadiz province.
Access Take the C381 from Jerez towards Medina Sidonia; the lagoon is 10km (6 miles) along this road.
Contact Sociedad Española de Ornitología (SEO), Melquiades Biencinto 34, E-28053 Madrid, Spain
Tel: 91 434 0910
Email: seo@seo.org
Web: www.seo.org

This lagoon has many Cattle Egrets, ducks including Red-crested Pochards (with a greater variety and higher numbers in winter), Whiskered Terns, Black-winged Stilts, Avocets, and Great Reed Warblers. A selection of very rare and localized birds includes White-headed Ducks, Marbled Teal, Purple Gallinules, and Crested Coots. Greater Flamingos are frequent in winter.

⑰ La Algaida and Bonanza

Location Part of the Coto Doñana wetland complex (see above) near the town of Sanlúcar de Barrameda.
Access From Sanlúcar de Barrameda take the small road to Bonanza.
Contact Sociedad Española de Ornitología (SEO), Melquiades Biencinto 34, E-28053 Madrid, Spain
Tel: 91 434 0910
Email: seo@seo.org
Web: www.seo.org

The saltpans and associated channels are good in summer. There are Greater Flamingos, Night and Purple Herons, Spoonbills, Marbled Teal, excellent birds of prey, Avocets, Collared Pratincoles, Slender-billed Gulls, Great Spotted Cuckoos, Red-necked Nightjars, Rollers, Spectacled Warblers, and Short-toed, Lesser Short-toed, Calandra, and Crested Larks. The pine forests have Red Kites, Spanish Imperial Eagles, Great Grey Shrikes, and Azure-winged Magpies.

⑱ Gibraltar

The Rock of Gibraltar.

Location Close to the southernmost tip of Spain, approximately 100km (62 miles) southwest of Malaga.
Access You can drive in from San Roque on the N340 to La Linea (N351); it is easiest to leave your car at La Linea, walk through the border, and then use a bus or taxi to get around on the Rock.
Contact Gibraltar Ornithological and Natural History Society, Gibraltar Natural History Field Centre, Jews' Gate, Upper Rock Nature Reserve, PO Box 843, Gibraltar
Tel: (+350) 200 72639
Email: enquiries@gonhs.org
Web: www.gonhs.org

In summer, Gibraltar has one great attraction – the Barbary Partridge. At other times, you can watch Cory's Shearwaters, Gannets, Arctic Skuas, and

Little, Mediterranean, and Yellow-legged Gulls passing offshore. The best times are March, April, and September to October, when big numbers of birds migrate across Gibraltar. Expect Black and White Storks, Honey Buzzards, Black Kites, Egyptian Vultures, Short-toed and Booted Eagles, harriers, buzzards, and a host of small birds, including Rufous Bush Robins, chats, wheatears, Pied Flycatchers, shrikes, and a variety of warblers. The Cable Car Top Station is the best spot for migrant raptors and storks; try the Mediterranean Steps for the Barbary Partridge.

View across the Cabo de Gata.

🅙 Ronda

Location 70km (43 miles) west of Malaga.
Access Easily reached by the A366 from airports on the Costa del Sol.
Contact Sociedad Española de Ornitología (SEO), Melquiades Biencinto 34, E-28053 Madrid
Tel: 91 434 0910
Email: seo@seo.org
Web: www.seo.org

The main road through Ronda town crosses a bridge above a gorge. Here you can watch birds of prey and Blue Rock Thrushes, while Crag Martins, Alpine, Pallid, and Common Swifts dash by at head height. Roads in the surrounding hills are scenically appealing, with chances to see Golden, Bonelli's, Booted, and Short-toed Eagles, Griffon Vultures, Woodchat Shrikes, Hoopoes, Bee-eaters, and many larks and warblers. The woods have Firecrests, Bonelli's Warblers, Iberian Chiffchaffs, and Crested Tits; the open areas Red-necked Nightjars and Black Wheatears.

Woodchat Shrike

🅚 Cabo de Gata, Almería

Location Cabo de Gata is 40km (25 miles) southeast of Almería.
Access Almeria has an airport; Cabo de Gata lies east off the N332.
Contact Sociedad Española de Ornitología (SEO), Melquiades Biencinto 34, E-28053 Madrid, Spain
Tel: 91 434 0910
Email: seo@seo.org
Web: www.seo.org

This large cape has good saltpans, an interesting coastline, and arid areas inland. The lagoons are best, with Greater Flamingos all year, as well as Avocets, Black-winged Stilts, and Yellow-legged Gulls. Cliffs inland have Bonelli's Eagles and Peregrines. You may also find Trumpeter Finches in their only European site. In summer, Lesser Kestrels, Collared Pratincoles, and Alpine Swifts are found.

🅛 Alicante and El Hondo

Location Alicante is at the centre of the Costa Blanca. El Hondo is along the coast just south of the town.
Access Alicante is a busy city on the A7; to the south on the N332 are wetlands including El Hondo and the Santa Pola salt pans near Elche.
Contact Sociedad Española de Ornitología (SEO), Melquiades Biencinto 34, E-28053 Madrid, Spain
Tel: 91 434 0910
Email: seo@seo.org
Web: www.seo.org

The coastal road gives good views of the coastal wetlands south of Alicante; you may see Greater Flamingos, Little Egrets, Red-crested Pochards, Lesser Short-toed Larks, and Moustached Warblers. In summer, there are Marbled Teal as well as Whiskered and Gull-billed Terns. Audouin's Gulls are likely on migration. Reservoirs at El Hondo have Cattle and Little Egrets, Marbled Teal, Red-crested Pochards, Squacco and Purple Herons, Collared Pratincoles, Whiskered Terns, and often Greater Flamingos. You may be lucky and see White-headed Ducks.

🅜 Mallorca: Albufera

Marshland in Albufera, Mallorca.

Location An extensive wetland just southeast of Alcudia.
Access Reached by footpaths from the coast road; nearby salinas are overlooked from the road farther east.
Contact The Environmental Organisation of the Balearics (GOB), C / Manuel Sanchis Guarner, Palma 1007004, Mallorca
Tel: (+34) 971 49 60 60
Email: info@gobmallorca.com
Web: www.gobmallorca.com

Exciting birds can be seen on this marsh, especially in the early morning and evening (but mosquitoes can be a menace). In summer, Eleonora's Falcons feed over the reeds. In the reedbeds proper, there are Moustached and Great Reed Warblers, while any patch of sand or water is likely to have Kentish Plovers. Migrants are good here, with harriers, storks, waders, and terns, and a few Greater Flamingos turn up on the salinas. There is a visitor centre, nature trails, and hides.

🅝 Mallorca: Formentor

Location In the north of the island, 20km (12½ miles) from Puerto Pollensa.
Access By road or foot north of Pollensa.
Contact The Environmental Organisation of the Balearics (GOB), C / Manuel Sanchis Guarner, Palma 1007004, Mallorca
Tel: (+34) 971 49 60 60
Email: info@gobmallorca.com
Web: www.gobmallorca.com

The northern tip of Mallorca's mountain spine is best explored on foot. The cliff tops have Marmora's Warblers and the lighthouse at the end is a good place to see Eleonora's Falcons. Offshore, you can see Mediterranean Shearwaters, Cory's Shearwaters, and possibly an Audouin's Gull. The road to the headland cuts through good countryside for Woodchat Shrikes, Hoopoes, Bee-eaters, Crag Martins, Blue Rock Thrushes, and a variety of Mediterranean warblers. The woods also have the dull-coloured local Crossbills and often good migrants in spring and autumn. Watch the skyline for birds of prey, including Black Vultures venturing north from the mountains (especially in the Bocquer Valley).

Italy

SWITZERLAND   AUSTRIA

EUROPE

Milan ②
③

ITALY

④

Rome ⑦
⑤ ⑧ ⑨

⑥

Taranto
⑩

N

⑪
⑫

WITH ITS LONG REACH from the highest Alps to the centre of the Mediterranean, Italy covers almost the whole range of European bird habitats. Its birds are hunted and trapped by the million, but it remains a great country to see birds if you know where to go. Such places include dramatic coastal headlands, inland lakes, and many coastal wetlands. Some sites, still almost undiscovered as far as northwest Europeans are concerned, vie with the best in Europe for the number and variety of exciting birds to be seen.

❶ Gran Paradiso national park

Spectacular slopes of Gran Paradiso.

Location About 55km (34 miles) northwest of Torino, in northwest Italy.
Access There are several routes in on the Piedmont side, from Pont, Noasca, Ceresole Reale, and Ronco.
Contact Park headquarters, Via della Rocca 47-10123 Torino
Tel: +39- (011) -8606233
Email: info@pngp.it
Web: www.pngp.it

Here you have superb Alpine habitats, from high peaks to forested slopes, pastures, and open valleys. The birds are exciting too: look for Choughs and Alpine Choughs, introduced Lammergeiers, Rock Thrushes, Alpine Accentors, Snowfinches, and Ring Ouzels. Lower levels and woodlands hold Dippers, Nutcrackers, Bonelli's Warblers, Crested Tits, Citril Finches, and Rock Buntings. Black Redstarts are common in villages and on the cliffs. Wallcreepers are always present but elusive.

❷ Golfo di Venezia

Location The lagoon around Venice.
Access Best watched from the east side from a small road that runs between Cavallino in the south, through Valle Sacchetta and Valle Paleazza, to Ca'Savio in the north. Brussa Beach to the east is reached from Portogruaro towards Lugagnano; stop 1km (⅔ mile) short of Brussa to see large heronries at a lagoon.
Contact Venezia LIPU, Giacomo Matteotti, 26, 30020 Gaggio di Marcon, Venice
Web: www.lipuvenezia.org

The city of Venice is built on islands in a shallow, brackish lagoon between the mouths of the Brenta and Piava Rivers. In spring, you will see the migration of ducks (including Garganeys), Little Gulls, and waders. In summer, Black-winged Stilts, Purple Herons, and Little Egrets breed. Autumn migrants may include Marsh and Hen Harriers and Buzzards, as well as many interesting waders. Great White Egrets are often present in the winter. The pine woods at Brussa are good for wintering birds and Nightingales; Long-eared Owls are known to breed here. A few hundred ducks can be found on lagoons behind the wood and on the sea, and Bean, White-fronted, and Greylag Geese winter there.

Wetlands adjacent to the Po Delta.

❸ Po Delta

Location On the coast, about 55km (34 miles) south of Venice.
Access The large delta area can be approached from the S309 south of Venice. There are good walks near Marina di Romea in the Valle Mandriole, and at the Punte Alberete WWF reserve by the Fossatone canal. At the mouth of the Po, try the Casoni and Comacchio marshes; a boat trip from Casone Foce is excellent too. The Valle Zavelea (Fossa di Porto reserve) is best viewed from a canalside path from Fosa di Porto on the Anita road.
Contact LIPU, Via Trento n.49, 43100 Parma
Tel: 0521 273043
Email info@lipu.it
Web: www.lipu-uk.org

This extensive area, crisscrossed by numerous small roads and tracks, is a tangled complex of wetland, woodland, river, and stream systems, including shallow estuaries, sandbanks, and salt-marsh. Breeding birds include herons and egrets, Spoonbills, Black-winged Stilts, and Avocets. The Boscoforte reserve adds Mediterranean Gulls, Gull-billed Terns, and Ferruginous Ducks. Migration is always exciting with a great variety of waders, including Marsh Sandpipers, gulls, terns, Pygmy Cormorants, Great White Egrets, Marsh Harriers, and other birds of prey in spring. Collared Flycatchers may sometimes be seen in the nearby woods.

④ Laguna di Orbetello

Location Just behind a headland at Orbetello, 105km (65 miles) northwest of Rome.

Access From route S1, 30km (19 miles) south of Grosseto, turn towards Orbetello and take a road along a long spit between lagoons. A small road completes a full circuit of the lagoon area, skirting the foot of Monte Argentario on the south side.

Contact WWF warden
Tel: 0564 870198
Email: oasiorbetello@wwf.it
Web: www.wwf.it/orbetello.nt

In winter, this is a great spot for Cormorants, Coots, Teal, Wigeon, Pintails, Shovelers, and Pochards, plus a few Greater Flamingos, Cranes, Spoonbills, and geese. Marsh and Hen Harriers are replaced in summer by Montagu's Harriers. Black-winged Stilts breed but waders are better in late winter and spring, when thousands pass through, especially Black-tailed Godwits and Ruffs, and a few rarities, such as Terek and Marsh Sandpipers. Keep an eye out for Collared Pratincoles, White-winged Black, Whiskered, and Caspian Terns, and Golden Orioles.

⑤ Circeo national park

Location Between Rome and Naples, 35km (22 miles) southeast of Latina.

Access Good views from the coastal road. Enter the forested areas from Strada Mediana, following signs to Cerasella Refuge.

Contact National Park Visitor Centre, Via Carlo Alberto, 104/107 – 04016 Sabaudia (LT)
Tel: +39 0773/512240
Email: segreteria@parcocirceo.it
Web: www.parks.it/parco.nazionale.circeo/Eindex.php

Try this little reserve with its limestone cliffs, oak forest, winter floods, Mediterranean heath and scrub, deep lakes, and beaches. In winter, you will see many Cormorants, Wigeon, Teal, and Pochards, hundreds of Black-necked Grebes, Black-throated Divers offshore, and a selection of waders. In spring, look out for Lanners, Black Kites, Cory's Shearwaters offshore, Alpine and Pallid Swifts, Rollers, Tawny Pipits, Blue Rock Thrushes, Subalpine, Sardinian, Melodious, Great Reed, Moustached, and Cetti's Warblers, and Penduline Tits.

Black-headed Bunting

⑥ Capri

Location An island 35km (22 miles) south of Naples in the Gulf of Naples.

Access By hourly ferry from Naples. On the island, minibuses take you to good areas, such as Barbarossa Castle, Mount Solaro, and the southwest coastal cliffs. The Axel Munthe Foundation in Anacapri has an excellent reserve and organizes guided tours.

Contact Axel Munthe Foundation
Tel: 081 8371401
Web: www.capri.net/home/en/index.php

Capri is best visited in spring, before the hectic tourist season enters full swing; you should have many good walks almost to yourself. It is a great island for migrants of all kinds. Specialities include Spectacled Warblers, Collared and Semi-collared Flycatchers, Black-headed Buntings, and various birds of prey, such as Honey Buzzards, Red-footed Falcons, and Eleonora's Falcons. In winter, Wallcreepers are relatively easy to spot on the coastal cliffs. Any summer visit might produce good sightings of Golden Orioles, Black-eared Wheatears, Red-backed and Woodchat Shrikes, Sardinian Warblers, Yellow-legged Gulls, Peregrines, and other typical Mediterranean species.

⑦ Tremiti Islands

Location In the Adriatic Sea, 30km (19 miles) north of the Gargano peninsula, which is situated on the "spur" on the east coast, northeast of Foggia in central Italy.

Access By ferry from Termoli all year round. A ferry from the main island of San Nicola also reaches San Domino.

Contact Azienda Autonoma di Soggiorno di Termoli
Tel: 0875 706754

The main islands of San Nicola, San Domino, and Capraia, and the islets of Cretaccio and Vecchia have good spots along their coasts. These are limestone islands with rugged crags inland and cliffs along the shore, and are best visited from March to June. There are interesting land birds in the scrubby areas, but much of the interiors are stony and bare. A wood on San Domino has Sardinian, Subalpine, and other warblers, Pied Flycatchers, Red-backed Shrikes, migrant Honey Buzzards, and sometimes Red-footed Falcons. Seabirds breed on the islands and can be seen offshore; these include Cory's and Mediterranean Shearwaters, and Yellow-legged Gulls.

⑧ Abruzzo national park

Location 100km (62 miles) east of Rome in central Italy.

Access This huge park is reached on the S83, from the A25 motorway from Rome to Pescara. There are many other good places to explore; try Monte Meta, approached from the S83; Monte S Nicola, reached from the S509 from Opithen via several well-marked footpaths; and Valle Sangro, accessed on paths from the La Camosciara road.

Contact Centro Parco Nazionale d'Abruzzo, Boulevard Saint Lucia - 67032 Pescasseroli (AQ)
Tel: +39 0863/91131
Email: info@parcoabruzzo.it
Web: www.parks.it/parco.nazionale.abruzzo or National Park Office

The Abruzzo national park is heavily forested but rises to high peaks above the tree line, giving scope for all the usual Alpine species, including Golden Eagles, Alpine Accentors, Snowfinches, and Alpine Choughs. In early spring, Eagle Owls are calling and eagles and Goshawks displaying. Wallcreepers, Peregrines, Crag Martins, Black Redstarts, White-backed Woodpeckers, Orphean and Bonelli's Warblers, Hoopoes, Collared Flycatchers, Hawfinches, and Red-backed Shrikes are just a few of the attractions here. In winter, try for Rock Partridges, which come lower down and closer to the roads, but are generally hard to see.

The impressive Mainarde Mountains in Abruzzo national park.

Pine-topped cliffs at Gargano.

❾ Gargano peninsula

Location Northeast of Foggia.
Access Explore inland from the S528 and on the coast from 15km (9½ miles) north of Mattinata.
Contact Ufficio dell'Amministrazione dell Foreste Demaniali del Gargano, Foresta Umbra
Tel: 0884 560944

This limestone peninsula has inland peaks reached by twisting roads, as well as craggy cliffs and coastal gorges, and is a good habitat for Short-toed Eagles, Lanners, Honey Buzzards, Peregrines, and Eagle Owls. In the forested areas in spring there are five kinds of woodpeckers, Short-toed Treecreepers, and Firecrests. More open areas give a chance of Alpine and Pallid Swifts, Blue Rock Thrushes, Rüppell's and Subalpine Warblers, Rock Buntings, and Red-backed Shrikes. It is possible to sample crag, heath, beech and pine forest, and coast in one day.

❿ Capo d'Otranto

Location In the far southeast of Italy, 40km (25 miles) southeast of Lecce.
Access Good road access.
Contact LIPU, Via Trento n. 49, 43100 Parma
Tel: 0521 273043
Email: info@lipu.it
Web: www.lipu-uk.org

This is a large, low plateau above indented coastlines, with Mediterranean scrub and some saline lakes. Spring migrants are plentiful: Cranes come over in March and April, followed by birds of prey, with Marsh, Pallid, and Montagu's Harriers, Hobbies, Kestrels in hundreds, Lesser Kestrels, kites, Long-legged Buzzards, and Ospreys. Honey Buzzards are abundant in May; Eleonora's Falcons and White and Black Storks join the show. Small birds on migration include Red-rumped Swallows, Red-throated Pipits, wheatears, chats, flycatchers, and warblers. Sardinian and Spectacled Warblers nest in the lowest scrub. In winter, the lakes attract wildfowl and Ospreys.

⓫ Straits of Messina

View over the Straits of Messina.

Location The narrow straits separating Sicily from mainland Italy.
Access On the eastern (Calabrian) side, take the A3 motorway to Pilone di Santa Trada and follow a narrow road uphill to an open viewing area, which is excellent during the spring migration.
Contact LIPU, Reggio di Calabria
Email: lipurc@libero.it

Thousands of birds wait for good weather conditions before setting out on their long migratory flights from Africa to Europe over the Mediterranean. By the time they reach Messina in Sicily they are tired, and they typically cross this last stretch of water flying low overhead. For this reason, birdwatching over the straits in spring is a fantastic experience. It is seriously marred, however, by the ominous presence of illegal hunters who make watching difficult and disturbing. The birds are marvellous, with numerous Honey Buzzards, frequent White and Black Storks, and many smaller migrants, including Bee-eaters. You may find it best to join the April–May LIPU research and observation camp.

⓬ Sicily: Messina and Mt Etna

The northern slopes of Mount Etna.

Location Sicily is off the "boot tip" of Italy. Messina lies on the Sicilian side of the Straits, and Mount Etna looms 60km (37 miles) to the southwest.
Access Road access is good. Try Via Palermo uphill from Messina town to the Peloritani. The lower slopes of Etna can be explored by car.
Contact LIPU Palermo
Tel: 091 320506

Illegal shooting of birds of prey has mostly been eradicated on the Sicilian side of the Straits and birdwatching is easier and more pleasant than on the northern side. Between 20,000 and 30,000 birds of prey fly over in spring in huge variety with Honey Buzzards (in May), Black Kites (in April), and sometimes Red-footed Falcons most numerous. Black and White Storks also move through and rarities are sometimes noted. Look for Collared Flycatchers in nearby woods, and Golden Orioles, Dartford Warblers, Bee-eaters, and other birds in the general vicinity of Messina and Mt Etna.

⓭ Sardinia: Gulf of Cagliari

Location A bay at the southern end of Sardinia, which includes the city of Cagliari.
Access The Molentargius Marsh is a few minutes from Cagliari by car or bus. Other good sites are the Quartu marshes (near Poetto Beach), and Santa Gilla and Macchiareddu marshes, 6km (3½ miles) along the S195 towards Pula.
Contacts LIPU Cagliari
Tel: 070/837458
Email: lipu.sardegna@tiscalinet.it
Web: www.lipu.it

These wetlands, set in the industrial suburbs of Cagliari, are better for birds than they are for scenery. Never mind: they have breeding Purple Gallinules, Glossy Ibises, Cattle Egrets, Black-winged Stilts, Red-crested Pochards, and Slender-billed Gulls (a couple of thousand pairs) among many other species. In winter, they are home to Avocets, Greater Flamingos, and Cormorants, (several thousands of each), and occasional rarities, such as Broad-billed Sandpipers and Red-necked Phalaropes. You should also be able to find Audouin's Gulls.

⓮ Sardinia: Gulf of Oristano

Location The west coast of Sardinia, 80km (50 miles) northwest of Cagliari.
Access The Sale Porcus LIPU reserve lies north of Oristano, off the S292.
Contact LIPU Oristano
Web: www.lipu-uk.org/Oasi/SalePorcus.htm
Tel: 0783 211058

This area of Sardinia is a secret, undiscovered treasure. The Sale Porcus LIPU reserve is especially important, with several thousand Greater Flamingos in winter and breeding birds as diverse as Purple Gallinules, Black-winged Stilts, Avocets, Slender-billed Gulls, Red-crested Pochards, Montagu's Harriers, Collared Pratincoles, several species of larks, chats, warblers, and shrikes, Rock and Spanish Sparrows, and Fan-tailed Warblers. Audouin's Gulls are regular and Glossy Ibises appear on migration.

Slovenia, Croatia, and Yugoslavia

This region has suffered wretchedly from conflict in recent years. Nevertheless, many of its birdwatching areas are safe and accessible, and Slovenia, in particular, is a dream for the all-round naturalist. There are great birds throughout, from White and Dalmatian Pelicans to White-tailed Eagles. Lesser Grey Shrikes, Bee-eaters, Rollers, and many warblers, larks, and other Mediterranean species are widespread. The effects of war on the birdlife here have not yet been fully assessed.

❶ Lake Cerknica

Location About 45km (28 miles) southwest of Ljubljana, Slovenia.
Access Take the E63/E70 from Ljubljana and turn off southeast at Rakek to Cerknica. The lake and flooded meadows can be viewed from small roads.
Contact Bird Study Association of Slovenia, Prvomajska 9, SI-1000 Ljubljana, Slovenia
Email: dopps@dopps-drustvo.si

This shallow lake is surrounded by reeds, scrub, meadows, and a peat bog. Breeding birds include Little Bitterns and Corncrakes. Good numbers of Black Terns and a few White-winged Black Terns appear on migration. Little Crakes and Ferruginous Ducks are other possibilities; the recent status of birds here is not well recorded and there may be interesting discoveries to be made.

❷ Krakovska Forest

Location About 70km (43 miles) southeast of Ljubljana, Slovenia.
Access Adequate roads off the E70 lead through this large region. Northeast Slovenia also has excellent wetlands around the Ormož and Ptuj reservoirs on the River Drava between Maribor and Zavrč, and on the River Mura near Gibina. A riverine forest along the River Lendava is reached from Maribor.
Contact Bird Study Association of Slovenia, Prvomajska 9, SI-1000 Ljubljana, Slovenia
E-mail: dopps@dopps-drustvo.si
Slovenian Tourist Board
Web: slovenija.turistika.net

This region is a remnant of the once huge Pannonian oak forest. The forest reserve is protected and has breeding Black Storks and Collared Flycatchers, which are numerous and widespread, while the riverine forests and wetlands can be good in summer for breeding White Storks, Rollers, and River Warblers. Middle Spotted Woodpeckers are present in small numbers.

Black Stork

❸ River Sava

Wetlands beside the River Sava.

Location About 70km (43 miles) southeast of Zagreb, Croatia.
Access The floodplains of the Sava, Lonja, and Struga rivers are close to the towns of Sunja and Dubica.
Contact Croatian Tourist Board (UK)
Tel: +385 (0) 1 4699 333
Web: www.croatia.hr

These floodplains include seasonally-flooded forests, marshes, meadows, fish-ponds, and lagoons, all of which are threatened by agricultural intensification. In recent times, they had many breeding Cormorants, Night Herons, Little Egrets, Purple Herons, Spoonbills, Honey Buzzards, White-tailed Eagles, Lesser Spotted Eagles, Corncrakes, and Whiskered Terns. The forests are good for Middle Spotted Woodpeckers and Collared Flycatchers. Migrant terns and waders add to the interest in spring and autumn.

❹ Plitvice Lakes national park

Location 140km (87 miles) south of Zagreb, Croatia, close to the border with Bosnia-Herzegovina.
Access 10km (6 miles) by road east of Bihać.
Contact Mr Stjepan Dujmović, The Plitvice Lakes Public Establishment, NP Plitvička Jezera, 53231 Plitvička Jezera
Tel: +385 (0)53 751 015, or +385 (0)53 751 014
Email: info@np-plitvicka-jezera.hr
Web: www.np-plitvicka-jezera.hr

This area has a few Brown Bears and Wolves, as well as exciting birds including Eagle Owls and Capercaillies. Some 126 species of birds have been recorded, of which 70 breed in the area. Woodland and upland species include typical Balkans birds, such as Sombre Tits and Lesser Grey Shrikes. There are good facilities in and around the park, with hotels, restaurants, information centres, and guided tours inside the area.

Lesser Grey Shrike

209

❺ Paklenica national park

Location Near Zadar on Croatia's Adriatic coast.
Access Only a short hop from Trieste in Italy, the national park is reached along the the coastal road (Jadranska cesta) from Rijeka or Zadar.
Contact 23244 Starigrad-Paklenica, Hrvatska, Croatia
Tel: 00385 / 23 / 369-155, 369-202, 369-803 (Park Reception)
Email: np-paklenica@zd.t-com.hr, or prezentacija@paklenica.hr
Web: www.paklenica.hr/paklenica_en/index_en.html

This is a scenically beautiful area, with inland mountains and shingle beaches on the coast. Almost 100 species nest within the national park, including Peregrines at Velika and Mala Paklenica; Red-backed Shrikes are common. Bee-eaters, Sombre Tits, Syrian Woodpeckers, Rock and Cirl Buntings, and many other species may be found here.

Syrian Woodpecker

❻ Fruska Gora national park

Location 50km (31 miles) east of Belgrade, Yugolavia.
Access Easily reached from Belgrade and Novi Sad, these hills run east–west just south of the Danube.
Contact Fruska Gora national park, 21208 Sremska Kamenica, Zmajev trg 1, Yugoslavia
Tel: 021 463 666; 021 463 667
Web: www.npfruskagora.co.rs

This Park covers forested hills where Imperial Eagles, Lesser Spotted Eagles, and Saker Falcons breed. White Storks,

Black Storks, Honey Buzzards, Eagle Owls, Red-backed and Lesser Grey Shrikes, and Ortolan Buntings also add interest. The status of the larger birds is now uncertain; hunting and recreational use had already threatened the site before the wars and political upheavals.

❼ Belgrade

Banks of the river Sava in Belgrade.

Location The capital city of Yugoslavia.
Access Belgrade Airport is connected to the major European airports and rail connects Belgrade and Novi Sad with all European capital cities.
Contact Tourist Organization of Belgrade, Masarikova 5/IX, 11000 Belgrade, Serbia
Tel: +381 11 30 61 400
Web: www.tob.rs

Belgrade is where the River Sava meets the Danube, with the Pannonian Plains in the north and wooded hills to the south. In and around the city are Pygmy Cormorants, Black Storks, Ferruginous Ducks, White-tailed Eagles, Saker Falcons, White-winged Black Terns, and Syrian Woodpeckers. Also try Veliko Ratno Ostrvo Island and Pančevacki Rit Wetlands in the Belgrade area.

❽ Dalmatian coast

Location The coastal region of Croatia.
Access Numerous tourist resorts strung along the coast road make exploration easy.
Contact Croatian Tourist Board (UK)
Web: www.croatia.hr

This varied stretch of Balkan coast has limestone crags, cliffs, gorges, scattered wetlands, and big hills inland. Its birds are equally varied: Lesser Grey and Woodchat Shrikes, Penduline and Sombre Tits, Nightingales, Red-rumped Swallows, Blue Rock Thrushes, numerous warblers, and birds of prey make even a short visit exciting. Migrants include Collared and Red-breasted Flycatchers, Honey Buzzards, and storks. In winter, there are Wallcreepers low down and Rock Nuthatches are resident in many gorges.

❾ Uvač and Mileševka Griffon Vulture sanctuary

Location: In the central Balkans near the town of Nova Varoš, about 250km (155 miles) south of Belgrade.
Access: From Belgrade, take the Ibarska Magistrala road to Nova Varoš, about 15km (9½ miles) from the reserve.
Contact: Birds of Prey Protection Fund, Despota Stefana 142, 11000 Belgrade, Serbia
Email: grifon@ibiss.bg.ac.yu

Most of Serbia is excellent for birds of prey. This is one of the best areas, with 19 diurnal and 9 nocturnal raptors recorded. The birds include Peregrines,

Levant Sparrowhawks, Golden, Booted, and Short-toed Eagles, Egyptian and Griffon Vultures, and Long-legged Buzzards. Others to look out for are Alpine Swifts, Crag Martins, Red-rumped Swallows, Wallcreepers, Black Storks, Rock Nuthatches, Shore Larks, Black-eared Wheatears, Sombre Tits, Water Pipits, Nutcrackers, and Alpine Choughs.

❿ Lake Skadar

Location Southeastern Montenegro, at the border with Albania.
Access Lake Skadar is easily reached by road south from Titograd.
Contact Bird report
Web: www.visit-montenegro.com/skadar-lake.htm

The pelican colony here (sometimes with a handful of Dalmatian Pelicans) was once very important. Though now degraded, the lake is still worth a visit: Little Bitterns, Night Herons, Purple Herons, Whiskered Terns, and Pygmy Cormorants can be seen. The general area is rich in birds such as Alpine and Pallid Swifts, Bee-eaters, Rollers, Penduline Tits, Woodchat Shrikes, Rock Nuthatches, Rock and Blue Rock Thrushes, Crag Martins, Alpine Choughs, and a great range of warblers. In winter, there are grebes and ducks and large numbers of Greylag Geese.

The rocky shores of Lake Skadar, on the Yugoslav–Albanian border.

Greece

For every birdwatcher who chooses Spain as Europe's best country, another will tip Greece. It lacks the numbers of birds of prey that can be seen in Spain, but its many eastern specialities – including pelicans – more than compensate. Its varied landscapes are tempting – mountains, lakes, forests, coastal lagoons and marshes, and endless hot, dry Mediterranean scrub, full of warblers, buntings, larks, and shrikes. However, Greece has a poor environmental record, particularly with regard to the hunting of migrant birds on some of the islands.

❶ Delphi

Breathtaking views from Delphi.

Location Opposite the north coast of the Peloponese, about 180km (112 miles) west of Athens.
Access A well-signposted destination on route 48.
Contact Hellenic Ornithological Society, Themistokleous 80, GR-10681, Athens, Greece
Tel: +30 210 8227937
Email: info@ornithologiki.gr
Web: www.ornithologiki.gr

Delphi is a revered historical site that can get very crowded, so a morning visit is best. Noisy Rock Nuthatches perch on the ruined columns; there are also Blue Rock Thrushes, Olive-tree and Rüppell's Warblers, Black-headed, Rock, and Cretzschmar's Buntings, and Orphean Warblers. Sombre Tits like the wooded slopes. Over the high crags there are birds of prey, although Griffon Vultures and Short-toed and Booted Eagles are less regular now. There may be White-backed Woodpeckers in the surrounding woods.

❷ Ioannina

Location In western Greece, close to the Albanian border.
Access The town is west of the Pindos Mountains, easily reached by routes 5, 6, and 20. There is a large and interesting lake, easily watched from the town itself.
Contact Hellenic Ornithological Society, Themistokleous 80, GR-10681, Athens, Greece
Tel: +30 210 8227937
Email: info@ornithologiki.gr
Web: www.ornithologiki.gr

The lake is used for water sports, so you might be greeted by the sight of a jet skier passing behind a White Pelican. Pygmy Cormorants drop in around spring and autumn and Moustached Warblers nest in the reeds. In the surrounding hills, there are Lanners and Wallcreepers, but Rock Nuthatches and Semi-collared Flycatchers are reliable sightings.

Lanner

The rugged and impressive Pindos Mountains are largely undisturbed.

❸ Pindos Mountains

Location Northwestern Greece, close to the Albanian border.
Access Best approached from route 6 between Trikkala and Ioannina. The Vikos-Aoos national park, which includes the stunning Vikos Gorge, is immediately south of the village of Konitsa on route 20 north of Ioannina.
Contact Hellenic Ornithological Society, Themistokleous 80, GR-10681, Athens, Greece
Tel: +30 210 8227937
Email: info@ornithologiki.gr
Web: www.ornithologiki.gr

These high, spectacular, and rugged mountains have a few roads and trails. Some of the best birds, such as the Lammergeier and Golden Eagle, are large and visible from afar, but not easy to find. You may, with persistence, come across Lanners, Rock Partridges, Wallcreepers, Alpine Accentors, Snowfinches and Cretzschmar's Buntings. Try a trail over very high ground from Papingo to see these high altitude specialists. This remote area is as near to wilderness as you'll get in southern Europe: be prepared.

❹ Prespa Lakes

The stunning view over Prespa Lakes.

Location Northwestern Greece on the borders with Albania and Macedonia.
Access Take the main road west from Florina; use minor roads to explore.
Contact Hellenic Ornithological Society, Themistokleous 80, GR-10681, Athens, Greece
Tel: +30 210 8227937
Email: info@ornithologiki.gr
Web: www.ornithologiki.gr

This special place, with golden reeds, blue water, and snowy mountains, is a magnificent setting for a colony of White and Dalmatian Pelicans. The birds can be seen closely from the road crossing a ridge to the northwest. The lake is also good for other water birds: you may find Glossy Ibises, Red-crested Pochards, Short-toed and Booted Eagles, Bee-eaters, Rollers, shrikes, and several interesting warblers.

❺ Porto Lago

Location About 250km (155 miles) east of Thessaloniki.
Access The village is easily reached from the main coastal road; turn to the village from Xánthi on route 2.
Contact Hellenic Ornithological Society, Themistokleous 80, GR-10681, Athens, Greece
Tel: +30 210 8227937
Email: info@ornithologiki.gr
Web: www.ornithologiki.gr

Walks along the tamarisk-lined beach and the south shore of the lagoon are recommended; you may see Spur-winged Plovers, Olivaceous Warblers, and Pygmy Cormorants. Regulars include Great White Egrets, White and Dalmatian Pelicans, Slender-billed Gulls, Glossy Ibises, Red- and Black-necked Grebes,

White Storks, and Bee-eaters. Mediterranean Shearwaters pass by offshore, and the area is known as a good site for Pygmy Cormorants.

❻ Evros Delta

Location About 25km (16 miles) east of Alexandroupolis.
Access From minor roads off route 2. A permit is needed to explore most of the delta.
Contact Hellenic Ornithological Society, Themistokleous 80, GR-10681, Athens, Greece
Tel: +30 210 8227937
Email: info@ornithologiki.gr
Web: www.ornithologiki.gr

This rather degraded wetland still has many good birds; in winter, Pygmy Cormorants and wildfowl may number in the tens of thousands. White and Dalmatian Pelicans are winter visitors, along with Spotted and White-tailed Eagles. Lesser Spotted Eagles, Long-legged Buzzards, and other birds of prey breed in the area. You should see Isabelline Wheatears, Gull-billed Terns, Slender-billed Gulls, Collared Pratincoles, White Storks, Olive-tree Warblers, and Rollers. A Ruddy Shelduck or a Spur-winged Plover is possible.

❼ Dadia-Soufli Forest Reserve

Location In far eastern Greece, 60km (37 miles) northeast of the town of Alexandroupolis.
Access East of Alexandroupolis, take route 51 north, then turn west at Provatonas to Lefkimi. Try tracks to the west and northwest. Farther north on route 51, a turning just beyond Likofos goes to Dadia, where there is a reserve information centre; a track from here leads south to a raptor feeding station.
Contact Community of Dadia
Tel: 554 32208 or Hellenic Ornithological Society, Themistokleous 80, GR-10681, Athens, Greece
Tel: +30 210 8227937
Email: info@ornithologiki.gr
Web: www.ornithologiki.gr

This reserve is best visited in summer, when there are Masked Shrikes in

Black Vulture

the bushes and Levant Sparrowhawks to be seen. The vulture feeding station (accessible by minibus) is worth a visit; you will see Black, Egyptian, and Griffon Vultures, and perhaps some Black Storks. Close-up views are excellent, and you should spend some time to appreciate these birds in the air. Golden and Lesser Spotted Eagles breed in the area too.

❽ Lesbos

The popular island of Lesbos.

Location A large island close to the Turkish coast.
Access Many ferries serve the island.
Contact Hellenic Ornithological Society, Themistokleous 80, GR-10681, Athens, Greece
Tel: +30 210 8227937
Email: info@ornithologiki.gr
Web: www.ornithologiki.gr

This rugged island is favoured by birdwatchers, especially in spring, but is large enough not to feel claustrophobic. It has resident Krüper's Nuthatches and breeding Cinereous Buntings, eastern species like Masked Shrikes, Olive-tree and Rüppell's Warblers, and Cretzschmar's Buntings, as well

as a good selection of typical Mediterranean birds including Red-footed Falcons, Red-backed Shrikes, Bee-eaters, and Hoopoes. Almost anything is possible, however, with Greater Flamingos, Ruddy Shelducks, Audouin's Gulls, Red-throated Pipits, Isabelline Wheatears, and Glossy Ibises among the migrants that could be observed in spring and autumn.

❾ Crete

Location A large island off southern Greece.
Access Crete is well served by roads. Interesting areas include Mt Koutroulis, the Rhodopos Peninsula, the Lefka Mountains, Mt Idi, Mt Kofinas, and Dia Island.
Contact Hellenic Ornithological Society, Themistokleous 80, GR-10681, Athens, Greece
Tel: +30 210 8227937
Email: info@ornithologiki.gr
Web: www.ornithologiki.gr

This gem of an island has some small but good wetlands, as well as inland mountains that support magnificent Griffon Vultures and Lammergeiers. Golden Eagles, Peregrines, Short-toed Eagles, and Eleonora's Falcons add further excitement for the raptor enthusiast in the blue summer skies. Chukar Partridges breed in the hills, and you may find Rüppell's Warblers in bushy places low down. Watch offshore for Cory's Shearwaters, slowly drifting by in summer.

Spectacular birds of prey are exciting sightings over the hills in Crete.

Turkey

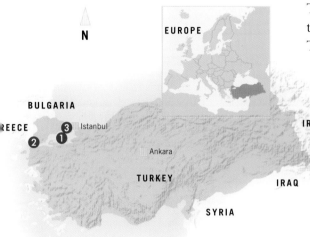

THE EUROPEAN REGION OF TURKEY, or Thrace, lies to the west of the Sea of Marmara and Istanbul. Though small in extent, the area has many of the birds which can be expected in Greece. Additionally, it boasts a magnificent spring and autumn passage of pelicans, storks, and birds of prey, which concentrate on the short sea crossing between Europe and Asia (and thence to Africa) that is so necessary to their survival. The sea itself is also interesting, with passing shearwaters and Mediterranean Gulls among the attractions.

❶ Sea of Marmara

Location The enclosed sea between the narrow straits of the Dardanelles and the Bosporus.
Access By road or bus from Istanbul.
Contact Doğal Hayati Koruma Derneği (DHKD)
Email: kelaynak@dhkd.org
or Ornithological Society of the Middle East (OSME)
Web: www.osme.org

Scenically this is a stunning and diverse region – a mix of Mediterranean landscapes and areas oddly reminiscent of northwest European coastal farmland. It is great for birds at any time, but is best in spring for local breeding species, including storks, Isabelline Wheatears, a wide selection of larks, Lesser Grey Shrikes, Hoopoes, Bee-eaters, Sombre Tits, Serins, and Ortolan and Black-headed Buntings. In autumn, birds of prey and White Storks are to be seen moving towards the narrow crossing points at each end of the wide Sea of Marmara. Yellow-legged Gulls, Mediterranean Gulls, and Mediterranean Shearwaters are common.

❷ Evros Delta

Location At the mouth of the Evros River on the border between Turkey and Greece.
Access The Turkish side of the delta is best approached from Enez; Gala Lake is nearby. This border region is potentially sensitive; check with the authorities before visiting.
Contact Doğal Hayati Koruma Derneği (DHKD)
Email: kelaynak@dhkd.org
or Ornithological Society of the Middle East (OSME)
Web: www.osme.org

The delta has diminished as a site for birds, but there are still interesting species to be found in its lagoons and meadows. Look for pelicans, storks, White-tailed Eagles, Long-legged Buzzards, Lesser Spotted Eagles, Isabelline and Black-eared Wheatears, Syrian Woodpeckers, Red-rumped Swallows, Masked and Lesser Grey Shrikes, Hoopoes, Bee-eaters, and various warblers. Many of the more colourful and larger species can be seen from roadsides, which should pose no problem with the authorities. Nevertheless, always be careful where you point your binoculars.

Bee-eater

The city of Istanbul and the shores of the Bosporus.

❸ Istanbul and the Bosporus

Location On the west shore of the Bosporus – the narrow straits between the Black Sea and the Aegean.
Access Anywhere around Istanbul can be good for birds; in autumn, the eastern side of the Bosporus is favoured, especially the famed Çamlica Hills.
Contact Doğal Hayati Koruma Derneği (DHKD),
Email: kelaynak@dhkd.org
or Ornithological Society of the Middle East (OSME)
Web: www.osme.org

Soaring birds migrate huge distances by gaining height on warm upcurrents of air (thermals). These rise only over land, so birds naturally seek the narrowest sea crossings, making Istanbul a great birdwatching site. Late August to October is the best time: Honey Buzzards peak in August but mid-September brings at least another 15 species of birds of prey. White Storks are most abundant of all, but raptors include thousands of Buzzards, Lesser Spotted Eagles, Black Kites, and Levant Sparrowhawks, smaller numbers of various eagles and vultures, and occasional rarities to be picked out from the throng. At the same time, Mediterranean Shearwaters constantly shoot through the strait, and you can see Laughing Doves and Mediterranean Gulls around the harbour.

Glossary

Adult A fully mature bird, that is able to breed and is in its final plumage that no longer changes pattern with age

Axillary A feather at the base of the underside of the wing; axillary feathers often form small, distinct patches

Barred With marks that cross the body, wings, or tail

Behaviour How a bird moves, calls, sings, nests, and carries out all aspects of its life, in a manner that is more or less characteristic of its species

Breeding plumage An imprecise but useful general term; usually refers to the plumage worn when birds display and pair (hence, in ducks, it is usually a winter, rather than summer, plumage)

Brood Young produced from a single clutch of eggs, and incubated together

Call Vocal sound, often characteristic of a single species, communicating a variety of messages

Clutch A group of eggs in a single nest, usually laid by one female, and incubated together

Colony A group of nests of a social species that has some social function, especially among seabirds, Sand Martins, Rooks, and various herons

Covert A small feather in a well-defined tract on the wing or at the base of the tail, covering the base of the larger flight feathers

Cryptic A plumage pattern or colouration that makes a bird more difficult to see

Dabble To feed in shallow water by sieving water and food through comb-like filters in the bill, hence "dabbling duck"

Dawn chorus The short-lived concentration of bird song around dawn, especially in spring

Declining A population undergoing a steady reduction over a period of years

Dimorphic Two forms of a single species; this can be according to sex (sexual dimorphism), or to a physical characteristic such as colours (skuas, for example, have two colour forms)

Display Ritualized, showy behaviour that is used in courtship and/or by a bird claiming a territory; other forms of display include, for example, distraction display, in which a bird attempts to lure a predator from its nest

Drumming An instrumental sound made by vibrating the bill against a branch (woodpeckers) or by vibrating outspread tail feathers through the air (Snipe)

Ear tuft A distinct tuft of feathers on each side of the forehead, but with no connection with the true ears

Eclipse Summer plumage of male ducks and some other species, helping their camouflage during moult

Endangered Found in very small numbers, in a small area, or in a restricted and declining habitat, so that the future survival of the species is in doubt

Eruption A large-scale movement of birds from their breeding area, when numbers are high but food is short; an "irruption" is this movement into another area, such as Waxwings, Bearded Tits, or Crossbills wandering widely across western Europe in some winters

Escape An individual bird that has wandered from a zoo or other collection to live in the wild

Eye patch An area of colour around the eye

Eyering A ring of colour around the eye

Eyestripe A stripe of colour running as a line through the eye

Family A category in classification, grouping genera that are closely related; also the family group of a pair (or single adult) with young

Feral Living wild, in a sustainable population, but derived from captive stock or from domestic stock that has escaped, or that has been introduced into an area where the species either does not naturally occur or, as in the case of the feral, or town, pigeon, from which it has disappeared as a truly wild bird

Flight feather A large quill feather on the wing

Forewing The front part of the spread wing, including the outer primaries, primary coverts, alula, and smaller secondary coverts

Gape The mouth of a bird or the angle at the base of the bill

Genus A grouping of species (or, sometimes, a single species if the genus is "monotypic") that are closely related, recognized by the same first word in the scientific name; plural "genera"

Hindwing The rear of the wing, including the inner primaries and the secondaries

Hybrid The result of cross-breeding between two species; rare in the wild

Immature Not yet fully adult or able to breed (although some species, such as the Goshawk, may breed while still in apparently immature plumage); some species, such as larger gulls, have a sequence of changing immature plumages for three or four years, while others (such as the Fulmar) are unable to breed for several years but show no sign of such immaturity in their plumage pattern

Inner wing The inner half of the wing inside the "wrist" joint, including the secondary coverts and secondaries

Juvenile The plumage of a bird in its first flight, before its first moult

Lek A gathering of birds at which the males display or fight to impress watching females

Localized With 90% or more of the population in ten sites or fewer

Moult The shedding of old feathers and growth of new replacements, in a systematic fashion that is characteristic of the species

Migrant A species that spends part of the year in one geographical area and part in another, "migrating" between the two

Order A category in classification, grouping families according to their presumed relationship

Outer wing The outer half of the spread wing, including the primaries and primary coverts

Orbital ring A thin, bare, fleshy ring around the eye, often of a distinctive colour

Passerine A bird that is a member of the Passeriformes, or songbirds or perching birds – largest order of birds; other species are commonly called "non-passerines"

Primary One of the large outer wing feathers, growing from the digits of the "hand"

Race A more or less distinct group within a species, defined by geographical area; also "subspecies"

Rare Found in very small numbers or low densities, or an individual bird found outside its normal range (a "rarity" or "vagrant")

Roost A place where birds sleep, or the act of sleeping; this is typically at night, but in many coastal species, is determined by the tides (such as waders that feed at low tide and roost, in secure places, at high tide when feeding places are inundated). "A roost" infers a communal nature

Scapular One of a more or less oval tract of feathers growing at the base of the wing, to each side of the back

Secondary One of the row of long, stiff feathers at the trailing edge of the inner wing

Seawatching Watching for passing seabirds from a fixed point on the shore (such as a headland)

Secure A population that is not currently or foreseeably threatened

Song A vocal performance with a pattern characteristic of the species; may attract a mate, or repel intruders from a territory

Song flight A special and usually distinctive flight in which the song is performed; often short (as in warblers) but is sometimes prolonged (as in larks)

Species A group of living organisms, individuals of which can breed and produce fertile offspring, but which do not or cannot usually breed with individuals of other species

Speculum A colourful patch on the secondaries (usually of ducks)

Streaked Marked with lines of colour aligned lengthwise along the body

Subspecies A more or less distinct group within a species, defined by geographical area; also "race"

Superciliary stripe A line of colour above the eye

Talon A claw (of a bird of prey)

Tarsus The longest, most obvious part of a bird's leg, between the "toes" and the "ankle joint" (often called the "knee", but points backwards)

Tertial One of a small group of feathers at the base of the wing, adjacent to the innermost secondaries

Twitcher A birdwatcher who travels to see a specific individual bird that has been discovered and whose whereabouts have been made known; not synonymous with birdwatcher

Under tail coverts Feathers at the underside of the base of the tail

Underwing The underside of the wing

Upper tail coverts Feathers at the base of the upperside of the tail

Upperwing The upper surface of the wing

Vagrant An individual bird that has accidentally strayed outside its normal range; also a species that is only found in such circumstances in a given area, such as the Northern Parula, a "vagrant" in Europe

Vent The area of feathers between the legs and the under tail coverts

Vulnerable A species potentially at risk due to dependence on a restricted habitat or range, or to small numbers

Wader A bird or species within a group of families, including plovers and sandpipers, which may or may not actually wade in water (for example, Lapwings will wade but typically nest and feed in drier areas, while Avocets habitually wade in shallow water); other species also wade (such as herons and flamingos) but are not included in this group; in the USA, called "shorebirds" (but as many live far inland, this is equally imprecise)

Wingpit The base of the underside of the wing, the "axillaries"

Wingbar A line of colour across the coverts on the closed wing (as on a Chaffinch), or along the extended wing as a bar or stripe (as on the Tufted Duck or Ringed Plover)

Young An imprecise term to indicate an immature bird, from a nestling to a full grown bird in immature plumage

Useful contacts

Organizations (UK and Ireland)

Royal Society for the Protection of Birds (RSPB)
Web: www.rspb.org.uk

UK Headquarters:
The Lodge, Sandy, Bedfordshire
SG19 2DL
Tel: 01767 680551

Northern Ireland Headquarters:
Belvoir Park Forest, Belfast BT8 4QT
Tel: 028 9049 1547

Scotland Headquarters:
2 Lochside View, Edinburgh Park
Edinburgh EH12 9DH
Tel: 0131 317 4100

South Wales Office:
Sutherland House, Castlebridge, Cowbridge
Road East, Cardiff CF11 9AB
Tel: 02920 353000

The British Trust for Ornithology (BTO)
The Nunnery, Thetford, Norfolk IP24 2PU
Tel: 01842 750050
Web: www.bto.org

Scottish Ornithologists' Club
Waterston House, Aberlady, East Lothian,
EH32 0PY
Tel: 01875 871 330
Web: www.the-soc.org.uk

Welsh Ornithological Society
30 Fairfield, Penperlleni, Pontypool,
Gwent, NP4 0AQ
Tel: 01873 880 165
Web: www.birdsinwales.org.uk

The Wildfowl & Wetlands Trust (WWT)
WWT Slimbridge, Gloucestershire
GL2 7BT
Tel: 01453 891900
Web: www.wwt.org.uk

The Wildlife Trusts
The Kiln, Waterside, Mather Road,
Newark, Nottinghamshire, NG24 1WT
Tel: 01636 677711
Web: www.wildlifetrusts.org

Bird Watch Ireland
Unit 20, Block D, Bullford Business
Campus, Kilcoole, Co. Wicklow, Ireland
Tel: 353 (0)1 2819878
Web: www.birdwatchireland.ie

BirdLife International
Wellbrook Court, Girton Road, Cambridge
CB3 0NA, United Kingdom
Tel: 01223 277318
Web: www.birdlife.org

International organizations

Austria:
BirdLife Austria
Web: www.birdlife.at

Belgium:
BirdLife Belgium
Web: www.natuurpunt.be

Denmark:
Dansk Ornitologisk Forening
Web: www.dof.dk

Finland:
BirdLife SUOMI-FINLAND
Web: www.birdlife.fi

France:
Ligue pour la Protection des Oiseaux (LPO)
Web: www.lpo.fr

Germany:
Naturschutzbund Deutschland (NABU)
Email: NABU@NABU.de
Web: www.nabu.de

Greece:
Hellenic Ornithological Society
Email: birdlife-gr@ath.forthnet.gr
Web: www.ornithologiki.gr

Hungary:
Hungarian Ornithological and Nature
Conservation Society (MME)
Email: mme@mme.hu
Web: www.mme.hu

Iceland:
Icelandic Society for the Protection of Birds
Email: fuglavernd@fuglavernd.is
Web: www.fuglavernd.is

Italy:
Lega Italiana Protezione Uccelli (LIPU)
Web: www.lipu.it

Netherlands:
Vogelbescherming Nederland
Web: www.vogelbescherming.nl

Norway:
Norsk Ornitologisk Forening
Email: nof@birdlife.no
Web: www.birdlife.no

Poland:
Polish Society for the Protection of Birds
Email: office@otop.most.org.pl
Web: www.otop.org.pl

Portugal:
Sociedade Portuguesa para o Estudo das Aves
Web: www.spea.pt

Romania:
Romanian Ornithological Society
Web: www.sor.ro

Slovenia:
Bird Study Association of Slovenia
Email: dopps@dopps-drustvo.si
Web: www.ptice.si

Spain:
Sociedad Española de Ornitología (SEO)
Web: www.seo.org

Sweden:
Swedish Ornithology Society
Web: www.sofnet.org

Switzerland:
SVS-BirdLife Suisse
Email: svs@birdlife.ch
Web: www.birdlife.ch

Turkey:
Ornithological Society of the Middle East
(OSME)
Web: www.osme.org

Web Resources

Fatbirder
Information about birdwatching worldwide.
Web: www.fatbirder.com

Eurobirding
Information about birdwatching in Europe,
North Africa, and the Middle East.
Web: www.eurobirding.co.uk

Index

Page numbers in **bold** refer to entries in the *Species by species* section; numbers in *italics* refer to illustrations.

Acknowledgments

Cobalt id would like to thank the following for assistance with this book: Richard Thomas for compilation of site information; Kathleen Rosewarne for proofreading; Hilary Bird for indexing; Christine Percy and all at Swarovski UK Ltd for providing images of optical equipment; Mel Kemp for patient guidance at Minsmere Reserve; Richard Chappell, Ennis Jones, and John Ferguson for their enthusiastic help in the photography of their special gardens; Dr Christoph Zöckler (WCMC), Gina Pfaff (BirdLife International), Chris Gomersall, David Tipling, and all at FLPA for invaluable guidance on image sources; and Rebecca Johns.

Commissioned photography: Peter Anderson
Commissioned illustration: Halli Verrinder

The publisher would like to thank the following for their kind permission to reproduce their photographs:
(**Key**: a-above; b-below/bottom; c-centre; f-far; l-left; r-right; t-top)

Alamy Images: 15cl.

BirdLife Austria: A Ranner 195cl, 196tl; E Karner 195br.

BirdLife International: 42bc Web image (http://www.worldbirds.org/mapportal/worldmap.php)

BirdLife Switzerland: 189cl, 189br.

Bruce Coleman Collection: Kim Taylor 22bl, 87tr.

Chris Gomersall: 54tr, 60r, 84bl, 90cr1, 90cr3, 95cl, 173tr, 203bl, 208cl, 22br, 104tl,106tl, 108tl, 111bl, 114bl, 124tl, 141cc.

Chris Knights: 90tl.

Christoph Zöckler: 186tl, 194tr.

David Tipling Photo Library: 45tc

Dorling Kindersley: Marcus Varesvuo 1c, 110bc, 117c

Eugene Hüttenmoser: 82bl.

FLPA: A Wharton 16bl; AR Hamblin 61bl; B Borrell 29tr, 67cb, 202cl; DA Robinson 29br; David Hosking 37tr, 180br, 211cl; Derek Middleton 62tr; Desmond Dugan 90cl3; E Woods 58br; E&D Hosking 10cr, 27bl, 27r, 46br, 52c, 59cl, 61cl, 71c, 90cl1, 199tr; F De Marco/Panda 197cl; Foto Natura Stock 19crb; Fritz Polking 70br, 190cr, 191tl; G Marcoaldi/Panda 19t, 204cr, 206cr; H Clark 32bl, 90cl2; H Hautala 70c, 15bc, 23bc; J Hawkins 23bl, 28br, 85c; J Watkins 22bc, 59bl; J&C Sohns 86cl; Jean Hosking 212 br; Lennart Norstrom 172cr; Liora & Ofer Bahat 19bl; Martin Withers 25br; MB Withers 29bl; MJ Thomas 62br, 67cb; P Perry 17tr, 18bl; R Mattio/Panda 206cl; R Tidman 90cr2; Richard Brooks 20crb, 23br; Robert Canis 39cr, 70tr, 94br, 95bl; Robin Chittenden 204tl; Roger Tidman 20crt, 39tr, 55cl, 56c; Roger Wilmshurst 24tr, 88bc, 88bl; Rv SC Brown 27clb; S Jonasson 54bl; S Maslowski 70cb; Silvestris 174cl; Steve Young 24br; Terry Adrewartha 28cr, 79cr, 198cr; Tony Hamblin 27cl; W Wisniewski 22tr; Yossi Eshbol 53cr.

Getty Images: 20cr.

Gunnar Oertel: 193br, 193bl, 193tr.

Marek Walisiewicz: 42bl1, 42bl2, 42bl3, 199cr.

masterfile.com: 96

Michel Decleer: 182cl, 182cr, 183cr, 183tl, 183tr.

Mike Lane: 52bc, 69bl, 175br, 177cr, 178cl, 212tl.
Mike Read: 62c, 63bc, 68tr, 184cl, 184cr, 185br, 186cr, 186cl, 186bl, 187cr, 188tl, 201cr, 202cr, 204bl.

Natural History Museum: 13cl.

NHPA: A Nardi 52br, 175tl, 191cl, 207br, 208tl; Alan Williams 181cr, 181ct; D Woodfall 66r; EA Janes 199br; Eric Soder 68br; John Buckingham 177cl; M Stelzner 200cr; Paal Hermansen 52tr; Roger Tidman 173cl, 202tl; Vicente Garcia Canseco 65c.

OSF: Alastair Hay 205tr; Berndt Fischer 178cr, 197br; Bob Gibbons 187tr; Caroline Brett 172br; Clive Bromhall 213cr; CW Helliwell 174cr; David Tipling 212cr; Dr R Cannon 211cr; Jorge Sierra 65bc; Jorge Sierra Antinolo 203tl; Martyn Chillmaid 64r; Peter Gathercole 205cr; TC Middleton 208cr, 188cr.

Panasonic: 36cl, 36c.

Roger Tidman: 107tl, 145bc.

RSPB Images: 73c; Chris Gomersall 16br; Chris Knights 121bc; David Kjaer 137bc; Gordon Langsbury 113tl; Mark Hamblin 151bc; Mike Lane 89br, 112tl, 119bl; Philip Newman 138tl; Richard Brooks 152tl; Andy Hay 25bc, 32tr, 42tr, 56br, 58bl, 156cl, 157cl, 157br, 158cr, 160cr, 162cla, 163cr, 164cr, 165cb, 166br; Barry Hughes 94cr; Bill Paton 84cb; Bob Glover 24bca, 43t, 84tr; Chris Gomersall 4, 5, 6, 11bl, 15cl, 56br, 80tr, 86cl, 157tcr, 158br, 160cl, 162cl, 162br, 164cl, 165tl, 166cl, 167tl; Chris Knights 84br, 92bl; David Broadbent 17bl; David Kjaer 86cl, 159tl, 159cl, 160tl, 163tr; David Tipling 165cr; Doug Allan/BBC Natural History Unit 38br; Ernie Janes 10bc, 74; Geoff Dore 158tcl; George McCarthy 24bc; Gerald Downey 39cr, 44tr; JL Roberts 89bc; Jan Halady 48tr; Laurie Campbell 8, 87cl, 88tr, 89tr; Malcolm Hunt 33bl, 161cl; Marianne Wilding 91br; Mark Hamblin 86cl, 156cr; Maurice Walker 28tr; Michael Gore 92tr; Mike Lane 11br; Mike Richards 33tl, 37bcr; Niall Benvie 39cr; Paul Doherty 21tr; Ray Kennedy 44bl, 73cb; Richard Brooks 85tl; Robert Smith 87bl; Roger Wilmshurst 26tr, 85cl, 93cl, 94cr; Steve Austin 161br; Tony Hamblin 47t, 87cl, 88bl.

Sue Cunningham Photographic: 209cr, 199cl.

Thomas W Johansen: 168cr, 169tr, 169br, 170cr, 170tr, 170tl.

Tim Loseby: 171cr.

Windrush Photos: Arthur Morris 21br, 36tr; David Tipling 34tr, 57br, 79br, 85br, 88br, 90bl, 90bc, 91cr, 91tr, 95cl, 166ccl, 167cr; DM Cottridge 54br, 58tr; G Downey 80bl; Göran Ekström 20crc; Jari Peltomaki 86b, 60cl, 176cl, 176br; John Gardner 55bc; Les Borg 38br; Pentti Johansson 10br; Peter Cairns 69cr; Richard Brooks 179br.

Jacket images: Front: **Alamy Images:** pronature crb; **Corbis:** Andrew Parkinson cb; **Dorling Kindersley:** Natural History Museum, London cra; **Fotolia:** Bombaert Patrick br; **NHPA / Photoshot:** Thomas Kitchin & Victoria Hurst fcrb; **rspb-images.com:** tl, tc, Nigel Blake bc; Back: **rspb-images.com:** fcl, Nigel Blake

Every effort has been made to trace the copyright holders. The publisher apologizes for any unintentional omissions and would be pleased, in such cases, to place an acknowledgment in future editions of this book.

All other images © Dorling Kindersley
For further information see: www.dkimages.com